JBoss AS 5 Development

Develop, deploy, and secure Java applications on this
robust, open source application server

Francesco Marchioni

PUBLISHING

BIRMINGHAM - MUMBAI

JBoss AS 5 Development

First published: December 2009

Production Reference: 1091209

Published by Packt Publishing Ltd.
32 Lincoln Road
Olton
Birmingham, B27 6PA, UK.

ISBN 978-1-847196-82-8

www.packtpub.com

Cover Image by Vinayak Chittar (vinayak.chittar@gmail.com)

Credits

Author
Francesco Marchioni

Reviewers
Edem Morny

Peter Johnson

Acquisition Editor
Sarah Cullington

Development Editor
Amey Kanse

Technical Editors
Gaurav Datar

Smita Solanki

Indexer
Hemangini Bari

Editorial Team Leader
Abhijeet Deobhakta

Project Team Leader
Lata Basantani

Project Coordinator
Joel Goveya

Proofreader
Chris Smith

Graphics
Nilesh R. Mohite

Production Coordinator
Aparna Bhagat

Cover Work
Aparna Bhagat

About the Author

Francesco Marchioni is a Sun Certified Enterprise architect employed by an Italian company based in Rome. He started learning Java in 1997 and since then he has followed the path to the newest application program interfaces released by Sun. He joined the JBoss community in 2000, when the application server was running release 2.X.

He has spent many years as a software consultant, where he has envisioned many successful software migrations from vendor platforms to open source products such as JBoss AS, fulfilling the tight budget requirements of current times.

In the past five years, he has authored technical articles for O'Reilly Media and is running an IT portal focused on JBoss products (`http://www.mastertheboss.com`).

I'd like to thank Packt Publishing for giving me this unique opportunity to write a book about a great product like JBoss. All the staff I have worked with has been very cooperative at giving their time in the arduous publishing process. I'd also like to thank the external reviewers Peter Johnson and Edem Morny who have offered their professional expertise for many parts of this book. And last but not the least, I want to pay my tribute to my family, my father in particular who has transmitted me the virus of programming when I was just a boy, my wife Linda who was so patient with my late nights and with my missing housework, and my 2 years old baby Alessandro who hasn't actually helped in writing this book but has been the inspiration of it.

About the Reviewers

Edem Morny has been involved in Enterprise Java technologies since he got introduced to Java in 2005, using tools and technologies encompassing both the standard Java EE stack and non-standard ones such as Hibernate and Spring. His experience with JBoss AS has also included porting clustered, fault-tolerant deployments of applications, from proprietary application servers to the open source alternative.

He has been an active promoter of Java EE, speaking at workshops and seminars on a national scale in Ghana. He is the cofounder of Ghana's first Java User Group, JAccra (http://groups.google.com/group/jaccra).

He is a senior developer at the application development center in Accra, Ghana, of an international biometric security solutions company, leading the development of Biocryptic Identity Management Systems for the global market.

Edem was a technical reviewer of *JBoss Tools 3 Developer Guide,* published by Packt Publishing in the year 2009. You'll find him blogging at http://edemmorny.wordpress.com.

Peter Johnson started his computer career in August, 1980, working for Burroughs, programming mainframes in COBOL and ALGOL. He started working with Java in 1998, and was a lead designer on projects such as a JDBC driver for the DMSII database that runs on Unisys mainframes.

For the past several years, he has been the chief architect of a team that does performance analysis of Java applications on large scale Intel-based machines (8 to 32 CPUs), and evaluates various open source software for Enterprise readiness.

In addition, Peter is a JBoss committer and is the coauthor of the book *JBoss In Action,* published by Manning. Peter often speaks on Java performance and various open source topics at industry conferences such as JBoss World and the annual Computer Measurement Group International Conference.

Table of Contents

Preface

The JBoss Application Server is a Java EE-certified platform for developing and deploying Java Enterprise applications. JBoss Application Server provides the full range of J2EE 1.5 features as well as extended Enterprise services including clustering, caching, and persistence. This book will show Java EE developers how to develop their applications using the JBoss Application Server. It covers topics such as:

- Setting up a development environment
- Customization
- Java EE programming modules
- Clustering
- Security

All these features will be explored by developing sample and intuitive applications built using the friendly interface of Eclipse and JBoss Tools.

What this book covers

Chapter 1: *Installing Core Components* covers the installation of the key components that will be needed throughout the rest of the book. The installation process will be completed by using intuitive wizards that will lead even inexperienced users through it.

Chapter 2: *What's New in JBoss AS 5.0* introduces the reader to the most significant changes brought by release 5.0 of the application server. The new server directory tree is analyzed in detail and possible variants in the server configuration are discussed in the latter part of this chapter.

Chapter 3: *Customizing JBoss Services* discusses the core configuration of the application server. The highlights of it include an introduction to JBoss AS monitoring services, the inner details about JBoss thread pool, how to configure logging services, and a detailed description of the transaction and Datasource service.

Chapter 4: *Developing EJB 3 Session Bean* introduces the reader to some concrete Java EE programming examples developed on JBoss AS 5. The focus of this chapter is on EJB 3 session Beans, including a section about their configuration for optimal results.

Chapter 5: *Developing JPA Entities* covers the development of an example based on the Java Persistence API (JPA). Here, we introduce an enterprise application named the Appstore, which will be a central theme of this book.

Chapter 6: *Creating a Web Application* is about developing and configuring web applications on JBoss AS 5.0 using the JSF cutting-edge technology. In the first part of this chapter we will enhance the Appstore Enterpirse application by adding a web layer to it. In the latter part, we explain in detail how to properly configure JBoss Web Server.

Chapter 7: *Developing Applications with JBoss Messaging Service* discusses JBoss Messaging provider by giving a short introduction to the new messaging system. The chapter then helps us set up some proof of concept programming examples.

Chapter 8: *Developing Applications with JBoss and Hibernate* covers the de facto standard object relational mapping tool, Hibernate, showing how to quickly set up a Hibernate project using the facilities provided by the JBoss tools interface.

Chapter 9: *Managing JBoss AS* covers the Java Management Extension (JMX), which still plays a vital role in the application server infrastructure. The chapter includes many examples that show how to write traditional MBeans services and the new POJO Services.

Chapter 10: *Developing Applications with JBoss Web Services* focuses on the JBoss Web Service implementation, JBossWS, showing how to create, deploy, and test Web Services on JBoss AS along with some advanced concepts such as Handler chains and SOAP debugging.

Chapter 11: *Clustering JBoss AS* covers the facts about JBoss AS clustering configuration, moving from cluster basics to detailed configuration of the individual services of the application server.

Chapter 12: *Developing a Clustered Application* continues the journey in the clustering arena by adding some concrete examples based on the abstract concepts covered in the earlier chapter.

Chapter 13: *JBoss AS Security* provides a systematic guide to JBoss security framework and the cryptographic interfaces available in the Java EE framework. This supplies the basis for concrete examples, which are delivered in the next chapter.

Chapter 14: *Securing JBoss AS Applications* continues the in-depth exploration of the JBoss security framework, adding concrete programming examples applied on the EJB and Web Services technologies.

Who this book is for

If you are a Java architect or developer who wants to get the most out of the latest release of the JBoss application server or a JBoss administrator who wants a clear and simple reference for JBoss services, this book is for you. You are not expected to have accumulated experience on the application server though you must know the basic concepts of Java EE.

Conventions

In this book, you will find a number of styles of text that distinguish between different kinds of information. Here are some examples of these styles, and an explanation of their meaning.

Code words in text are shown as follows: "Since release 5.1.0 of the application server, the admin console is bundled as a web application in the `deploy` folder of JBoss AS."

A block of code will be set as follows:

```
<mbean code="org.jboss.util.threadpool.BasicThreadPool"
    name="jboss.system:service=ThreadPool">
    <attribute name="Name">JBoss System Threads</attribute>
    <attribute name="ThreadGroupName">System Threads</attribute>
    <attribute name="KeepAliveTime">60000</attribute>
    <attribute name="MaximumPoolSize">10</attribute>
```

When we wish to draw your attention to a particular part of a code block, the relevant lines or items will be shown in bold sometimes with numbers in square brackets referring to notes in the text:

```
<attribute name="Log4jQuietMode">true</attribute>
    <attribute name="RefreshPeriod">60</attribute> [1]
    <attribute
        name="DefaultJBossServerLogThreshold">DEBUG</attribute>
</mbean>
```

Any command-line input or output is written as follows:

```
twiddle -s localhost invoke "jboss.system:type=ServerInfo"
  listThreadCpuUtilization > threadCpu.txt
```

New terms and **important words** are shown in bold. Words that you see on the screen, in menus or dialog boxes for example, appear in our text like this: "In the left frame expand the **Resources | Datasources** leaf and choose the suitable transaction option."

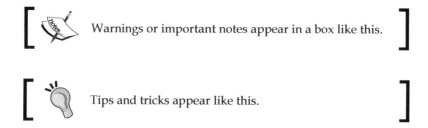

Warnings or important notes appear in a box like this.

Tips and tricks appear like this.

Reader feedback

Feedback from our readers is always welcome. Let us know what you think about this book—what you liked or may have disliked. Reader feedback is important for us to develop titles that you really get the most out of.

To send us general feedback, simply drop an email to feedback@packtpub.com, and mention the book title in the subject of your message.

If there is a book that you need and would like to see us publish, please send us a note in the **SUGGEST A TITLE** form on www.packtpub.com or email suggest@packtpub.com.

If there is a topic that you have expertise in and you are interested in either writing or contributing to a book, see our author guide on www.packtpub.com/authors.

Customer support

Now that you are the proud owner of a Packt book, we have a number of things to help you to get the most from your purchase.

Downloading the example code for the book

Visit http://www.packtpub.com/files/code/6828_Code.zip to directly download the example code.

The downloadable files contain instructions on how to use them.

Errata

Although we have taken every care to ensure the accuracy of our contents, mistakes do happen. If you find a mistake in one of our books—maybe a mistake in text or code—we would be grateful if you would report this to us. By doing so, you can save other readers from frustration, and help us to improve subsequent versions of this book. If you find any errata, please report them by visiting http://www.packtpub.com/support, selecting your book, clicking on the **let us know** link, and entering the details of your errata. Once your errata are verified, your submission will be accepted and the errata added to any list of existing errata. Any existing errata can be viewed by selecting your title from http://www.packtpub.com/support.

Piracy

Piracy of copyright material on the Internet is an ongoing problem across all media. At Packt, we take the protection of our copyright and licenses very seriously. If you come across any illegal copies of our works in any form on the Internet, please provide us with the location address or website name immediately so that we can pursue a remedy.

Please contact us at copyright@packtpub.com with a link to the suspected pirated material.

We appreciate your help in protecting our authors, and our ability to bring you valuable content.

Questions

You can contact us at questions@packtpub.com if you are having a problem with any aspect of the book, and we will do our best to address it.

1
Installing Core Components

Prologue

From: Acme Head Offices

To: Francesco Marchioni

Hi Francesco,

Can you meet at 4 PM in the boardroom? We are going to interview a few guys for the new JBoss Enterprise project.

Regards,

Monty Burns

JBoss Application Server has been around since the beginning of the new millennium and, in personal resumes, it is common to find people who have acquired some experience on it.

Before every job interview, I have the expectation that high caliber Java/Java EE candidates surely know the core concepts of JBoss AS. Often, companies don't consider hiring just the best techie guy, but a well-rounded profile with a "situation-action-result" mind.

One thing I personally like to ask to identify smart developers is: *Why have you chosen to learn JBoss and not XYZ? How does it differentiate from the competitors?* The most habitual answer is: *JBoss is free, so I chose to learn Java EE on this platform.* Although there is some truth in this answer, I think it's a partial truth and the concept needs to be elaborated.

First, let's define what is *free*. Today there's a common misconception of open source products being like "free lunch". They can be so for a student who's learning these technologies, but for the real world, open source means you don't pay a license fee to develop/roll in production certain software.

This obviously doesn't mean that the software hasn't got a cost. Moreover, if you don't want to risk breaking your service level agreement, you usually sign a contract with the owner of the open source software so that it guarantees quick and decisive support.

From the financial point of view, this is the first important difference with a commercial product. If you start a project, running a product such as JBoss AS, you don't have an immediate entrance fee. You can even dispense with commercial assistance if you are confident that your technicians will be able to solve any issue. Whatever you choose, this policy is much more flexible than a commercial contract, which requires an immediate financial commitment.

That's better than simply saying: *I like JBoss because it's free*.

The second and, in my opinion, the most important reason is the worldwide spread of the product. Today JBoss is the most used application server and it has been not only built with the collaborative efforts of many developers around the world, but also with simple contributions of users who request new features. This boils down to the actual nature of the success of JBoss. The real driving force of this product is its community of users, while vendor products are usually designed around commercial or marketing schemas.

As an example of this, you can see that JBoss Application Server is a Java EE compatible server, but you can freely add or remove modules from the application server, thus creating a customized product for your specific needs. It is the flexibility and willingness to adapt that has brought JBoss AS this far, and it will be this trait that will drive the application server full speed into the future.

What you will get in this book

This book is an intense guide to creating professional Java EE applications with JBoss AS 5.0. Packed with example code and written in a friendly, earthy style, this book will act as a handy guide to take you from the basics to the skills that will make you a JBoss developer to be reckoned with.

We think that studying good code samples is one of the best ways to learn, so we included as many as we could. We also wanted this book to be a quick reference to solve most common issues—a book you can have on your desk and turn to when you have a doubt.

JBoss big bang

JBoss AS is an open source Java EE-based application server. The project's first milestone dates back to early 1999, when Marc Fleury developed an open source product named JBoss that was a simple EJB 1.0 container. Since then, the project has been incorporated in a company named JBoss Group. In April 2006 the company was acquired by Red Hat Inc., which started providing professional services to the product. As a matter of fact, you now have two main references for JBoss products—`http://www.jboss.org`, which is the community of developers where you can freely download products and join forums, and the commercial site `http://www.jboss.com`, which is targeted at commercial support for the product.

Introduction

This is where our journey begins. In this chapter, we'll learn how to set up our environment for developing applications on JBoss AS correctly. Installation of the components is not particularly tricky, but it needs a few steps to be performed and quite a lot of Kbytes to be downloaded.

This is our checklist:

- Install the appropriate **Java Development Kit (JDK)** for running JBoss AS
- Install JBoss AS 5.0
- Install the **Eclipse** development environment
- Install the JBoss Tools plugins needed for developing applications

The products listed in this chapter are the latest versions at the time of writing and we diligently updated it at every new release. Don't worry if a new stable release of these products is released in the next months; all you have to do is adapt the chapter instructions to the newest file names.

Installing the Java environment

JBoss is a pure Java application server, so as you might imagine it needs a virtual machine for the Java Platform to run on.

At the time of writing, JBoss AS 5 is distributed in two flavors, one that is suited for Java 1.5 and another version that has been specifically designed for Java 1.6.

The choice of **Java Virtual Machine (JVM)** is yours otherwise, but we do recommend considering the Java 1.6, that has just undergone the 16th update at the time of writing. Most benchmarks available on the Internet exhibit a roughly 40 percent performance improvement by upgrading from Java 1.5 to Java 1.6. Additionally, Java SE 5.0 reached its **End of Service Life (EOSL)** on November 3, 2009, which is the date of the final publicly available update of version 5.0. So you are highly encouraged to design your applications with Java 1.6.

Java 1.6 has enhanced performance in many areas of the platform. Improvements include synchronization, performance optimizations, compiler performance optimizations, the new Parallel Compaction Collector, better ergonomics for the Concurrent Low Pause Collector, and application startup performance.

(http://java.sun.com/performance/reference/whitepapers/6_performance.html)

So let's move on to the Sun download page: http://java.sun.com/javase/downloads/index.jsp.

Choose to download the latest JDK/JRE, which is for JDK 1.6 Update 16.

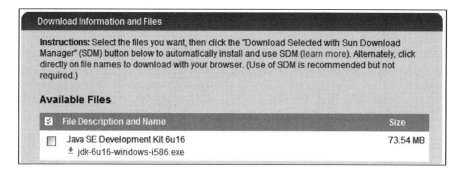

Is JRE enough ?

Yes! JBoss 5 ships with a set of libraries called **Eclipse Java development tools (JDT)** that allow dynamic compilation of classes at runtime. However, we still suggest you to download the full JDK installation, in case you need to compile your classes with plain *javac* anywhere else.

Once the download is complete, run the executable file to start the installation.

```
jdk-6-windows-i586.exe       # Windows
sh jdk-6u12-linux-i586.bin   # Linux
```

If you are installing on a Linux/Unix box, you can safely accept all the defaults given to you by the setup wizard. Windows users should stay away from the default C:\Program Files that leads to some issues when you are referencing the core libraries. An installation path such as C:\Software\Java or simply C:\Java is a better alternative.

When the installation is complete, we need to update a couple of settings on the computer so that it can interact with Java.

The most important setting is **JAVA_HOME** that is directly referenced by JBoss startup script.

Windows XP/2000 users should right-click on **My Computer** and select **Properties** from the context menu. On the **Advanced** tab, click the **Environment Variables** button. Then, in the **System variables** box click **New**. Give the new variable a name of **JAVA_HOME**, and a value of the path to your JDK installation, probably something like **C:\Java\jdk1.6.0_16**.

For Windows Vista users

Because of increased security in Windows Vista, standard users must have **User Account Control** (UAC) turned on to change environment variables and the change must be completed through **User Accounts**. In the **User Accounts** window, under **Tasks**, select **Change my environment variables**. Use the **New**, **Edit**, or **Delete** buttons to add, change, or delete environment variables.

Now it's the turn of the **Path** variable. Double-click on the **Path** system variable. In the box that pops up, navigate to the end of the **Variable value** line, add a semicolon to the end, then add the path to your JDK. This will be something like %JAVA_HOME% \bin.

Unix/Linux users can add the following commands in the user's profile scripts:

```
export JAVA_HOME=/installDir/jdk1.6.0_16
export PATH=$JAVA_HOME/bin:$PATH
```

As a final note, you should consider setting the JBOSS_HOME environment variable, which points to the root of the application server. (In our case, it would be C:\jboss-5.0.0.GA for Windows users.)

If you don't set this variable, the startup script simply guesses the location of JBoss AS by climbing one step up from the bin folder.

Installing JBoss AS 5

JBoss Application Server can be freely downloaded from the community site:

http://www.jboss.org/jbossas/downloads/.

Then, you'll soon be redirected to the SourceForge site where the project is hosted.

JBoss 5 is released in two different versions: **jboss-5.0.0.GA.zip** and **jboss-5.0.0-jdk6.zip**. The former version is the appropriate distribution if you are using JDK 1.5; the latter is the targeted release for JDK 1.6. Choose the appropriate distribution and start downloading.

At the time of writing, the newer stable release 5.1.0 of JBoss AS is available. The most important changes introduced by the new release include a new **web administration console** and the reactivation of the **cluster farming** option. For the purpose of running the examples of this book, you can safely use both the releases 5.0.0 and 5.1.0.

The installation of JBoss is simply a matter of extracting the compressed archive. Windows users can simply use any uncompressed utility, such as WinZip or WinRAR, taking care to choose a folder which doesn't contain empty spaces. Unix/Linux should use the `unzip` shell command to explode the archive:

```
$ unzip jboss5.0.0.GA-jdk6.zip
```

Security warning:

Unix/Linux users should be aware that JBoss AS does not require root privileges, as none of the default ports used by JBoss are below the 1024 privileged port range. To reduce the risk of users gaining root privileges through the JBoss AS, install and run JBoss as a non-root user.

Starting up JBoss AS

After you have installed JBoss, it is wise to perform a simple startup test to validate that there are no major problems with your Java VM/operating system combination. To test your installation, move to the `bin` directory of your `JBOSS_HOME` directory. Once there, issue the following command:

```
run.bat    # Windows users
$ run.sh    # Linux/Unix users
```

Here's a sample JBoss AS 5 startup console:

```
C:\WINDOWS\system32\cmd.exe

16:56:13,486 INFO  [ConnectionFactory] org.jboss.jms.server.connectionfactory.Co
nnectionFactory@1ca2026 started
16:56:13,517 INFO  [QueueService] Queue[/queue/DLQ] started, fullSize=200000, pa
geSize=2000, downCacheSize=2000
16:56:13,517 INFO  [ConnectionFactory] Connector bisocket://127.0.0.1:4457 has l
easing enabled, lease period 10000 milliseconds
16:56:13,517 INFO  [ConnectionFactory] org.jboss.jms.server.connectionfactory.Co
nnectionFactory@129a7d started
16:56:13,533 INFO  [QueueService] Queue[/queue/ExpiryQueue] started, fullSize=20
0000, pageSize=2000, downCacheSize=2000
16:56:13,533 INFO  [ConnectionFactory] Connector bisocket://127.0.0.1:4457 has l
easing enabled, lease period 10000 milliseconds
16:56:13,533 INFO  [ConnectionFactory] org.jboss.jms.server.connectionfactory.Co
nnectionFactory@96cf2f started
16:56:13,892 INFO  [ConnectionFactoryBindingService] Bound ConnectionManager 'jb
oss.jca:service=ConnectionFactoryBinding,name=JmsXA' to JNDI name 'java:JmsXA'
16:56:14,064 INFO  [TomcatDeployment] deploy, ctxPath=/, vfsUrl=ROOT.war
16:56:14,408 INFO  [TomcatDeployment] deploy, ctxPath=/jmx-console, vfsUrl=jmx-c
onsole.war
16:56:14,736 INFO  [Http11Protocol] Starting Coyote HTTP/1.1 on http-127.0.0.1-8
080
16:56:14,814 INFO  [AjpProtocol] Starting Coyote AJP/1.3 on ajp-127.0.0.1-8009
16:56:14,829 INFO  [ServerImpl] JBoss (Microcontainer) [5.0.0.GA (build: SVNTag=
JBoss_5_0_0_GA date=200812041714)] Started in 1m:32s:361ms
```

The previous command starts up JBoss AS and binds the application server to the localhost network interface. This means JBoss cannot be accessed from another machine in your network. The first thing you should learn is how to bind JBoss to the IP address of your machine; this can be achieved with the -b option as follows:

```
run.bat -b 192.168.10.1      # Windows Users
run.sh -b 192.168.10.1       # Unix/linux Users
```

Here the server is bound to the IP address 192.168.10.1.

 Using the IP address of the machine will also exclude the "localhost" network interface, which will no longer be accessible. If you want to bind your server to all available network interfaces, you can use -b 0.0.0.0.

You can verify that the server is reachable from the network by simply pointing the browser to http://192.168.10.1:8080.

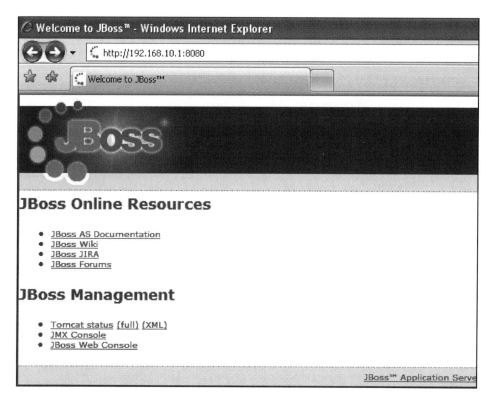

Introducing the twiddle utility

One useful command-line utility that ships with JBoss is **twiddle**. This is a needful shell command located inside the JBOSS_HOME/bin folder. It can be used if you don't have a graphical terminal where you can manage JBoss, or if you want to control JBoss with shell scripts.

The syntax of twiddle is basically built into 3 pieces:

```
twiddle [options] <command> [command_arguments]
```

Here's an example command line for checking JBoss status:

```
twiddle -s 192.168.0.1 get "jboss.system:type=Server"
Started
```

Stopping JBoss

Probably the easiest way to stop JBoss is sending an interrupt signal with the *Ctrl + C* key combination.

However, if your JBoss process was launched in the background or is running on another machine (see the next section), then you have to use the shutdown command from the bin folder:

```
shutdown -S            # Windows Users
./shutdown.sh -S       # Unix/Linux Users
```

Stopping JBoss on a remote machine

The shutdown script can also be used to shut down a remote JBoss server, contacting the **JBoss naming provider** on the remote host.

```
./shutdown.sh -s jnp://remoteHost:1099
Shutdown message has been posted to the server.
Server shutdown may take a while - check logfiles for completion
```

Unexpected shutdown?

Unix users sometimes reported unexpected shutdown of JBoss server.

For those who are not familiar with the Unix environment, when the terminal hangs up (drops the connection) the operating system sends a SIGHUP signal to all the programs that are launched from that terminal.

As Sun JVM monitors for SIGHUP signal, it can be interpreted as a signal to shut down. The workaround is to add the -Xrs option when launching JBoss. This is an option of the JVM, which reduces the use of operating system signals by the Java Virtual Machine.

Installing Eclipse

Eclipse is the most popular environment for developing Java Enterprise applications. You can explore the Eclipse universe at `www.eclipse.org`.

The download area is reachable at `http://www.eclipse.org/downloads/`.

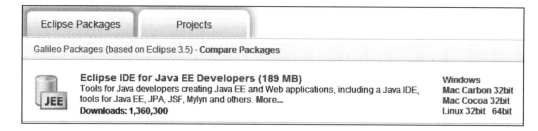

As you can see, there are several distributions available—what we suggest for your best programming experience is the **Eclipse IDE for Java EE Developers**. This will cost your hard disk a bit more in terms of space, but your productivity will benefit a lot from it.

Now choose the distribution that's appropriate for your OS. Once the download is complete, Windows users can simply unzip the `eclipse-jee-galileo-win32.zip`, while Linux users can use the `tar` command to uncompress the `.tar.gz` archive.

```
tar -zxvf eclipse-jee-galileo-linux-gtk.tar.gz
```

Unzipping the archive will create a root directory named `eclipse`. In that folder, you will find the Eclipse application (a big blue dot). We recommend that you create a shortcut on the desktop to simplify the launching of Eclipse.

Running Eclipse is simply a matter of executing the following command:

```
eclipse
```

This command is executed from the root directory of Eclipse.

When you launch Eclipse, you'll be prompted to enter your workspace location. That's the repository where your projects are stored. If you check the option **Use this as the default and do not ask again**, Eclipse will not bother asking you about your workspace location every time you launch Eclipse. However, you can change it from the menu at anytime, by going to **File | Switch Workspace | Other**.

How much memory should I give to Eclipse?

By default, Eclipse will allocate up to 256 megabytes of Java heap memory. This should be enough for most development tasks. However, depending on the JRE that you are running, the number of additional plugins you are using, and the number of files you will be working with, you could conceivably have to customize Eclipse settings.

Open the `eclipse.ini` file located under the Eclipse home directory, and add the following lines before starting Eclipse:

```
-vmargs -Xms512m -Xmx512m -XX:PermSize=128m -XX:
MaxPermSize=128m
```

The above configuration is suggested for a machine running 1024 MB of memory. As performance boost, you should consider also turning off some inessential options such as:

- Uncheck the **Enable Capture** option in **Window | Preferences | Usage Data Collector**.

- Still under Eclipse **Preferences**, in the **Validation** menu, turn on the **Suspend all validators** option.

- Ignore the spell checking features by checking out the **Enable spell checking** option in **Window | Preferences | General | Editors | Text Editors | Spelling**.

Plugins: The heart of Eclipse

The most important architectural characteristics of Eclipse is the plugin architecture. A **plugin** in Eclipse is a component that provides a certain type of service within the context of the Eclipse workbench. The Eclipse IDE itself is built with a number of plugins, which are dependent on each other, so that you can customize your development environment exactly for your needs.

Installing JBoss Tools plugins

JBoss plugins for Eclipse are part of the JBoss suite. You can find them in the JBoss Tools project, which is an umbrella project for all the JBoss developer plugins. JBoss Tools plugins can be downloaded from:

```
http://www.jboss.org/tools
```

The installation of the JBoss tools can be performed in two ways—one is directly from your Eclipse IDE, the other choice (covered in the next section) is the manual installation of single plugin files.

So, once you have started Eclipse, move onto the last menu option **Help**, and select **Install New Software** (former releases of Eclipse name this menu option **Software Updates**). In the upper combo box, you need to select the repository for your Eclipse plugins. JBoss Tools is not installed by default, so you need to add a link to JBoss Tools trunk. The list of available update sites can be found at `http://www.jboss.org/tools/download`.

Once there, select the release that matches with your Eclipse distribution. For example, if you have downloaded the Eclipse 3.5 (Galileo) release, there's a development update available at `http://download.jboss.org/jbosstools/updates/development/`.

 For learning, it is appropriate to use a development update. However, consider sticking to a stable release of JBoss Tools for your cutting-edge software projects.

Once added, expand the JBoss Tools update site and you'll see the list of available plugins. For the purpose of this book, all you need is the JBoss AS plugin, the Hibernate plugin, and JBoss Tools RichFaces plugin.

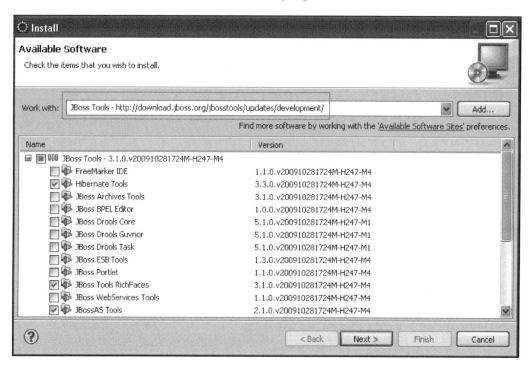

Check them and click on the **Next** button, which will confirm your selections. Finish and wait for the time necessary to download the tools. Once the download is completed you will be prompted to restart Eclipse.

Installing JBoss Tools plugins manually

You can mimic the behavior of the **Update Manager** by installing the JBoss Tools plugins manually into your Eclipse installation.

The list of JBoss Tools plugins is available at `http://www.jboss.org/tools/download`.

Download the single JBoss AS plugin and Hibernate plugin zip files.

The structure of the single plugin's archive resembles the same structure of your Eclipse installation:

```
eclipse/

    features/

    plugins/
```

Once the download completes, you simply need to extract the plugins into the Eclipse installation directory.

For example, if you are using the command line and your Eclipse installation directory is named `eclipse`, navigate to the directory above your Eclipse installation and extract the archive using the `unzip` command.

```
unzip JBossTools-2.1.2.GA-ALL-linux-gtk.zip
```

Automatic versus manual installation

Automatic installation is the easiest solution because the wizard takes care to place all the necessary files in the right place, so we recommend it for developers who are approaching Eclipse with JBoss. However, manual setup is the preferred choice if you have to perform lots of installations for your developers because you can easily create a script that simply extracts the required files on multiple partitions. Manual installation is also the preferred choice when you need to change the plugin versions because switching from one release to another merely requires a file substitution.

If you are not too confident with shell commands, you might consider a third alternative of downloading the `.zip` files containing the plugins, and pointing to the archive from the **Software Updates** menu as **New Local Site**.

Connecting Eclipse with JBoss

We're almost done with the configuration. The last piece of the puzzle is connecting Eclipse with our installation of JBoss. Eclipse enterprise provides some out of the box facets to manage most application servers. However, we'll use the features of **JBoss Perspective**, which offers a richer set of options.

What is an Eclipse perspective?

A perspective is a visual container for a set of views and editors. These components are specific to that perspective and are not shared with other perspectives. You can think about it like a page within a photo book.

Therefore, the JBoss Perspective is a special view designed specifically for JBoss AS.

You can reach it from the menu. Select **Window**, then **Open Perspective** and **Other**. Select **JBoss AS** from the next menu.

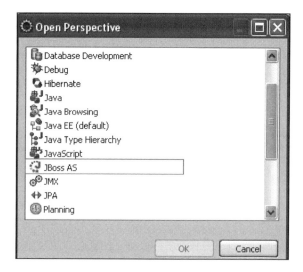

Now a tiny little panel will appear in left-corner section of the screen. This panel holds the **JBoss Server View**. Right-click on it and select **New | Server**.

You'll be guided by an intuitive wizard that will at first ask you to select the **Server's host name**, the **JBoss Community AS release**, and the **Runtime Environment**.

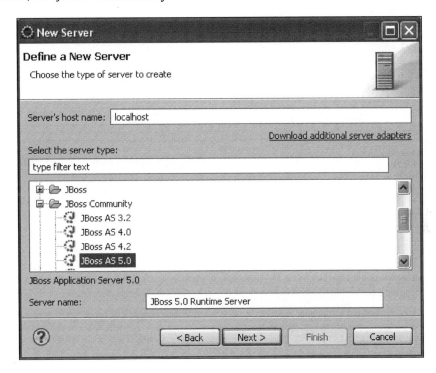

 Deploy-only servers

Notice that among the available servers there's a **Deploy-Only** option that will simply point to the deploy directory. You can use this option if you don't need to start/stop/debug your AS, but simply deploy applications.

In the next window, you will have to complete your server configuration by adding a JBoss Runtime.

What is a Runtime Environment ? Put it simply, it is a pointer to the JBoss server installation. It provides to Eclipse all classpath information that is required for each kind of project. It also communicates to the server's components, all the necessary information to start and stop the server.

Basically, we need to choose a **Name** for our environment, point to the **Home Directory** where JBoss AS has been unpacked, and finally select the location where JDK/JRE has been installed.

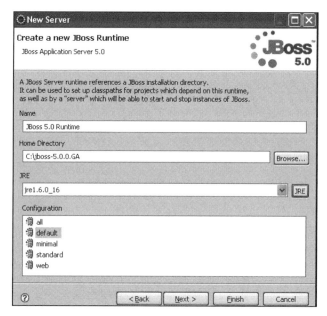

More is better

It is a good idea to create several runtime environments if you are going to test your project across different configurations. Remember to give a meaningful description to your runtime environment. For example, it's better to have a "JBoss Development" and "JBoss Production" rather than "JBoss Runtime 1" and "JBoss Runtime 2"

Once you have completed the selections, click **Finish** and your new runtime will be added to the list and can now be targeted by a JBoss server. Right-click on your new server icon and verify that the application server starts correctly.

Summary

In this chapter, we've completed all the required steps to set up our environment. Most of the installation process was completed using intuitive wizards and so should be accessible to inexperienced users.

Your initial configuration will be suited for an initial tour of JBoss. However, in real-world projects you may benefit from proper customization of the application server. In the next chapter, we will dissect JBoss Application Server structure.

2
What's New in JBoss AS 5?

Smooth seas do not make skillful sailors — an African saying

Java Enterprise middleware has matured a lot in the last few years. The current release (1.5) of the Enterprise Specification signifies the end of Java's era of Enterprise arrogance — "We are complex because we are powerful" — and the beginning of a new era based on simplicity. This has created new opportunities for some open source products that provide state-of-the-art technology but at a lower cost.

JBoss AS is the leader of the open source application servers and, according to a recent survey, the most used application server by the community of developers. What is the reason for this success? First of all, JBoss AS makes it easy for developers to leverage Enterprise features without undue complexity by focusing on "transparent middleware". This means providing services such as **JBoss Clustering**, which requires no changes or design-time modifications to the code in order to benefit from.

The second important reason is that JBoss AS is widely recognized for supporting the latest standards. Actually, it is the first open source application server to achieve J2EE 1.4 certification with JBoss AS version 4.0. This demonstrates the strength and speed of its Professional Open Source development model.

Increasingly, JBoss is not only setting the pace in implementing standards, but is also becoming a leader in setting industry standards. JBoss was recently elected to the executive committee of the **Java Community Process (JCP)**. In the latest years, JBoss has been driving the development of Java Enterprise including voting on all **Java Specification Requests (JSRs)**. Indeed, JBoss sits on the expert group for **Enterprise Java Beans (EJB)** version 3.0 and was one of the first application servers to release a compliant EJB 3.0 release.

The current stable release of JBoss is 5.1.0 (at the time of writing), but we will refer to 5.0.0, which was released on December 5, 2008, after a three year long marathon. The new application server was long awaited by the community of developers and, as with all major refactorings, its release took a bit longer than expected. However, the effort needed to release the new version was justified by the number of innovations. Changing the internal architecture and replacing the guts of the application server, while maintaining backward compatibility with the majority of the existing services, was a cumbersome task.

The application server kernel has been rewritten completely based on the **JBoss Microcontainer** project. JBoss Microcontainer is a refactoring of the earlier JBoss **Java Management Extension (JMX)** kernel and delivers something that the competitors tried to produce for a long time—a completely modular and scalable POJO-based foundation. Support for JMX in JBoss AS 5 remains strong, and MBean services written against the old Microkernel are expected to work.

The Microcontainer integrates with JBoss AOP—a programming paradigm that increases modularity by allowing the separation of concerns. In fact, JBoss AS 5 is one of the first application servers that intensively uses AOP. The new deployment layer of the application server is heavily influenced by AOP too.

As a matter of fact, JBoss AS 5 is designed around the advanced concept of a **Virtual Deployment Framework (VDF)**, which applies aspect-oriented design to the deployment layer.

Aspect-oriented deployers operate in a chain over a **virtual file system (VFS)**, analyze deployments, and produce metadata to be used by the JBoss Microcontainer, which in turn instantiates and wires together the various pieces of a deployment, controlling their life cycle and dependencies. This helps you to have have full control over the deployment cycle of your application. For example, you can customize the structure of your application so that a non-standard Java EE application can be deployed on JBoss. We'll see this later.

Application server features

We'll divide our journey into the new features of JBoss in a few steps. First, we'll inspect the core modules, which are the foundation of the application server. Then we shall analyze the directory structure of the application server. At this point we will have enough elements to draw some conclusions.

The core modules of JBoss AS 5

JBoss AS 5 is a combination of stable technologies. Some of these have been adopted by earlier 4.x releases such as the EJB 3.0 technology, others are a substitute like the new messaging system that replaces the older JBoss MQ.

JBoss AS 5 puts in your hands the lastest generation of Java Enterprise frameworks without the need to install additional libraries. In the next chapters, you'll learn how this can greatly improve things from a productivity standpoint—developing Java Enterprise applications has never been easier!

Cutting edge EJB container

JBoss AS was one of the first application servers to adopt EJB 3.0 specifications. The EJB 3.0 model simplifies development by removing the requirements for home interfaces, deployment descriptors, and callback methods, and by adopting regular Java classes and business interfaces as EJBs.

JBoss EJB 3.0 framework uses, behind the scenes, Hibernate 3.x. as persistence engine. Hibernate's **Entity Manager** implements the programming interfaces and life cycle rules as defined by the EJB 3.0 persistence specification. You may use a combination of EJB 3 interfaces or even pure native Hibernate, depending on the business and technical needs of your project. You can, at all times, fall back even to native JDBC while adopting the EJB 3 paradigm.

> In the third quarter of 2009, an EJB 3.1-compliant release of the JBoss EJB stack is planned, which will add many new features such as asynchronous session beans, optional session bean interfaces, singleton EJBs, and much more. For more details, check out the EJB 3 project home page at: http://www.jboss.org/ejb3.

The new messaging provider

JBoss Messaging is the new high-performance JMS provider included with JBoss AS 5 as the default messaging provider. It replaces the old JBossMQ, which was shipped with JBoss AS 4.x series. JBM supports clustered queues and topics out of the box, along with transparent fail-over and intelligent message redistribution. Messages can be replicated in memory across nodes avoiding disk I/O, or be persisted to any popular relational database using paging techniques with support for very large messages. You will hardly find any other Java open source messaging implementation that can beat that level of functionality and performance.

Rock solid transaction manager

JBoss AS 5 ships with **JBossTS** (the transaction manager purchased from Arjuna). This transaction engine is rock solid with more than 20 years of expertise in transaction management. It was the first **JTA (Java Transaction API)** and the first **JTS (Java Transaction Service)** transaction management implementation on the market, and its implementation fully supports recovery and logging. So, it's an amazing expertise there.

Enhanced web container

JBoss Web is the web container in JBoss AS 5, which is based on the Apache Tomcat 6.0 project and includes the **Apache Portable Runtime (APR)** and Tomcat native technologies to achieve scalability and performance characteristics that match and exceed the Apache HTTP server. The "web" configuration is now also one out of the box server configurations that ships with the application server. It aims at providing a lightweight JBoss HTTP Container, along with additional features such as **Java Persistence API (JPA)**, and JTA or **J2EE Connector Architecture (JCA)**.

JBoss Web Services 3.0

JBoss AS comes with JBossWS 3.0, which fully supports **JAX-WS/JAX-RPC** standards, attachments with **XOP** and **SwA**. JBossWS has been designed as a pluggable architecture, which allows the replacement of the underlying Web Services stack that had several compatibility issues, so you can swap JBossWS Native with Sun Metro or Apache CXF. Thus, you should be able to use the web services stack best suited to the problem at hand.

Improved clustering support

One big improvement in the clustering area is the use of the new Hibernate/JBoss Cache integration for second-level caching that was introduced in Hibernate 3.3. Used along with JBoss AS 5's new **CacheManager** service, this combination provides a flexible framework that allows use of separate caches for entities (invalidation cache) and queries (replication cache).

The application server structure

The structure of the application server has changed quite a lot from the 4.x release. Let's first have a look at the new server directory tree and the corresponding JBoss system properties:

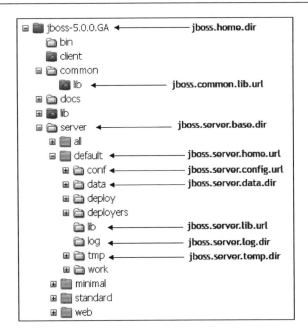

Impressed by all stuff we've got here? If you are not familiar with the JBoss Application Server, you might feel a bit disoriented. However, the following tables will be your initial reference to the application server. The first table scratches the surface of the root directory structure, giving a short description of the content of the individual folders:

Directory	Description
bin	This directory contains the scripts necessary to manage the startup and shutdown of the server. Along with these scripts, there are a few utilities for Web Services and server management.
client	This directory contains the client libraries needed to run client applications (such as EJB clients and Web Service clients).
common	This directory hosts the lib folder, which is the new repository for the common libraries used by all application server configurations.
docs	In spite of its name, this folder doesn't contain JBoss documentation. It hosts the XML schemas used by the various XML configuration files and useful JMS, JTA, and DataSource configuration examples that can be used as templates.
lib	This is the repository for all JBoss bootstrap libraries. Here is the new Microcontainer along with the earlier JMX kernel.
server	This directory is the home of all server configurations. Here you can find the built-in server configurations (minimal, default, standard, web, and all). Each server configuration contains the set of directories that are mentioned in the next table.

Drilling down further into each server configuration, we see yet another common hierarchy below. The directory `server` contains all the code and configuration information regarding the services provided by the particular configuration. The following table resumes the content and description of the directory:

Directory	Description
conf	This is the configuration directory of the single server configurations. Configuration files will be discussed in detail in the chapter *Customizing JBoss AS Services*.
data	The `data` directory is a location available for use by services that want to store content in the filesystem.
deploy	The `deploy` directory is the default location for deployment of JBoss services.
deployers	The `deployers` directory contains all of the JBoss AS services that are used to recognize and deploy different application and archive types.
lib	This folder contains the common libraries of all applications. You can still use this directory for storing configuration-specific libraries. For example, in the "all" configuration this folder contains some clustering-specific libraries such as JGroups and JBoss Cache.
log	The `log` directory is the default directory into which the bootstrap logging service places its logs.
tmp	The `tmp` directory is the location to which deployments are copied for local use.
work	Used by JBoss Web Server (the web container that comes prepackaged with JBoss AS) to store compiled JSP files and other temporary data.

The next generation application server

The major innovations in the AS 5.0 converge into the following four areas:

- The introduction of the new Microcontainer kernel
- The new library configuration
- The addition of new server configurations
- The introduction of the virtual file system and the `deployers` folder

Let's see them all in detail.

From JMX to the Microcontainer

Change is the law of life. And those who look only to the past or present are certain to miss the future. – J.F.Kennedy.

Before the 5.0 release, the backbone of the JBoss AS was the JMX API, which provided a modular way to integrate components, containers, and plugins. In order to provide a new service, you had to declare the service as an MBean service, provide some configuration, and then load it into JBoss. The JMX components might subsequently be administered using the JMX API or some utilities such as **twiddle** or a web application named **jmx-console**.

This approach was an important milestone in the JBoss project; however, it suffers from a major drawback: actually services deployed to the JMX kernel are tightly coupled with the application server and can hardly be tested outside of the container.

The answer to this issue is in the JBoss Microcontainer kernel that allows the services to be created using **Plain Old Java Objects** (**POJOs**), which can be deployed into a Java Platform, Standard Edition (Java SE) runtime environment in a controlled manner to create a customized environment for your applications. These services, as well as MBean services, are fully managed to ensure that new services cannot be deployed until the services they depend on have first been deployed. Also, undeploying a service causes all dependent services to be undeployed first in order to maintain the integrity of the system.

One great advantage of the Microcontainer approach is that you can build every Java service on top of it (and of course remove the unwanted services). These services, being POJO, can be moved onto any other environment such as Tomcat or Glassfish without hassle.

In common with other lightweight containers, JBoss Microcontainer uses dependency injection to wire individual POJOs together to create services. Configuration is performed using either annotations or XML, depending on where the information is best located. Finally, unit testing is made extremely simple, thanks to a helper class that extends JUnit to set up the test environment, allowing you to access POJOs and services from your test methods using just a few lines of code.

The new library configuration

The release 5.0 of the application server introduces some important changes in the location of the client and server libraries. Starting from the client libraries, the `jbossall-client.jar` library that used to bundle the core JBoss client libraries is now an empty archive that references the client libraries through the `Class-Path` entry in the manifest file. This allows swapping included libraries (for example, `jboss-javaee.jar`) without having to repackage `jbossall-client.jar`.

The downside of this new configuration is that most IDEs don't scan the libraries indicated in the manifest entry, so you have to manually insert all the JARs needed.

Which are the libraries used by my project?

This issue has been a headache for most developers, and it is generally solved empirically by adding the required libraries to your project at every `ClassNotFoundException`. If you want to save time and health, then consider downloading the **JBoss Tattletale tool** (`http://www.jboss.org/tattletale`), which is a simple web application that identifies dependencies of any application along with many other features.

However, the most important change to the application server structure is the introduction of a common repository for the server configuration. This repository is located in the `common/lib` folder of your `JBOSS_HOME` directory.

Copying a library into the `common/lib` folder will make it available **to all server configurations** (except for the "minimal" configuration). This prevents your JBoss AS installation from inflating your hard disk with duplicate libraries for each server configuration.

The earlier location of libraries, `server/xxx/lib`, can still be used, but it is advised to use it only for libraries that are specific for a server configuration.

Moving to the `JBOSS_HOME/lib` folder, which hosts the bootstrap classes, we notice some changes here. This directory contains the classes needed to start the new kernel of JBoss with the introduction of the Microcontainer. As you can see from the libraries in this folder, JBoss AS 5 relies heavily on the AOP model. Along with the new kernel, the common libraries used by the kernel have also swapped from `jboss-common.jar` to `jboss-common-core.jar`.

The following screenshot summarizes the new library configuration:

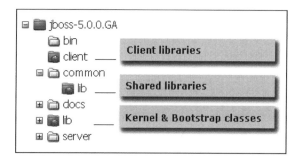

JBoss AS 5 server configurations

JBoss AS 5 contains five different out of the box server configurations: minimal, default, all, standard, and web. Out of these, the standard and web configurations have been introduced with the new release of the application server, so we will first have a look at them and then we will briefly recap the preexisting server configurations.

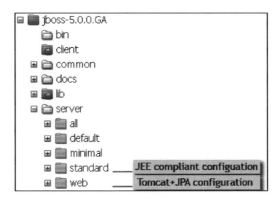

The "standard" configuration

The standard folder hosts the configuration that has been tested for Java EE 5.0 compliance. The major differences with the other server configurations is that call by value and deployment isolation are enabled by default, along with support for **RMI-IIOP** and **jUDDI**.

If you feel confused by all these weird words, here's a quick drill:

Call by value: It is a requirement of the EJB specification that parameters passed during the method call be passed **by value,** so that the EJB receives a copy of any object parameters (and the caller receives a copy of the return object, if applicable).

The use of call by value, however, is very inefficient. With call by value, each method invocation is **marshalled** — the parameters are turned into **ObjectStream**. Once the invocation reaches the EJB container, the result is unmarshalled and the return value is turned back into **ObjectStream**.

 In terms of percentage, it typically means that method invocations **take 10 times more cpu** than call by reference.

RMI-IIOP: This is a protocol developed by Sun and IBM to deliver CORBA distributed computing to the Java platform. The middleware that promotes communication between systems by transforming data structures from and to byte sequences is called an object request broker (**ORB**). JBoss AS ships with a free implementation of CORBA standard named **JacORB**.

jUDDI: This is an XML-based registry for publishing and discovering services or software applications over the Internet. A web application is built-in with the standard configuration for testing, publishing, and inquiring of Web Services. You can have a look at it by pointing your browser to: `http://localhost:8080/juddi`.

The changes related to RMI-IIOP and jUDDI support are reflected in the following files:

- `conf/jndi.properties`

  In the default server configuration this file references the `NamingContext-Factory`, which is a factory implementation for connecting to the JNDI service. When using Sun's CORBA services it is necessary to set the global context factory to `org.jboss.iiop.naming.ORBInitialContextFactory`, which sets the ORB to JBoss's ORB.

- `conf/jacorb.properties`

  This file contains the JacORB configuration file.

- `lib/jacorb.jar`

  These are the libraries needed for JacORB applications.

- `deploy/iiop-service.xml`

  This service provides IIOP invocation support.

- `lib/avalon-framework.jar`

  These Avalon libraries are a required dependency, so they are added in the `lib` folder.

The "web" configuration

The web configuration is a new experimental lightweight configuration created around JBoss Web that will follow the developments of the Java EE 6 web profile. Besides being a servlet/JSP container (and this is the most relevant difference with a pure Tomcat Web Server), it provides support for JPA and JTA/JCA.

Therefore, with this configuration you are now able to deploy your persistence layer and access it from the web container.

The major limitation of this configuration is that its applications can be accessed only through the HTTP channel. Bear in mind that this configuration is not Java EE certified and will most likely change in the following releases.

The former server configurations

The other configurations were introduced in the early releases of JBoss, so they should be known to majority of developers. Let's again take a glimpse at the `server` directory:

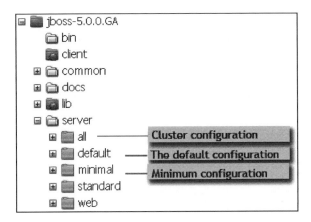

As shown in the screenshot, the pre-existing server configurations are as follows:

- **minimal**: This is the minimal configuration—the bare minimum services required to start JBoss. It starts the logging service, a JNDI server, and a URL deployment scanner to find new deployments. This is what you would use if you want to use JBoss to start your own services without any other Java EE technologies. This is just the bare server. There is no web container, no EJB or JMS support. This is not a Java EE-compatible configuration.

- **default**: This is the basic JBoss configuration containing a default set of services. It has the most frequently used services required to deploy a Java EE application. It does not include the **Java API for XML Registries (JAXR)** service, the **Internet Inter-ORB Protocol (IIOP)** service, or any of the clustering services.
- **all**: This configuration is a full Java EE server profile with Enterprise extensions, such as clustering and RMI-IIOP.

Creating a custom server configuration

JBoss AS 5.0 offers a wide choice of server configurations. However, you are not limited to the existing built-in configurations. You can create your own custom configuration that suits your needs best.

You have two choices. You can either add an empty directory under JBOSS_HOME\server and create all the infrastructure beneath, or preferably (as we suggest) start from the existing configuration that is closest to your needs and then add/remove the services.

The following table summarizes the modules installed in the single server configurations, so you can decide which configuration is closest to the one you have in mind:

Module	minimal	web	default	standard	all
Microcontainer	X	X	X	X	X
Naming service	X	X	X	X	X
Log4j	X	X	X	X	X
Deployment scanner	X	X	X	X	X
JPA		X	X	X	X
EJB container			X	X	X
JCA support		X	X	X	X
JMS			X	X	X
Mail service			X	X	X
HSQL DB		X	X	X	X
JBoss WS			X	X	X
XA transactions		X	X	X	X
Monitoring services			X	X	X
Quartz service			X	X	X
Clustering support					X
RMI-IIOP and jUDDI				X	X

The name of the new directory you created matches the name of the server configuration. You will need to pass the server configuration name to instruct JBoss to use the new configuration. For example, if your new configuration directory is named `performance` then you would need to start JBoss using:

```
run  -c performance          # Windows users
$ ./run.sh -c performance        # Unix users
```

The starting point: JBoss AS service map

If you need to customize your server configuration, the first step is identifying which are the libraries and configuration needed to start a specific service. This serves different purposes, such as adding new services to your JBoss AS or simply skimming your configuration by reducing unwanted services.

Here you have a comprehensive list of core JBoss AS services and the corresponding libraries:

Service	server/<node>/deploy	server/<node>/deployers/
EJB 3	`ejb3-connectors-jboss-beans. xmlejb3-container-jboss-beans. xml ejb3-interceptors-aop.xml`	`jboss-ejb3-endpoint-deployer. jar`
	`ejb3-timerservice-jboss-beans. xmlprofile-service-secured.jar` (JBoss 5.1.0)	
EJB 2	`ejb2-container-jboss-beans.xml`	
	`ejb2-timerservice.xml`	
JBoss WS	`jbossws.sar` [D]	`jbossws.deployer` [D]
Messaging	`messaging` [D]	`messaging-definitions-jboss-beans.xml` (JBoss 5.1.0)
	`jms-ra.rar`	
jUDDI	`juddi-service.sar`	
Key Generator	`uuid-key-generator.sar`	
JBoss Mail	`mail-service.xml`	
	`mail-ra.rar`	
Scheduling	`scheduler-manager-service.xml`	
	`scheduler-service.xml quartz-ra.rar`	
Hypersonic DB	`hsqldb-ds.xml`	
Bsh deployer	`bsh.deployer`	
Hot deployment	`hdscanner-jboss-beans.xml`	

How do you read this table? In the first column (Service) you can find the list of JBoss AS core services. The next two columns describe the files and folders (marked with "D") that need to be added or removed in order to activate or deactivate the service. We have split the file list into two columns, so that the reader can immediately find the right folder location.

Custom configuration sample: Adding JMS to the web configuration

The web configuration is an interesting configuration option. It enables you to run web applications that use the Java Persistence API and Java Transaction API. Let's say it's like a Tomcat + JPA configuration. One thing that could be added with little effort is the JMS server.

Adding the JMS server is not a complicated matter. Let's start from a web configuration: we'll duplicate the web directory structure as follows:

```
$ cd $JBOSS_HOME/server
$ cp -R web webAndJMS
```

Windows users simply need to cut and paste the folder web and rename it to webAndJMS

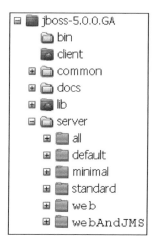

Looking back at our service map, we discover that we need to add the following files to the `deploy` folder:

- `messaging` (folder)
- `jms-ra.rar`

We add the files as follows:

```
$ cp -r $JBOSS_HOME/server/default/deploy/messaging $JBOSS_HOME/server/
webAndJMS/deploy
```

```
$ cp $JBOSS_HOME/server/default/deploy/jms-ra.rar $JBOSS_HOME/server/
webAndJMS/deploy
```

 If you were to use JBoss AS 5.1.0, it would also be required to copy `messaging-definitions-jboss-beans.xml`, which contains the messaging profile definitions, into the `server/xxx/deployers` folder.

So now your `deploy` folder should look like this:

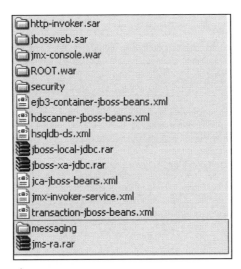

That's all. You now are able to add JMS capabilities to your web applications.

Start the server with the `-c` option:

```
$ cd $JBOSS_HOME/bin
$ run.sh -c webAndJMS
```

This configuration enables your web application to send/receive JMS messages configured on the application server. However, you cannot deploy MDB components as you don't have the EJB container. If you need to further expand this server configuration adding EJB support, then it's likely easier to start from the "default" configuration and maybe remove the services you don't require.

JBoss virtual file system

Deploying an application can be imagined as being similar to when you drop a coin in your office coffee machine—lots of sounds *clatter* in the room but what you see is only the cup of coffee coming out.

What happens when you deploy an application to JBoss ? Well, a few checks need to be done, a first check being on the structure of the deployment. This means finding out if it contains any deployment descriptors and/or classes, and if so where they are located.

Once the structure of a deployment has been determined, then a **DeploymentContext** is built for handling information such as the location of the classes, references to other components, and the location of deployment descriptors.

At this point the actual process of deployment starts. This activity goes through several steps:

- PARSE: Deployment descriptors are parsed into deployment metadata
- DESCRIBE: Dependencies on other deployments or runtime components are determined
- CLASSLOADER: A classloader for the deployment is created
- POST_CLASSLOADER: Any action to be performed after classloader creation
- REAL: Components are deployed into runtime

Once the REAL phase is completed successfully, the application is fully deployed to JBoss. Knowing a bit of theory will help you to understand how the deployment can be tuned to your needs. The actual deployment configuration is located in the new `server/xxx/deployers` folder.

You'll notice this folder is populated with many `*-deployer-beans.xml` files. These files make up the **application deployers**, which are used to deploy a specific type of application. For example, the `ear-deployer-jboss-beans.xml` file contains all the deployment logic for EAR applications.

On the other hand, the `.deployer` folders contain the actual POJO, which are in charge of managing the deployment process for the specific needs of your server.

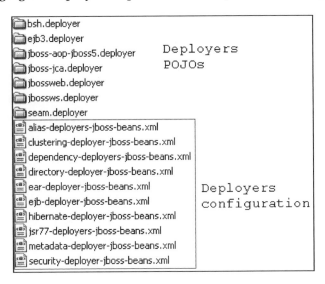

Besides this, the `.deployer` folders can hold some special metadata files in the `META-INF` folder. What are these metadata files? They are some configuration files that can help customize your server configuration. For example, the `jboss-scanning.xml` file can be used to customize the scanning path of the application server, and the `jboss-structure.xml` file allows you to deploy applications with a different filesystem structure. For example, it can be used to deploy on JBoss applications that don't have a standard Java EE structure. If you are interested in some inner details about the new deployer metadata files, you can have a look at `http://www.jboss.org/community/wiki/JBoss5custommetadatafiles`.

Summary

This chapter was an introduction to new JBoss AS 5 functionalities. JBoss AS 5.0 has a completely new architecture based on the Microcontainer with POJOs and AOP, which support dynamic loading and unloading of services on the top of it.

The structure of the application server also had some significant changes with the introduction of the new common/lib repository for the application classes and the add on of the deployers directory, which is the foundation for the new deployment framework, designed around the concept of a virtual file system.

JBoss AS 5.0.0.GA introduces two new configurations—the standard and the web configuration. The standard configuration is the configuration that has been tested for Java EE compliance. The web configuration is a new experimental lightweight configuration created around JBoss Web that provides support for servlet/JSP container, as well as JTA/JCA and JPA.

In the next chapter, we're going to install the components needed to develop an application with JBoss AS 5. Setting up your environment doesn't require particular sysadmin skills; however, it will require about half an hour (depending on how fast your network is) to complete all the necessary steps.

3

Customizing JBoss
AS Services

Try not to become a man of success, but rather try to become a man of value – A. Einstein

What do you want to write on your next resume? JBoss developer? Dare to write JBoss *specialist*! In today's highly competitive workplace, you need outstanding skills. Being a developer is only part of your duty. What makes you different from the queue of competitors is the ability to solve critical situations. Mastering JBoss services requires time and devotion. You don't have the coolest widgets in the market; most of the time you have to edit the configuration files, either manually or by using a raw web interface. However, in this chapter we'll try to make your journey through JBoss services as pleasant as can be. This chapter discusses the following topics:

- An introduction to JBoss AS monitoring services
- All about JBoss thread pool
- How to configure logging services
- Configuring connections to the database
- Configuring the transaction service

How to monitor JBoss AS services

JBoss has several options for monitoring your services, spanning from web interfaces to command-line tools. Most developers are familiar with the **JMX console** web application. It provides a raw view of the microkernel of the JBoss Application Server by listing all active registered services (MBeans).

Another available option is the **Web console**. This is quite similar to the JMX console, except that it contains an interactive applet that can be used to capture system metrics.

The Web console is not covered in this book as it has not been upgraded since a long time and so de facto is going to be deprecated. Rather, we would like to encourage the reader to learn about the newer web-based **admin console** that is an offshoot of the **Jopr** project. This project aims at producing administrative, monitoring, alerting, and operational control on JBoss AS and related projects. Since release 5.1.0 of the application server, the admin console is bundled as a web application in the `deploy` folder of JBoss AS.

The last monitoring option that we will discuss is the `twiddle` command execution tool that provides access to registered services using a command line.

The JMX console

The JMX console is the most widely used tool for inspecting JBoss MBeans components. It requires nothing but a standard web browser. The default URL for the console is `http://localhost:8080/jmx-console/`.

What are MBeans?

MBeans are single, manageable components that are plugged into JBoss by registering on a central server (MBean server). MBeans were the foundation of JBoss Kernel in pre 5.0 releases.

The console is divided into two frames — the left frame contains the list of **domains** of the JBoss Server, while the right frame is called the **agent view** and exhibits the list of all MBeans that are registered for the selected domain (at start up it just contains all MBeans registered grouped for every domain). In the top-right corner, you can filter on domains and agents.

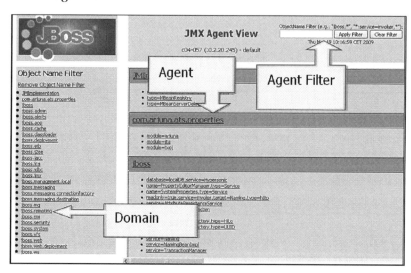

By **domain**, we just mean a logical group of components (MBeans) that are related to a certain service. So, we have a domain **jboss.system** that handles the system parameters such as `jboss.jdbc`, which is about datasource configuration, and so on.

When you select one of the MBeans, you will be taken to the **JMX MBean View**. In this panel, you can view and edit the MBean's attributes, as well as invoke operations on it.

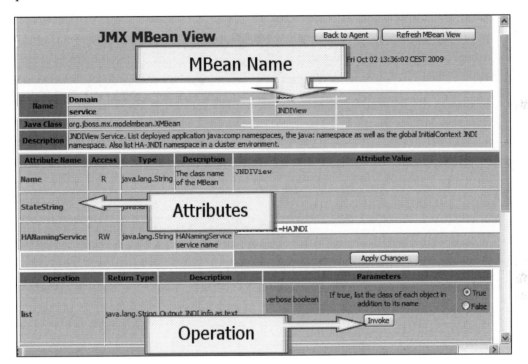

Security warning

 The JMX console doesn't require any authentication to log on. This might expose your system to severe vulnerability. Check out how to secure the JMX console in Chapter 13, *JBoss AS Security Architecture*.

An example: Using the JMX console to display the JNDI tree

Here is a typical scenario where the JMX console is really required. Somehow it happened that you failed to retrieve one object from the JNDI tree. Chances are that the object was registered in the wrong namespace; however, don't panic, the first aid is a **JNDI tree dump**.

Navigate to the `jboss` domain and in the next view select `service=JNDIView` MBean. Follow the link and you'll be taken to the MBean view. Once there, scroll down to the **list** operation.

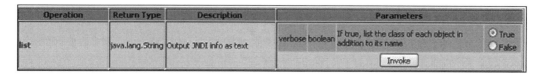

Operation	Return Type	Description	Parameters	
list	java.lang.String	Output JNDI info as text	verbose boolean — If true, list the class of each object in addition to its name	○ True ○ False
			Invoke	

By clicking **Invoke**, you should be able to see a page dump of your JNDI tree:

```
java: Namespace
+- securityManagement (class:
      org.jboss.security.integration.JNDIBasedSecurityManagement)
+- comp (class: javax.namingMain.Context)
+- XAConnectionFactory (class:
      org.jboss.jms.client.JBossConnectionFactory)
+- TaskListEar (class: org.jnp.interfaces.NamingContext)
|   +- TaskListSessionBean (class: org.jnp.interfaces.NamingContext)
|   |   +- remote (class: Proxy for:
|   |         sample.ejb.manager.TaskListSession)
|   |   +- remote-sample.ejb.manager.TaskListSession (class: Proxy
|   |         for: sample.ejb.manager.TaskListSession)
Global JNDI Namespace
+- UserTransactionSessionFactory (proxy: $Proxy150 implements
      interface org.jboss.tm.usertx.interfaces.
      UserTransactionSessionFactory)
+- UUIDKeyGeneratorFactory (class:
      org.jboss.ejb.plugins.keygenerator.uuid.UUIDKeyGeneratorFactory)
+- HiLoKeyGeneratorFactory (class:
      org.jboss.ejb.plugins.keygenerator.hilo.HiLoKeyGeneratorFactory)
+- XAConnectionFactory (class:
      org.jboss.jms.client.JBossConnectionFactory)
+- topic (class: org.jnp.interfaces.NamingContext)
+- ClusteredConnectionFactory (class:
      org.jboss.jms.client.JBossConnectionFactory)
+- ProfileService (class: AOPProxy$0)
```

The JNDI tree is divided into several sections, each one gathering information for a specific **namespace**. If you cannot look up an object from the JNDI tree, it is likely that it is an issue with namespaces. For example, if you look at the JNDI tree, you can see a component `TaskListSessionBean` registered in the `java:` JNDI namespace. Registering a component in the `java:` namespace is perfectly valid; however, bear in mind that the component will not be accessible outside the JBoss server JVM. If your objects need to be looked up from remote clients too, then you should rather register them in the global namespace.

The admin console

The newer admin console ships with JBoss AS, since the release of 5.1.0. If you are running an earlier version of JBoss AS, then you should check and install a compatible release of the the **Embedded Jopr** project. The downloads available are listed at `http://www.jboss.org/community/wiki/EmbeddedJoprDownloads`.

If your JBoss AS is bound at localhost, then you can access the admin console at the following URL: `http://localhost:8080/admin-console`. You can log in with the default administrator credentials: **admin/admin**.

> These credentials come from the **jmx-console** security domain, which by default is configured through `JBOSS_HOME/server/xxx/conf/props/jmx-console-users.properties`. Security domains are discussed in detail later in Chapter 13, *JBoss AS Security Architecture*.

The web application is basically divided into two frames—the left frame provides the navigation between the resources available on the application server, while the central frame is your **Control Panel** where you can manage the single resource.

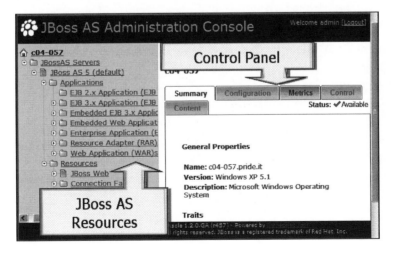

The **Control Panel** is composed of the following options:

- **Summary**: This option summarizes the general properties of the resource (for example, JNDI name) along with the most relevant metrics.

- **Configuration**: This option allows editing or creation of new resources. For example, it can be used to add a new service without the need to edit the configuration file.

- **Metrics**: As the name implies, this option displays the available metrics collected for the resource.

- **Control**: If this option is enabled, you can use some special actions that are related to the resource. For example, in a connection pool, you might want to flush the connections from the pool.

We will see some of these options in more detail as we approach the configuration of AS resources.

The twiddle utility

JBoss provides a simple command-line tool called **twiddle** (for twiddling bits using JMX) that allows interaction with a local or remote JMX server instance. This tool is located in the `bin` directory of the distribution. It can be executed using either `twiddle.sh` (Unix/Linux) or `twiddle` (Windows). Passing a `-h` (`--help`) argument provides the basic syntax, and the `--help` command shows what you can do with the tool.

This is the basic syntax of twiddle:

```
$ ./twiddle.sh -h
A JMX client to 'twiddle' with a remote JBoss server.
usage: twiddle.sh [options] <command> [command_arguments]
```

The list of available commands that can be passed to twiddle is presented in the following table:

Command	Description
jsr77	Print out JSR77 related information
xmbean	Print out MBean metadata as an XMBean descriptor
info	Get the metadata for an MBean
get	Get the values of one or more MBean attributes
invoke	Invoke an operation on an MBean

Command	Description
`create`	Create an MBean
`setattrs`	Set the values of one or more MBean attributes
`unregister`	Unregister one or more MBeans
`query`	Query the server for a list of matching MBeans
`set`	Set the value of one MBean attribute
`serverinfo`	Get information about the MBean server

So, for example, the equivalent `twiddle` command to dump the JNDI tree can be written as follows:

```
./twiddle.sh invoke jboss:service=JNDIView list true
```

If you want to contact a remote JBoss server, you have to use the `-s` option as follows:

```
./twiddle.sh -s 192.168.0.1 invoke jboss:service=JNDIView list true
```

JBoss AS thread pool

The Java platform is designed from the ground to support concurrent programming, with basic concurrency support in the Java programming language and the Java class libraries. Application servers, however, maintain a pool of worker threads available, rather than creating a thread for every request. This improves performance because thread creation (as well as destruction) does have a significant overhead that is better avoided, especially if your application creates many short-lived threads.

A second advantage of maintaining threads in a pool is that you can control (and possibly limit) the number of threads in your application. Without a centralized pool manager, your system will be heavily dependent on the client requests. Suppose you are running a heavy-duty EJB application that manages about 5,000 requests at the same time. If the number of requests goes up to 10,000, then your system will not be prepared to handle so much load and therefore is likely to crash.

Using a centralized pool manager in this scenario causes the server response to degrade (for example, by queuing requests) and maintains the maximum number of threads optimal for the server system.

Application server thread pool anatomy

The JBoss thread pool is defined in `JBOSS_HOME/server/xxx/conf/jboss-service.xml` (you need to replace `xxx` with your server configuration). This is the core section of it:

```
<mbean code="org.jboss.util.threadpool.BasicThreadPool"
    name="jboss.system:service=ThreadPool">
    <attribute name="Name">JBoss System Threads</attribute>
    <attribute name="ThreadGroupName">System Threads</attribute>
    <attribute name="KeepAliveTime">60000</attribute>
    <attribute name="MaximumPoolSize">10</attribute>
    <attribute name="MaximumQueueSize">1000</attribute>
    <attribute name="BlockingMode">run</attribute>
</mbean>
```

Each of these parameters is described as follows:

- `MinimumPoolSize`: The minimum number of threads that can be active. By default it is `0`.

- `MaximumPoolSize`: The maximum number of threads that can be active. By default it is `100`.

- `KeepAliveTime`: How long to keep threads alive, when there is nothing to do. Time is expressed in milliseconds. By default it is `60000` (which equals 1 minute).

- `MaximumQueueSize`: The maximum number of requests that are waiting to be executed. By default it is `1024`.

- `Blocking Mode`: If all your threads are busy and the waiting queue has also reached the `MaximumQueueSize`, then this parameter lets you configure the behavior of JBoss thread pool in this circumstance.

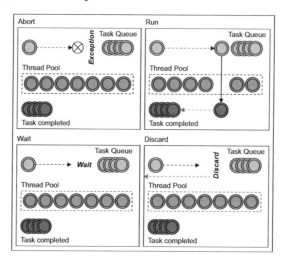

The last diagram shows the different behaviors of the `Blocking Mode` parameter.

Setting `Blocking Mode` to `abort` will determine a `RuntimeException`, when a new request attempts to enter the busy thread queue. On the contrary, the default `run` will give priority to the calling thread, which will be able to execute the task. Setting the parameter to `wait` will force the calling thread to wait until the thread queue has room, while the option `discard` will simply discard the calling thread. There is a last option `discardOldest` that does a scan of the thread pool to see if a thread is about to complete and tries to enqueue the newest thread wherever possible.

For simple applications, the default settings of the thread pool will work well. However, if your server has to handle lots of requests (usually the playground of web applications), then you should check your thread pool carefully. You have several monitoring options, the simplest of which is by means of the JMX console.

Open the JMX console and look for the object name `jboss.system`. Click on the link and the inner frame of the console will display all the MBeans that are registered under that domain. The information we look for is in the MBean `jboss.system:service=ThreadPool`.

This object contains all the attributes and operations relative to the thread pool. You can set new attributes for your pool, as well as check the current size of the queue, which is displayed as **QueueSize**.

Name		Domain	jboss.system
		service	ThreadPool
Java Class		org.jboss.util.threadpool.BasicThreadPool	
Description		Management Bean.	

Attribute Name	Access	Type	Description	Attribute Value
Name	RW	java.lang.String	MBean Attribute.	JBoss System Threads
Instance	R	org.jboss.util.threadpool.ThreadPool	MBean Attribute.	JBoss System Threads (1
QueueSize	R	int	MBean Attribute.	0
BlockingMode	RW	org.jboss.util.threadpool.BlockingMode	MBean Attribute.	run
PoolNumber	R	int	MBean Attribute.	1
MaximumPoolSize	RW	int	MBean Attribute.	20
KeepAliveTime	RW	long	MBean Attribute.	60000

Is QueueSize the tip of the iceberg?

QueueSize is a fundamental parameter and it should be on the top of your checklist if your application yields poor response time. If you have a steady (or worse, an increasing) QueueSize on your server, then you should consider raising the MaximumPoolSize pool size attribute.

However, simply incrementing the queue size might not be enough to solve your problems—analyze at first where your application is slowing down. For example, a very common scenario is that your threads are busy because they are handling slow or stuck JDBC connections. Here, merely increasing the MaximumPoolSize would only move the bottleneck into another area. In this scenario, you should first tune your queries or increase the JDBC connection pool.

How many threads for your applications?

We have just learned that setting an insufficient value for the MaximumPoolSize can cause severe performance degradation of the application; however, a grossly exaggerated value can be a problem as well.

Why? Because of the mechanics of thread switching, an application with a growing number of threads will tend to saturate the CPU. Switching from one thread to another involves suspending the current thread, saving its state into registers, and then restoring the state of the thread that is being switched to. All these operations are CPU intensive and must be considered while setting the minimum/maximum pool size.

Therefore, there is no magic number of threads that will be appropriate for all applications. We suggest you to start with the default values and then monitor the QueueSize. If you discover that there's a waiting queue, then you can just increase the MaximumPoolSize to that amount plus a little extra just to handle peaks of requests. Let's say you have configured a pool of 50 threads and you have a QueueSize of 5, then the next optimal amount of threads in the pool might be around 60.

Analyze what your threads are doing

Tweaking the pool parameters can be a quick winning strategy. However, it is really important that you understand where your application consumes most of the time. As we'll see in the next chapters, with Eclipse IDE it's relatively easy to debug a server application.

However, if you do not have a chance to debug your application step-by-step, you can still find useful information from a simple server thread dump. JBoss JMX console will again be our first choice here. Navigate to the `jboss.system:type=ServerInfo` MBean, where you'll find a button with an action **listThreadDump**.

Clicking on the button will produce a full thread dump of the application server. Here is a small excerpt from it:

```
Total Threads: 89
Total Thread Groups: 10
Timestamp: 20090311100332
Thread Group: system : max priority:10, demon:false
Thread: Reference Handler : priority:10, demon:true, threadId:2,
    threadState:WAITING
Thread: WorkerThread#0[127.0.0.1:1704] : priority:5,
    demon:false, threadId:193, threadState:TIMED_WAITING
    java.lang.Thread.sleep(NativeMethod)test.SleeperBean.
    doSomething(SleeperBean.java:9)sun.reflect.
    NativeMethodAccessorImpl.invoke0(Native Method)
Thread: WorkerThread#1[127.0.0.1:1703] : priority:5,
    demon:false, threadId:195, threadState:RUNNABLE test.
    RunnerBean.getConnection(RunnerBean.java:16)sun.reflect.
    NativeMethodAccessorImpl.invoke0(Native Method)
```

We have created and deployed a couple of remote components, namely **Enterprise Java Beans (EJB)** that are performing some time-consuming operations. As you can see from the output, the first EJB (`SleeperBean`) is in a `TIMED_WAITING` state, as we have intentionally added some `Thread.sleep` in its `doSomething` method. The second EJB (`RunnerBean`) is also suspended, but in this case it's in a `RUNNABLE` state. So, it's likely to be waiting for a response from an external system.

The same information can be obtained with the `twiddle` command-line utility:

```
twiddle -s localhost invoke "jboss.system:type=ServerInfo"
  listThreadDump > threadDump.txt
```

This shell command redirects the thread dump to the file `threadDump.txt` (Unix/Linux users only have to substitute `twiddle` with `twiddle.sh`).

Another useful option available on the same page of the console is the **listThreadCpuUtilization** action.

listThreadCpuUtilization	java.lang.String	MBean Operation.	[no parameters] Invoke

Clicking on the **Invoke** button shows the breakdown of the CPU usage on the machine by individual threads, as follows:

```
Thread Name    CPU (milliseconds )
HDScanner 921
WorkerThread#0 546
WorkerThread#1 343
DestroyJavaVM  140
Finalizer      125
Reference Handler 62
Total 2154
```

Again the equivalent operation with `twiddle` is:

```
twiddle -s localhost invoke "jboss.system:type=ServerInfo"
  listThreadCpuUtilization > threadCpu.txt
```

Configuring logging services

Logging messages is a common requirement in all server applications. Many developers interact during the creation of applications, and it is likely that every user will approach logging in their own style. There is also the burden of adding/removing logging information when you shift from early stage development to production.

Log4j is a reliable, fast, and extensible framework for handling log messages. The configuration file of log4j is located at JBOSS_HOME/server/xxx/conf/jboss-log4j.xml.

The three main components of log4j infrastructure are **appenders**, **layouts**, and **categories**. Let's see them in detail.

Appenders

An appender is an output destination of log messages. In your configuration file, you register all the available appenders to your application. In the default configuration file, you have two appenders enabled—the **console** file appender that outputs information to the AS command window (or wherever you have redirected the stout stream), and the **server** file appender that writes a more verbose log to the log/server.log file.

Console file appender

This is the definition of the console file appender:

```
<appender name="CONSOLE" class="org.apache.log4j.ConsoleAppender">
    <errorHandler class="org.jboss.logging.util.
        OnlyOnceErrorHandler"/>
    <param name="Target" value="System.out"/>
    <param name="Threshold" value="INFO"/>
    <layout class="org.apache.log4j.PatternLayout">
        <param name="ConversionPattern" value="%d{ABSOLUTE} %-5p
            [%c{1}] %m%n"/>
    </layout>
</appender>
```

As you can see, this appender is targeted on `System.out`, so it's equivalent to plain `System.out` statements. By changing the `Threshold` parameter, you can set a different level of verbosity for your logs. The set of possible log levels is (in order of gravity): TRACE, DEBUG, INFO, WARN, ERROR, and FATAL.

For example, when you're setting up JBoss for production, it is advised to increase the log level:

```
<param name="Threshold" value="WARN"/>
```

This will evict all log messages from the console that are concerned with the debugging, initialization, and deployment of components.

Changing the configuration at runtime

What happens if you change this file when the server is running? JBoss checks the log4j configuration every 60 seconds by default, so you can modify your configuration at runtime. You can also set the time between checks by changing the `RefreshPeriod` of the MBean `org.jboss.logging.Log4jService`. This attribute can be set in the `conf/jboss-service.xml` configuration file, as highlighted in the following code:

```
<mbean code="org.jboss.logging.Log4jService"
    name="jboss.system:type=Log4jService,service=Logging"
    xmbean-dd="resource:xmdesc/Log4jService-xmbean.xml">
    <attribute name="ConfigurationURL">resource:jboss-
        log4j.xml</attribute>
    <attribute name="Log4jQuietMode">true</attribute>
    <attribute name="RefreshPeriod">60</attribute>
    <attribute
        name="DefaultJBossServerLogThreshold">DEBUG</attribute>
</mbean>
```

File appenders

Next section is the **rolling file appender,** which is controlled by the `org.jboss.logging.appender.DailyRollingFileAppender` class. A working sample of this appender can be found at the top of the `jboss-log4j.xml` configuration file:

```
<appender name="FILE"
    class="org.jboss.logging.appender.DailyRollingFileAppender">
    <errorHandler
        class="org.jboss.logging.util.OnlyOnceErrorHandler"/>
    <param name="File" value="${jboss.server.log.dir}/server.log"/>
    <param name="Append" value="false"/>
    <param name="Threshold" value="${jboss.server.log.threshold}"/>
    <param name="DatePattern" value="'.'yyyy-MM-dd"/>
    <layout class="org.apache.log4j.PatternLayout">
        <param name="ConversionPattern" value="%d %-5p [%c] (%t)
            %m%n"/>
    </layout>
</appender>
```

The rolling schedule is specified by the `DatePattern` option. This parameter enables date-based rollover at these intervals—monthly, weekly, daily, twice a day at midnight and noon, and at the start of every hour and every minute. For example, the following pattern switches log once a week:

```
'.'yyyy-ww
```

This pattern switches log twice a day (at noon and midnight):

```
'.'yyyy-MM-dd-a
```

This pattern switches log every hour:

```
'.'yyyy-MM-dd-HH
```

>
> You may have noticed, in the appender configuration, the use of JBoss system properties to change the log level (`jboss.server.log.threshold`), as well as the directory where the file is written (`jboss.server.log.dir`).
>
> You can override these properties at startup using `-D` option, as follows:
>
> `run -Djboss.server.log.dir=C:/Documents/log`

Rolling the file by size

If you want to schedule file rolling using the size criterion, then you can replace the `DailyRollingFileAppender` with the `RollingFileAppender`. A template for the `RollingFileAppender` is located just a few lines thereafter:

```
<appender name="FILE"
    class="org.jboss.logging.appender.RollingFileAppender">
        <errorHandler
            class="org.jboss.logging.util.OnlyOnceErrorHandler"/>
        <param name="File"
            value="${jboss.server.home.dir}/log/server.log"/>
        <param name="Append" value="false"/>
        <param name="MaxFileSize" value="500KB"/>
        <param name="MaxBackupIndex" value="10"/>
        <layout class="org.apache.log4j.PatternLayout">
            <param name="ConversionPattern" value="%d %-5p [%c]
                %m%n"/>
        </layout>
</appender>
```

This will create up to 10 `server.log` files and each one of them has a maximum file size of `500KB`. When the `MaxBackupIndex` is reached, log4j will start erasing older files.

Other appenders

You are not limited to file and console loggers. In the `log4j.xml` configuration file, you can find some useful appenders for other protocols such as JMS, SMNP, SYSLOG, or JMX. By default, these appenders are commented. Therefore, if you want to enable them, all you have to do is remove the comment markers and provide the resource that is in charge of handling the logs. For example, if you want your ERROR logs published to a JMS topic, you have to create `topic/MyErrorsTopic` and add the following snippet to your log4j configuration:

```
<appender name="JMS" class="org.apache.log4j.net.JMSAppender">
    <errorHandler
        class="org.jboss.logging.util.OnlyOnceErrorHandler"/>
    <param name="Threshold" value="ERROR"/>
    <param name="TopicConnectionFactoryBindingName"
        value="java:/ConnectionFactory"/>
    <param name="TopicBindingName" value="topic/MyErrorsTopic"/>
</appender>
```

Layout of logs

Have you noticed the PatternLayout class and its parameter ConversionPattern? The goal of this parameter is to format a logging event and return the results as a string. The patterns are made up of a sequence of characters that can be used to retrieve information about the application, the server, or the calling client.

For example, if you want to enhance the log output with the client host information (useful in web applications), you can simply add the %X{host} option as follows:

```
<layout class="org.apache.log4j.PatternLayout">
    <param name="ConversionPattern" value="%d{ABSOLUTE} %-5p
        [%c{1},%X{host}] %m%n"/>
</layout>
```

Another interesting add-on could be the thread name that produced the log message. The pattern layout option for the thread name is %t. The relative ConversionPattern could be like:

```
<param name="ConversionPattern" value="%d{ABSOLUTE} %-5p [%c{1}]
    (%t) %m%n"/>
```

For a full reference to the PatternLayout string, consult the log4j official documentation at http://logging.apache.org/log4j/1.2/apidocs/org/apache/log4j/PatternLayout.html.

Logging categories

The amount of logging is controlled by categories. Categories are named entities, which follow a hierarchical naming rule similar to Java packages. For example, the category named com.sample is a parent of the category named com.sample.Test. Similarly, java is a parent of java.util and an ancestor of java.util.Vector.

Let's see some samples of categories:

```
<category name="org.apache">
    <priority value="INFO"/>
</category>
<category name="org.jgroups">
    <priority value="WARN"/>
</category>
```

The first element limits the verbosity of org.apache packages to INFO, which means that this category will capture all logs in the priority — INFO, WARN, ERROR, and FATAL, but not TRACE and DEBUG levels.

The second one, WARN, is concerned with `org.jgroups` packages and starts capturing WARN, ERROR, and FATAL messages.

As we said, categories are hierarchical, so a category inherits its configuration from parent categories (unless it defines its own configuration). Similar to Java classes, which are extensions of the object class, all categories inherit from the root logger that resides at the top of the logger hierarchy.

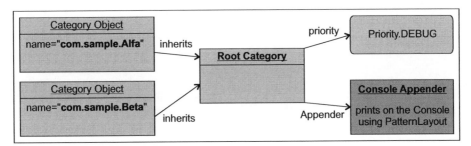

This is the default root category configuration:

```
<root>
    <appender-ref ref="CONSOLE" />
    <appender-ref ref="FILE" />
</root>
```

The `appender-ref` elements tell the category which appenders will be used to send the log messages. By default, JBoss is configured to capture the CONSOLE and FILE appenders.

Configuring your own logger

Keeping your application logs separated from the server log is a requirement for every application. As we have learned, the configuration of a new logger is a two-step process. First you need to create a new appender that points to a destination; the next step is setting up a category that collects the logs. For example, if you want to send your application logs to the file `application.log`, then this might be a good template:

```
<appender name="APPLICATION"
    class="org.jboss.logging.appender.DailyRollingFileAppender">
<errorHandler
    class="org.jboss.logging.util.OnlyOnceErrorHandler"/>
<param name="File"
    value="${jboss.server.home.dir}/log/application.log"/>
<param name="Append" value="false"/>
```

```
<param name="DatePattern" value="'.'yyyy-MM-dd"/>
    <layout class="org.apache.log4j.PatternLayout">
        <param name="ConversionPattern" value="%d %-5p [%c] %m%n"/>
    </layout>
</appender>
```

If you want to generate logs, you just need to add a category that gathers data from this appender:

```
<category name="packtpub.sample">
    <priority value="INFO" />
    <appender-ref ref="APPLICATION"/>
</category>
```

The element `appender-ref` instructs log4j to send messages for that category to the appender named `APPLICATION`.

Managing logs through JMX agents

If you don't have access to your configuration files, you can use the JMX console to get/set the logging parameters.

JBoss logging service is managed by `Log4jService` (`service=Logging`, `type=Log4jService`) in the `jboss.system` domain. Open up the JMX agent view pointing to `Log4jService`.

Besides changing the `ConfigurationURL` (that is where `log4j.xml` is placed) a useful parameter is the `DefaultJBossServerLogThreshold`, which lets you define a default log threshold for your applications.

Name	Domain		jboss.system
	service		Logging
	type		Log4jService
Java Class	org.jboss.mx.modelmbean.XMBean		
Description	This MBean allows to get and set Log4j specific options. See also resource:log4j.xml		

Attribute Name	Access	Type	Description	Attribute Value
RefreshPeriod	RW	int	The time in seconds between checking for new config.	60
DefaultJBossServerLogThreshold	RW	java.lang.String	The value to assign to system property jboss.server.log.threshold if it is not already set. This system property in turn controls the logging threshold for the server.log file.	DEBUG

As you can see in the previous screenshot, by default this level is set to **DEBUG**. In the **Operation** view, you can manage your **loggers** through the following actions:

Operation	Return Type	Description	Parameters		
getLoggerLevel	java.lang.String	Displays the log level of a given logger.	logger java.lang.String	The name of the logger to display.	
					Invoke
setLoggerLevel	void	Sets the log level for a given logger.	logger java.lang.String	The name of the logger to set.	
			level java.lang.String	The log level to set.	
					Invoke
setLoggerLevels	void	Sets the levels of each logger specified by the given comma seperated list of logger names.	loggers java.lang.String	The list of loggers	
			level java.lang.String	The log level to set	
					Invoke

For example, suppose you want to retrieve the logger level for the category `org.apache`, simply insert the category in the textbox for the operation `getLoggerLevel`. You can also modify logger limits by inserting both the category and the log level in the `setLoggerLevel` textboxes. You can also perform multiple variations with the `setLoggerLevels`, specifying the list of loggers and levels separated by a comma.

Configuring the connection to the database

The **Java Connector Architecture (JCA)**, part of **Java Platform, Enterprise Edition (Java EE)**, specifies a standard architecture for accessing resources in diverse **Enterprise Information Systems (EIS)**.

The connector architecture is implemented both in the application server and in an EIS-specific **resource adapter**.

What is a resource adapter?

Put it simply, a resource adapter is a system library specific to an EIS that provides connectivity to the EIS. You can imagine it like a JDBC driver. The following diagram depicts the Java Connector Architecture's main components:

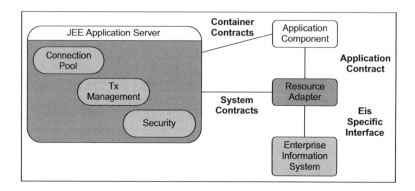

As you can see, the JCA API is based on the following contracts:

- System-level contracts between the resource adapter and the application server
- The **Common Client Interface (CCI)** that provides Java applications and development tools to a client API so as to access the resource adapter
- A standard packaging and deployment facility for resource adapters

Connection management is a system-level contract that allows the application server to pool resource connections. The purpose of the pool management is to achieve scalability. Resource connections are typically expensive objects to create, and pooling them allows for more effective reuse and management. From the developer point of view, this mechanism is *transparent*, as applications only need to pick up connections from a datasource registered on the **Java Naming and Directory (JNDI)** API.

Configuring a datasource in JBoss AS

You don't need to know low-level details of the resource adapter to configure JBoss connectivity—configuring a datasource in JBoss simply requires creating a file with the *-ds.xml extension in the deploy folder of your JBoss server configuration.

The configuration file for the datasource can contain the following elements:

- no-tx-datasource: This datasource uses the NoTxConnectionManager service. Such a transaction manager does not take part in JTA transactions. It can be used safely, for example, in a scenario where your application has a read-only view of the data.

- local-tx-datasource: This element uses the LocalTxConnectionManager, which supports JTA transactions but does not support two-phase commit. You can use this datasource if your transactions do not span across multiple RDBMSs.

- xa-datasource: This element uses the XATxConnectionManager, which supports two-phase commit.

- mbean: This element can be contained multiple times, and it states the MBean that can be used to configure services used by the datasources.

JBoss comes bundled with an embeddable open source database called **Hypersonic SQL**. When JBoss starts up, the Hypersonic database MBeans initialize the in-memory database reading the following configuration file hsqldb-ds.xml.

```xml
<?xml version="1.0" encoding="UTF-8"?>
<datasources>
    <local-tx-datasource>
        <jndi-name>DefaultDS</jndi-name>
        <connection-url>jdbc:hsqldb:${jboss.server.data.dir}$
            {/}hypersonic${/}localDB</connection-url>
        <driver-class>org.hsqldb.jdbcDriver</driver-class>
        <user-name>sa</user-name>
        <password></password>
        <min-pool-size>5</min-pool-size>
        <max-pool-size>20</max-pool-size>
        <idle-timeout-minutes>0</idle-timeout-minutes>
        <track-statements/>
        <security-domain>HsqlDbRealm</security-domain>
        <prepared-statement-cache-size>32</prepared-statement-cache-
            size>
        <metadata>
            <type-mapping>Hypersonic SQL</type-mapping>
        </metadata>
        <depends>jboss:service=Hypersonic,database=localDB</depends>
    </local-tx-datasource>
    <mbean code="org.jboss.jdbc.HypersonicDatabase"
      name="jboss:service=Hypersonic,database=localDB">
        <attribute name="Database">localDB</attribute>
        <attribute name="InProcessMode">true</attribute>
    </mbean>
</datasources>
```

The `jndi-name` property sets the JNDI name of the datasource. In our example it is registered into the global namespace with the name `DefaultDS`. The `connection-url` and `driver-class` are the same arguments that you used in plain JDBC connections.

The initial size and the maximum size of the connection pool can be configured with `min-pool-size` and `max-pool-size`.

With `idle-timeout-minutes` you can indicate the maximum time a connection may be idle before being closed and returned to the pool. If not specified it is `15` minutes by default.

`track-statements` is an important debugging feature. It checks that all statements are closed when the connection is returned to the pool—remember to disable it in the production environment.

`security-domain` indicates that connections in the pool should be characterized by **Java Authentication and Authorization Service (JAAS)** subject-based information. The content of the `security-domain` is the name of the JAAS security manager, which will handle authentication. This name corresponds to the JAAS `login-config.xml` descriptor `application-policy` name attribute.

`prepared-statement-cache-size` is the number of prepared statements per connection to be kept open and reused in subsequent requests. They are stored in an **LRU** cache. The default is `0` (zero), meaning no cache.

The `depends` element specifies the JMX service that the connection manager services depend on. The connection manager service will not be started until the dependent services have been started.

Additional datasource properties

Besides the standard properties just covered, a number of additional properties are available. We will explore a few handy ones:

- `transaction-isolation`: The presence of this element specifies the `java.sql.Connection` transaction isolation level to be used. The constants defined in the connection interface are the possible element content values and include the following:
    - `TRANSACTION_READ_UNCOMMITTED`
    - `TRANSACTION_READ_COMMITTED`
    - `TRANSACTION_REPEATABLE_READ`
    - `TRANSACTION_SERIALIZABLE`
    - `TRANSACTION_NONE`

For a detailed explanation about transaction isolation levels, check the *Configuring the transaction service* section later.

- `no-tx-separate-pools`: Setting this element to `false` indicates that JBoss will create two separate connections pools—one to be used with a JTA transaction and one for a non-JTA transaction. The pools are lazily constructed on first use. This attribute has been added because Oracle's XA (and possibly other vendors') datasource cannot reuse a connection outside a transaction, once enlisted in a global transaction and vice versa.

The following three properties are available only in the `XAdatasource` context:

- `xa-datasource-class`: This is the fully qualified name of the `javax.sql.XADataSource` implementation class (for example, `com.informix.jdbcx.IfxXADataSource`).

- `xa-datasource-property`: This element allows specification of custom properties to assign to the `XADataSource` implementation class. Each property is identified by the `name` attribute, and the property value is given by the `xa-datasource-property` element content. This element is fundamental if you need to switch on specific vendor properties. For example, the following property activates an Oracle database feature, which is used to control whether a statement will *auto-bind* in memory:

  ```
  <xa-datasource-property name="CURSOR_SHARING">FORCE</xa-
      datasource-property>
  ```

- `isSameRM-override-value`: This Boolean flag allows you to override the behavior of `javax.transaction.xa.XAResource.isSameRM(XAResource xaRes)`. It is suggested to leave the default `false`.

Setting up a new datasource

Setting up a new datasource is a two-step process. First, because you don't want to write the configuration file from scratch, you need a template. This is a pretty simple task—the `JBOSS_HOME/docs/example/jca` directory contains sample files for a wide selection of databases and it is a good idea to use one of these as a starting point. Second, you need a JDBC driver so that the `ConnectionFactory` is able to instantiate new connections. The JDBC drivers can be downloaded from your database site; however, you can find a useful gateway on Sun network for downloading the appropriate driver:

`http://developers.sun.com/product/jdbc/drivers`.

Here, you can query the driver archive choosing from among many different search criteria. Once you have downloaded the driver .jar file, it's time to copy it into the common/lib of JBoss. As application libraries are loaded at bootstrap, you need to restart JBoss in order to make the classes available to the ConnectionFactory.

Here's for example, an XA MySQL datasource file:

```xml
<?xml version="1.0" encoding="UTF-8"?>
<datasources>
    <xa-datasource>
        <jndi-name>jdbc/MySQLDS</jndi-name>
    <xa-datasource-class>com.mysql.jdbc.jdbc2.optional.
        MysqlXADataSource</xa-datasource-class>
    <xa-datasource-property
        name="URL">jdbc:mysql://localhost/jbpm</xa-datasource-property>
    <user-name>admin</user-name>
    <password>admin</password>
    <transaction-isolation>TRANSACTION_READ_COMMITTED</transaction-
        isolation>
    <no-tx-separate-pools />
    <track-connection-by-tx />
    <exception-sorter-class-name>
        com.mysql.jdbc.integration.jboss.ExtendedMysqlExceptionSorter
    </exception-sorter-class-name>
    <valid-connection-checker-class-name>
        com.mysql.jdbc.integration.jboss.MysqlValidConnectionChecker
    </valid-connection-checker-class-name>
    <metadata>
      <type-mapping>mySQL</type-mapping>
    </metadata>
    </xa-datasource>
</datasources>
```

The highlighted section shows some differences between an xa-datasource and local-tx-datasource. Apart from the different root element (which is now xa-datasource), the element xa-datasource-class replaces driver-class. The former connection-url is now coded as xa-datasource-property.

Gathering connection pool statistics

All the datasource-related objects can be inspected through the jboss.jca domain. You can find them by searching through the JMX console page, or by using jboss.jca:* as the query filter.

Suppose you want to monitor your `jdbc/MySQLDS` datasource from the previous example. You could use a more specific filter, such as `jboss.jca:name=jdbc/MySQLDS,*`, to see only the `MySQLDS` entries. In either case, the following four MBeans will result from your query:

```
name=jdbc/MySQLDS,service=DataSourceBinding
name=jdbc/MySQLDS,service=ManagedConnectionFactory
name=jdbc/MySQLDS,service=ManagedConnectionPool
name=jdbc/MySQLDS,service=XATxCM
```

While each plays a critical role in providing the datasource functionality in JBoss, you are most likely to need to interact with the `ManagedConnectionPool`. Click the **ManagedConnectionPool** MBean to expose its management attributes and operations.

Changing connection pool settings

From the JMX console, you can specify new settings for the connection pool. However, these changes will persist only in memory. To change the configuration permanently, you need to update the datasource file or use the new admin console, as we will see in a minute.

If you want to change some pool attributes as part of a script, then you can use the `twiddle` command-line utility. All you need to know is which MBean controls the connection pool and the attribute we want to change. In our case, we will operate on the `ManagedConnectionPool` MBean, if we want to change the pool `MaxSize`:

```
twiddle -s hostAddress set "jboss.jca:name=MySQLDS,serv
ice=ManagedConnectionPool" MaxSize 50
```

The `ConnectionCount` attribute shows how many connections are currently open to the database. However, open connections are not necessarily in use by the application code. If you want to inspect how many connections are being used by your application, then check the `InUseConnectionCount` attribute. Another key attribute is `AvailableConnectionCount`, which shows how much room is left in the pool.

Name	Domain	jboss.jca			
	service	ManagedConnectionPool			
	name	jdbc/JbpmDS			
Java Class	org.jboss.resource.connectionmanager.JBossManagedConnectionPool				
Description	Management Bean.				

Attribute Name	Access	Type	Description	
StateString	R	java.lang.String	MBean Attribute.	Started
AvailableConnectionCount	R	long	MBean Attribute.	10

If you need to track connection pool usage in its lifetime, you would probably inspect the `ConnectionCreatedCount` and `Connection-DestroyedCount` that keep counting the total number of connections created and destroyed by the pool. Setting the attribute `IdleTimeout` with a value greater than zero will cause your connections to eventually time out, be destroyed, and be replaced by fresh connections.

Be aware that setting a time-out for your connections will cause the created and destroyed counts to rise constantly. The `MaxConnectionsInUseCount` attribute keeps track of the highest number of connections in use at a time.

The MBean exhibits a `flush` operation that can be used to reset the connection pool statistics. This will cause a new connection pool to be created, abandoning the previous connections.

Managing datasources from the admin console

Setting up a new datasource and managing the existing configurations can be performed in the admin console as well. This can be particularly useful if you need to add a persistent resource from a remote location.

In the left frame expand the **Resources** | **Datasources** leaf and choose the suitable transaction option. In the main frame, you can operate on your selection:

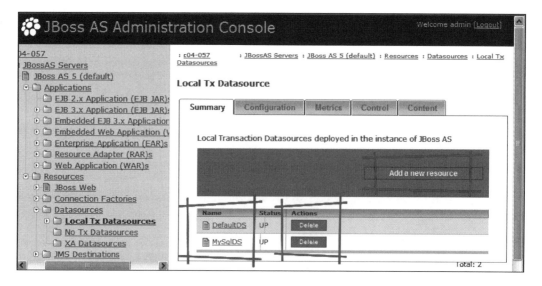

As you can see from the last screenshot, you can add or delete a resource by choosing the appropriate button. Clicking on a datasource in the list will enable the upper tab list, with a wider set of choices. Here for example is a snapshot of the **Metrics** for **DefaultDS**:

Summary	Configuration	Metrics	Control	Content	Status: ✔ Available

View the numeric metrics and traits for this resource.

Run State: RUNNING   **Pool JNDI Name:** DefaultDS   **Local Transaction:** true

Numeric Metrics

Name	Value	Description
Category: performance		
Available Connection Count	20	the maximum number of connections that are available
Connection Count	5	the number of connections that are currently in the pool
Connection Created Count	5	the number of connections that have been created since the datasource was last started
Connection Destroyed Count	0	the number of connections that have been destroyed since the datasource was last started
In Use Connection Count	0	the number of connections that are currently in use
Max Connections In Use Count	1	the most connections that have been simultaneously in use since this datasource was started
Max Size	20	Max Size
Min Size	5	Min Size

Refresh

Using statistics to tune the connection pool

Choosing the right pool size depends entirely on your application and the hardware you are running on. An optimal pool size is when the connection pool is just large enough to service requests without waits. If you need an easy starting point to determine the maximum number of connections, simply run a load test and measure the largest number of concurrently used connections (MaxConnectionsInUseCount). You can then work backwards from there to determine what values of minimum and maximum pooled connections give the best performance for your particular application.

Another key parameter in tuning your connection pool is the <prepared-statement-cache-size>. By using prepared statements, you are asking the database to parse the query only once, so that if the same query is executed again with different parameters, it saves the CPU resource to directly execute the queries without parsing. You are highly encouraged to use a <prepared-statement-cache-size> even if you need to know that prepared statements are cached per connection. The more connections you have, the more prepared statements you get (even when they are the same query). So, there's obviously a trade-off between performance and memory.

Be aware that statements in cache may reserve database cursors

When JBoss caches a prepared or callable statement, the statement may open a cursor in the database. If you allow JBoss to cache too many statements, you may end up exceeding the limit of open cursors for a connection. Carefully monitor the number of cursors in your database when you turn on this option, and when necessary, you can change the limit in your database management system or you can reduce the statement cache size for the datasource.

Deploying datasources at application level

When you drop a datasource file in the `deploy` folder, you will make it available to all your applications. This is a pretty simple job; however, it can be unpractical if the application server configuration is handled by a different group of people. Here, you need to pass the datasource file along with the application. This is not a big deal; however, in such a scenario it could be simpler to deploy the datasource along with the application.

All you need to do is add an extra configuration file named `jboss-app.xml`, which provides JBoss-specific deployment configuration.

```
<!DOCTYPE jboss-app PUBLIC "-//JBoss//DTD J2EE Application 1.4//EN"
"http://www.jboss.org/j2ee/dtd/jboss-app_5_0.dtd">
<jboss-app>
<module>
    <service>ApplicationDS-ds.xml</service>
</module>
</jboss-app>
```

This file needs to be placed in the `META-INF` folder of your application archive. On the other hand, your datasource file should be positioned at the root of your archive. This is how your EAR application should look like:

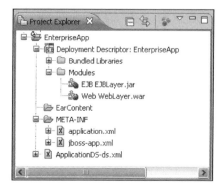

High availability datasources

A **high availability (HA)** datasource is an abstraction around a group of data sources that provides failover processing between a list of redundant resources. When you configure an HA datasource you have to provide a list of connection URLs, so that when the connection you are using is not available anymore, the connection factory will transparently choose another database connection URL.

The HA datasource configuration also requires that you indicate which delimiter is used to separate the list of connection URLs. Here's a high availability `local-tx` example:

```
<datasources>
<local-tx-datasource>
  <jndi-name>jdbc/HADatasource</jndi-name>
   <connection-url>
       jdbc:oracle:thin:@oraclehost:1521:SID|jdbc:oracle:
       thin:@oraclehost:1521:SID2
   </connection-url>
   <url-delimiter>|</url-delimiter>
   <driver-class>oracle.jdbc.driver.OracleDriver</driver-class>
   <user-name>user</user-name>
   <password>password</password>
   <check-valid-connection-sql>select count(*) from testable</check-
       valid-connection-sql>
</ha-local-tx-datasource>
</datasources>
```

HA datasources in earlier releases of JBoss

In earlier releases of JBoss, HA datasources used a different top level element. HA local datasources were nested in the `<ha-local-tx-datasource>`, while HA XA datasources were contained in `<ha-xa-tx-datasource>`. If you are porting your HA datasource files to JBoss 5, then you need to remove these elements.

Clustered RDBMS

Some database vendors (mainly Oracle and MySQL) provide built-in fault tolerance solutions that can guarantee high availability to your Enterprise tier. This is implemented by means of a clusterable database such as **Oracle Real Application Clusters (RAC)** or **MySQL Cluster** solution. In such scenarios, the only difference with a standalone database connection is the connection URL, which should contain the list of cluster members.

For example, if you need to configure a datasource connection to an **Oracle RAC** made up of host1 and host2, you should configure your datasource file with the following property:

```
<xa-datasource>
   <xa-datasource-property name="URL">
      jdbc:oracle:thin:@(DESCRIPTION=(ENABLE=BROKEN)(ADDRESS_LIST=
      (ADDRESS = (PROTOCOL = TCP)(HOST = host1)(PORT = 1521))
      (ADDRESS = (PROTOCOL = TCP)(HOST = host2)(PORT = 1521))
      (FAILOVER=on)(LOAD_BALANCE=off))(CONNECT_DATA=
      (SERVER=DEDICATED)(SERVICE_NAME=ORACLESERV)))
   </xa-datasource-property>
</xa-datasource>
```

The URL property contains a database-specific string for describing the Oracle RAC. We advise you to consult an expert database administrator for adapting the above statement to your RAC configuration. Anyway, you will need to focus on the key attributes, which are FAILOVER and LOAD_BALANCE. In this example LOAD_BALANCE is off due to the fact that pinging live nodes is a major bottleneck of the RAC.

Additional information about Oracle RAC can be found at http://www.oracle. com/technology/products/database/clustering/index.html.

On the other hand, if you were to use an open source cluster solution such as MySQL cluster, the connection string would be:

```
<xa-datasource>
   <xa-datasource-property name="URL">
      jdbc:mysql:loadbalance://host1,host2/database?
         loadBalanceBlacklistTimeout=5000
   </xa-datasource-property>
</xa-datasource>
```

Should you need further details about the MySQL Cluster option, here's the recommended link: http://www.mysql.com/products/database/cluster/.

Connecting from a remote client

Technically speaking, a datasource can also be accessed and used from a remote client, for example, a Swing GUI that displays tabular data the same way a JSP does. The only obstacle to using a datasource from a remote client is that it needs to be registered in the global JNDI namespace.

We will repeat it again—if a component is registered in the **global namespace**, it can be accessed from both the local and remote client, while components registered into the **java namespace** can only be looked up from the same JVM. In order to make your datasource available in the global namespace, you have to set `use-java-context` to `false` in your datasource `*-ds.xml` configuration file:

```
<datasources>
    <local-tx-datasource>
        <jndi-name>remoteDS</jndi-name>
        <use-java-context>false</use-java-context>
    </local-tx-datasource>
</datasource>
```

Configuring the transaction service

Transaction management is a **JCA system contract** between an application server and a resource adapter (and its underlying resource manager). The transaction management contract extends the connection management contract, which we just discussed. It provides support for the management of transactions.

What is a transaction? The authoritative definition of a transaction is a unit of work containing one or more operations involving one or more shared resources. Transactions are described in terms of **ACID** properties, which are as follows:

- **Atomicity** refers to the ability to guarantee that either all or none of the tasks of a transaction are performed.

- **Consistency** refers to the fact that when a transaction is completed, the system must be in a stable and consistent condition.

- **Isolation** refers to the requirement that other operations cannot access or see the data in an intermediate state during a transaction.

- **Durability** refers to the guarantee that once the user has been notified of success, the transaction will persist, and not be undone. This means it will survive system failure.

A transaction can be terminated in two ways—**committed** or **aborted** (rolled back). When a transaction is committed, all changes made within it are made durable (forced on to stable storage, for example, disk). When a transaction is aborted, all of the changes are undone. Atomic actions can also be nested; the effects of a nested action are provisional upon the commit/abort of the outermost (top-level) atomic action.

The ANSI/ISO SQL standard defines four levels of transaction isolation, which are as follows:

READ UNCOMMITTED: This isolation level allows dirty reads, that is, you're permitted to read uncommitted or dirty data. You can achieve this effect—for example, you could open an OS file that someone else is writing, and read whatever data exists in that file. Data integrity is compromised, foreign keys are violated, and unique constraints are ignored.

READ COMMITTED: This is the default isolation level in many RDBMS. When a transaction runs on this isolation level, a SELECT query sees only data committed before the query began. There are no dirty reads (reads of uncommitted data). There may be non-repeatable reads (that is, rereads of the same row may return a different answer in the same transaction) and phantom reads (that is, newly inserted and committed rows become visible to a query that were not visible earlier in the transaction).

REPEATABLE READ: The goal of REPEATABLE READ is to provide an isolation level that gives consistent and correct answers, and prevents lost updates. If you have REPEATABLE READ isolation, the results from a given query must be consistent with respect to some point in time.

SERIALIZABLE: This level provides the highest transaction isolation. It is called so because it emulates serial transaction execution, as if transactions had been executed one after another serially, rather than concurrently. However, applications using this level must be prepared to retry transactions in the event of serialization failures. When a transaction is on the serializable level, a SELECT query sees only data committed before the transaction began. It does not see uncommitted data nor does it see changes committed during transaction execution by concurrent transactions.

Preserving data integrity

Isolation is a strong requirement for transactions. In order to implement it, it is necessary to lock the portion of the database that is involved in a transaction. Locking can be implemented using two strategies—pessimistic locking and optimistic locking.

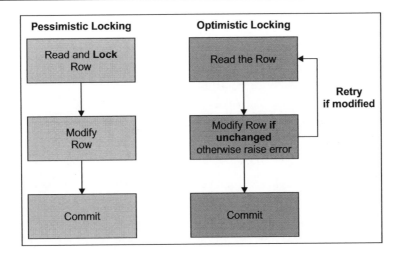

Pessimistic locking assumes that another transaction might change the data between the read and the update. In order to prevent that change and the data inconsistency that would result, the read statement locks the data to prevent any other transaction from changing it.

A pessimistic lock assumes a record will be held for an extended period of time; as in the case of, let's say, a news article being edited. In the case of the news article, you would need to apply a read-only lock.

Optimistic locking does not lock records when they are read, and proceeds on the assumption that the data being updated has not changed since the read. As no locks are taken out during the read, it doesn't matter if the user goes to lunch after starting a transaction, and all deadlocks are eliminated so that users never have to wait on each other's locks. An optimistic lock assumes that an update will be made soon after a record has been selected, as in the case of having to enter only a customer code.

One common strategy to implement optimistic locking is tagging each record with a version (that is, timestamp). If the record is updated, the timestamp is also updated. When a record is selected, the timestamp on the client will be compared to the timestamp on the server.

Global and local transactions

Whenever your application connects to a database using JDBC or any SQL interpreter, you are *de facto* creating a transaction. However, when the transaction involves only a single database, and all updates made to the database are committed at the end of these changes, we have a **local transaction**.

A **global transaction** involves a set of management objects. These global transaction objects (TransactionManager and Transaction) track all objects and resources involved in the global transaction. At the end of the transaction, the TransactionManager and Transaction objects ensure that all database changes are atomically committed at the same time.

One of the primary advantages for a global transaction is the number of objects and database resources managed as a single unit within the transaction. If your global transaction involves more than one database resource, you must specify a **two-phase commit engine**. The two-phase commit engine is responsible for ensuring that when the transaction ends, changes made to all of the databases are either totally committed or fully rolled back.

On the other hand, if your global transaction has multiple server objects, but only a single database resource, you don't need to specify a two-phase commit engine. The two-phase commit engine is required only to synchronize the changes for multiple databases. If you have only a single database, single-phase commit can be performed by the transaction manager.

Configuring JBoss transactions

JBoss implements the **Java Transaction API (JTA)**, which provides distributed transaction services for the Java EE platform. A distributed transaction involves a transaction manager and one or more resource managers. A resource manager is any kind of persistent datastore. The transaction manager is responsible for coordinating communication between all transaction participants.

JTA transactions are more powerful than JDBC transactions. While a JDBC transaction is limited to a single database connection, a JTA transaction can have multiple participants.

Java EE-compatible containers make the UserTransaction interface available through JNDI and then use it to demarcate transactions. Calling UserTransaction.begin() associates the calling thread with a new transaction context. Subsequent accesses of transactional resources implicitly enlist those resources into the transaction. A call to UserTransaction.commit() commits the transaction, transparently engaging the two-phase commit protocol, if necessary, while UserTransaction.rollback() aborts the transaction and rolls back all data updates.

By default, transactions live until they are terminated by the application that created them or if a failure occurs. However, it is possible to set a time-out (in seconds) on a per transaction basis, such that if the transaction has not terminated before the time-out expires, then it will be rolled back automatically.

The transaction time-out can be configured in the file `transaction-jboss-beans.xml`, which is located in the `deploy` folder of your server configuration:

```
<bean name="TransactionManager"
    class="com.arjuna.ats.jbossatx.jta.TransactionManagerService">
    <annotation>@org.jboss.aop.microcontainer.aspects.jmx.
        JMX(name="jboss:service=TransactionManager",
        exposedInterface=com.arjuna.ats.jbossatx.jta.
        TransactionManagerServiceMBean.class, registerDirectly=true)
    </annotation>
    <property name="transactionTimeout">300</property>
</bean>
```

By default, the `TransactionManager` is configured to time out after 300 seconds. However, if this value is not appropriate for your application, then you can change this parameter. You can even set it to 0, which means that transactions will be allowed to run indefinitely.

JBossTS uses a separate **thread reaper** that monitors all locally created transactions, and forces them to roll back if their time-outs elapse. To prevent this thread from consuming the application time, it runs only periodically. The default checking period is 120 seconds, but can be overridden by setting the `com.arjuna.ats.arjuna.coordinator.txReaperTimeout` property variable to another valid value, in microseconds.

Alternatively, if the `com.arjuna.ats.arjuna.coordinator.txReaperMode` is changed from the default (NORMAL) to DYNAMIC, the transaction reaper will wake whenever a transaction times out. This has the advantage of terminating transactions early, but may suffer from continually rescheduling the reaper thread.

The configuration file for the reaper thread is `jbossjta-properties.xml`, which is located in the `conf` folder of your JBoss AS.

```
<transaction-service>
    <properties depends="common" name="arjuna">
        <property
          name="com.arjuna.ats.arjuna.coordinator.txReaperTimeout"
          value="120000"/>
        <property
          name="com.arjuna.ats.arjuna.coordinator.txReaperMode"
            value="DYNAMIC"/>
    </properties>
</transaction-service>
```

Setting transaction time-out programmatically

A transaction time-out can also be set programmatically using the `UserTransaction` Object. For example:

```
UserTransaction ut = (UserTransaction)ctx.lookup("java:
comp/UserTransaction");
ut.setTransactionTimeout(100);
ut.begin();
ut.commit();
```

If you prefer, you can alternatively set the `Transaction` at class/method level using the annotation `@org.jboss.ejb3.annotation.TransactionTimeout`.

Monitoring transactions

The status of your transactions can be inspected from the JMX console. This information is contained in the `jboss` domain. From the agent view choose `service=TransactionManager`.

One handy attribute is the `RunningTransactionCount` that exhibits the number of transactions being executed, while the `TransactionCount` returns the total number of transactions started over the lifetime of the server.

Name	Domain	jboss		
	service	TransactionManager		
Java Class	com.arjuna.ats.jbossatx.jta.TransactionManagerService			
Description	Management Bean.			

Attribute Name	Access	Type	Description	
TransactionTimeout	RW	int	MBean Attribute.	300
TransactionCount	R	long	MBean Attribute.	2
RunningTransactionCount	R	long	MBean Attribute.	1

The self-explanatory attribute `CommitCount` returns the number of committed transactions, while `RollbackCount` returns the number of rolled back transactions.

If you want to know more details about the cause of rollback, you can check the following two attributes:

- `ApplicationRollbackCount`: Returns the number of transactions that have been rolled back by application request.

- `ResourceRollbackCount`: Returns the number of transactions that rolled back due to resource failure.

If you want to know the transactions that completed with a *heuristic* outcome, you need to check the `HeuristicCount` attribute.

Heuristic decisions

A **heuristic decision** occurs when a resource makes a unilateral decision during the completion stage of a distributed transaction to commit or rollback updates. This can leave distributed data in an indeterminate state. Network failures or resource time-outs are possible causes for heuristic completion.

Summary

In this chapter, we have completed our journey through the configuration of JBoss AS. We have logically separated the abstract container configuration from the EJB container and HTTP Connector configuration, which will be covered in the corresponding development chapter. We chose to do this mainly for two reasons—firstly, we didn't want to overwhelm the reader with too much information all at once, and secondly because it makes it easier for the reader to reach certain information if topics are not split in too many parts of the book.

However, once you have read through this chapter, you should have a sound knowledge of what it takes to get a customized JBoss environment based on our experience in the trenches. In the next chapter, we'll start designing Enterprise applications using Eclipse and JBoss plugins.

4
Developing EJB 3 Session Beans

The future has already arrived. It is just not evenly distributed yet – William Gibson.

In this chapter, we will introduce the reader to some concrete examples of Java Enterprise Programming developed on JBoss 5 application server. The sample code will be built using the Eclipse IDE and JBoss Tools that we have already installed, in order to meet the requirements of all developers.

In this chapter we will introduce the following topics:

- How to build business logic with Session Beans
- How to handle Session State with Stateful Session Beans
- How to configure the JBoss EJB container for optimal resource management

Java EE made easier

Developing a distributed, transactional, and secure application has traditionally been a complex task. If you have embraced the Java Enterprise platform before the new millennium, you should know that building even simple components required a certain amount of time. The Java EE 5 platform introduced a new simplified programming model. XML deployment descriptors are now optional. Instead, a developer can add the information as an annotation directly into a Java source file, and the Java EE server will configure the component at deployment and runtime.

Another useful innovation, borrowed from POJO frameworks, is **Dependency Injection**. This can be applied to all resources that a component needs, effectively hiding the creation and lookup of resources from application code. Dependency Injection can be used in EJB containers, web containers, and application clients, thus allowing the developer to easily insert references to other required components or resources with annotations.

What is Dependency Injection?

The term Dependency Injection has been coined by M. Fowler to describe the process of supplying an external dependency to a software component. Without Dependency Injection, an object that needs access to a particular service has to take the responsibility to access that service. In contrast, with Dependency Injection, an object simply provides a **property** that can hold a reference to that type of service; later, when the object is created, a reference to an implementation of that type of service will automatically be injected into that property by an external mechanism.

Developing Enterprise JavaBeans

Java EE applications are usually considered to be **three-tiered applications,** as they are distributed over three layers.

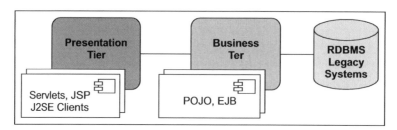

This diagram depicts a view of the three-layer architecture with the associated components. Here's a synthetic explanation:

- **Presentation Tier**: Built with dynamic pages and application clients, this layer is able to generate the user interface of the application.
- **Business Tier**: Also known as the middle tier, this layer contains the business logic of the application. All the business logic is centralized into this tier as opposed to client/server applications where the business logic is scattered between the frontend and the backend. The main benefit of having a centralized business tier is that the same business logic can support different types of clients.

- **Data Tier**: This provides the information infrastructure that is vital to the business processes of an Enterprise. This includes Enterprise infrastructure systems such as ERP, mainframe transactions processing, database systems, and other related legacy systems.

These layers provide an excellent model of how EJBs fit into a Java Enterprise system. EJBs provide both components for handling the application logic layer and JavaBeans-like abstraction of the data layer. There are actually three kinds of EJBs—**Session Beans**, **Entities**, and **Message-driven Beans**. In this chapter, we will discuss Session Beans and Entities. Message-driven Beans will be covered in Chapter 7, *Developing Applications with JBoss Messaging Service*.

Developing Session Beans

Session Beans are reusable components that contain the logic for business processes. For example, a stock trading application might have a Session Bean that contains logic for buying/selling futures. Another Session Bean might collect the line numbers in a telecom company. Every object that performs a relatively short-lived task on behalf of client code is a good candidate for a Session Bean.

There are two types of Session Beans—**Stateless Session Bean (SLSB)** and **Stateful Session Beans (SFSB)**. Each is used to model a different type of conversation between the client and the EJB.

Stateless Session Beans

A Stateless Session Bean does not maintain a conversational state for a particular client. When a client invokes the method of a Stateless Session Bean, the bean's instance variables may contain a state, but only for the duration of the invocation. When the method is finished, the state is no longer retained. Therefore, except for the duration of method invocation, all instances of a Stateless Session Bean are equivalent, allowing the EJB container to assign an instance to any client.

Life cycle of a Stateless Session Bean

The container creates instances of a Stateless Session Bean and keeps them in a **pool** of instances. When there is a method call from a client, the container checks if there is a handy instance in the pool. If the resource is available, the Bean is associated to the client for the duration of the call. Then it is returned to the pool.

If all Bean instances are busy, the container checks the Stateless Bean's `maxSize` attribute; if `maxSize` is smaller than the pool size, then a new Bean instance is created and immediately served to the client.

If the Container is not able to create any more Beans, the last chance for our client is that a new resource will be available before the EJB timeout. (See the section *Configuring Stateless Session Bean pool size* later in the chapter.)

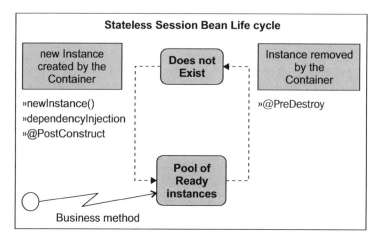

You can perform any initialization your Bean needs by tagging a method of your Bean with the @PostConstruct annotation.

```
@PostConstruct
public void init( ) {
   // Initialize some resources here
}
```

The @PreDestroy annotation can also be used to free allocated resources before the Bean is removed.

```
@PreDestroy
public void destroy( ) {
   // Deallocate resources acquired here
}
```

Use @PreDestroy with caution

We have tested the behavior of @PreDestroy even in critical situations such as a JBoss server crash. Before shutting down, JBoss 5 correctly invokes the callback method defined by the @PreDestroy annotation. However, this is not guaranteed to work the same in all application servers. When possible, evicting resources from an external application would be safer. For example, if you plan to restore a database structure before destroying the Bean, you could consider running an external script periodically.

Setting up a simple example

It is now time to put all this theory into practice. In this section, we are going to develop our first session Bean. First, we will walk through the Bean-creation code in a good bit of detail, reinforcing concepts we just covered and introducing new ones. Then we will explain how to run the example.

Launch Eclipse IDE and choose a workspace for our example. Once there, we need to create a new EJB Project. From **File**, select **New | Other | EJB | EJB Project**.

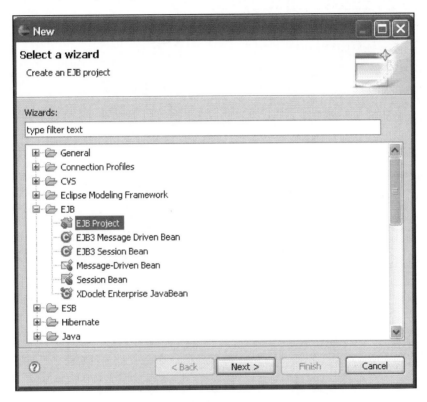

First, choose a name for this project. We will use **SessionBeanExample**. Then select the **Target Runtime** (JBoss 5). The **EJB Module version** is **3.0**. The **Configuration** used for this chapter will be the default JBoss configuration. For this example, we don't need to create an EAR package, so we leave that flag unchecked.

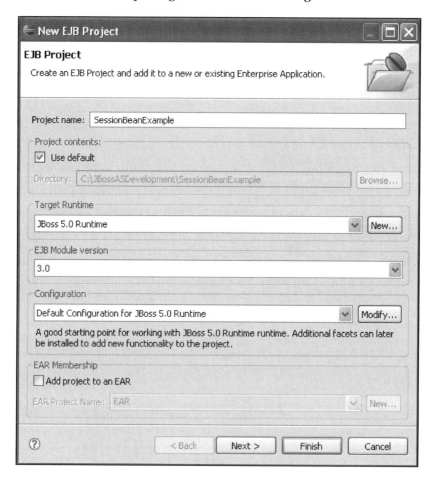

In the next menu, just leave the default **Source Folder** proposed (**ejbModule**). We have decided not to use an EAR packaging, so the wizard will not generate an EJB client JAR. The last option available is **Generate deployment descriptor**, which will create EJB deployment descriptors. We don't select this option in the following example:

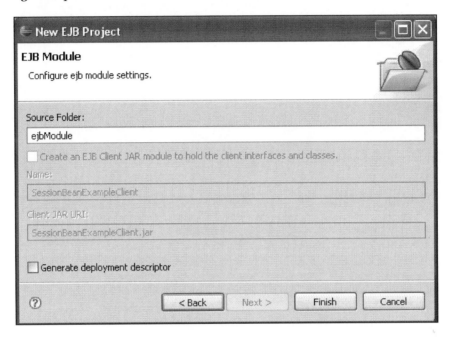

When you click **Finish**, Eclipse will suggest you to move to the Java EE perspective. Accept by clicking **Yes.** Let's have a glimpse at the **Project Explorer**:

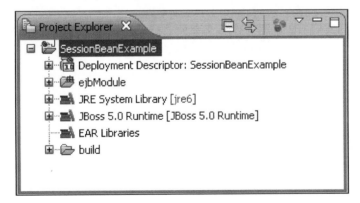

The folder `ejbModule` is the container for our EJB classes. You can see that Eclipse has automatically added both the **JRE System Library** and the **JBoss 5.0 Runtime** libraries. These libraries are automatically picked up from the JBoss 5 runtime configuration.

The first taste of EJB will be a simple Stateless Bean named **Mailer** that has a `sendMail` method for sending an e-mail.

Go to **File | New | Other**. Select the **EJB 3 Session Bean** option from the EJB folder. The **New Session Bean** wizard will appear. Choose **com.packtpub.ejb.example1** as the **Bean Package** and **Mailer** as the **Bean Name**.

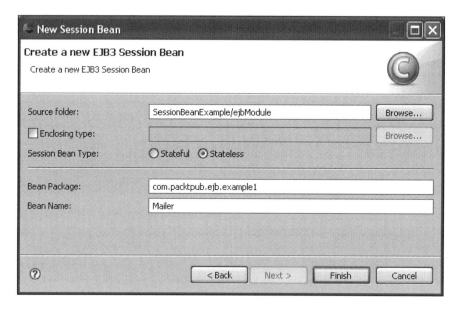

This image is slimmer than the actual wizard window; it has been intentionally resized to skim unused options from the page.

Leave the other options unchanged and click **Finish**.

You will see that the wizard has created a bare bones EJB with a remote interface named `Mailer` and an implementation class `MailerBean`. We are now going to add a method `sendMail` in the remote interface, which will be used to send an e-mail.

```
package com.packtpub.ejb.example1;

import javax.ejb.Remote;

@Remote
public interface Mailer {
```

```
    public void sendMail(String aToEmailAddr,
                    String aSubject, String aBody);
    }
}
```

Notice the @Remote annotation; it indicates that the interface Mailer is exposed as a remote service. If you would like to expose your EJB to local clients only, you would need the @Local annotation.

Most EJB 3 annotations are optional

If you don't specify the type of your interface, it's assumed that your EJB interface is a local interface. Actually, the EJB 3 specification mandates the use of a large set of default values for common EJB attributes.

Following is the concrete Bean implementation for the remote interface:

```
package com.packtpub.ejb.example1;

import javax.annotation.Resource;
import javax.ejb.*;
import javax.mail.*;

import com.packtpub.ejb.Mailer;

@Stateless [1]
@RemoteBinding(jndiBinding=»remote/MailerEJB»)

public  class MailerBean implements Mailer {

...@Resource(mappedName="java:/Mail")
...private javax.mail.Session session;
...
...public void sendMail(String aToEmailAddr,
                    String aSubject, String aBody)
......   {
...... MimeMessage message = new MimeMessage( session );
......     try {
......
......         message.addRecipient(
......           Message.RecipientType.TO, new
                                InternetAddress(aToEmailAddr)
......         );
......         message.setSubject( aSubject );
......         message.setText( aBody );
......         Transport.send( message );
......     }
```

```
......        catch (MessagingException ex){
......           throw new EJBException(«Cannot send email. « + ex);
......        }
......}
...
}
```

Here the `@Stateless` [1] annotation declares the EJB as a Stateless Session Bean. This is the only mandatory annotation for creating an SLSB.

Annotation shortcut

Fortunately, you don't have to remember all the annotations. Eclipse has a built-in shortcut key to display all annotations. Start typing "@" and press *Ctrl + Space* to browse between the available annotations. You can also use the same shortcut (*Ctrl + Space*) to retrieve the parameters of an individual annotation.

The annotation `@RemoteBinding` is used here to assign a custom JNDI binding to your Bean. If we don't use this annotation, a default JNDI binding will be assigned to your Bean (in our case it would be `MailerBean/remote`).

Default JNDI bindings

The default JNDI for your EJBs is determined by the archive name and the Bean name.

If you deploy your Bean in a JAR file, the JNDI name is `EJB-CLASS-NAME/local` for local interfaces and `EJB-CLASS-NAME/remote` for remote ones.

If the application is deployed in an **EAR** archive, the default JNDI name is the `EAR-FILE-BASE-NAME/EJB-CLASS-NAME/local` for the stub of the local interface. For the remote interface, it is `EAR-FILE-BASE-NAME/EJB-CLASS-NAME/remote`.

In this sample we are "injecting" the mail session as an `@Resource` in our EJB. The support for resource injection makes accessing resources significantly easier, avoiding the need to look up the resource, cast it, and handle exceptions.

Deploying your application

The last step is deploying your client and testing it. The quickest way to deploy an application to JBoss is copying the archive file (`.jar`, `.war`, `.ear`, and so on.) into the `deploy` folder of your configured server. Now we will see how to deploy your application from within the Eclipse environment.

Switch to the **JBoss Server View**, which can be reached from **Window | Open Perspective | Other**. Right-click on your JBoss Server label and select **Add and Remove Projects**. A little wizard will let you move your applications in or out of your JBoss server. Add the **SessionBeanExample** project and click **Finish**.

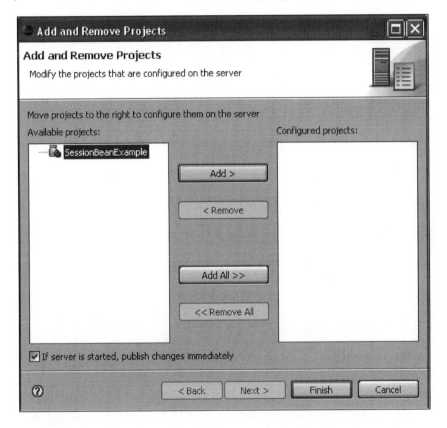

Now expand your JBoss label. It should contain your new deployment unit **SessionBeanExample**; right-click on it and select **Full Publish**.

Now it's time to start JBoss AS, if you haven't already. Right-click on the **JBoss 5.0 Server** and choose **Start**. JBoss will start to throttle, your CPU will peak as well; however, don't panic but check on the console to see if your EJB has been deployed correctly.

```
C:\WINDOWS\system32\cmd.exe

17:25:10,937 INFO  [JBossASKernel]      jboss.ejb:service=EJBTimerService
17:25:10,937 INFO  [JBossASKernel]   and supplies:
17:25:10,937 INFO  [JBossASKernel]      jndi:MailerBean/remote-com.packtpub.ejb.
example1.Mailer
17:25:10,937 INFO  [JBossASKernel]      Class:com.packtpub.ejb.example1.Mailer
17:25:10,937 INFO  [JBossASKernel]      jndi:remote/MailerEJB
17:25:10,937 INFO  [JBossASKernel]      jndi:MailerBean/remote
17:25:10,937 INFO  [JBossASKernel] Added bean(jboss.j2ee:jar=Example.jar,name=Ma
ilerBean,service=EJB3) to KernelDeployment of: Example.jar
17:25:10,937 INFO  [EJB3EndpointDeployer] Deploy AbstractBeanMetaData@51e191(nam
e=jboss.j2ee:jar=Example.jar,name=MailerBean,service=EJB3_endpoint bean=org.jbos
s.ejb3.endpoint.deployers.impl.EndpointImpl properties=[container] constructor=n
ull autowireCandidate=true)
17:25:11,031 INFO  [SessionSpecContainer] Starting jboss.j2ee:jar=Example.jar.na
me=MailerBean,service=EJB3
17:25:11,031 INFO  [EJBContainer] STARTED EJB: com.packtpub.ejb.example1.MailerB
ean ejbName: MailerBean
17:25:11,062 INFO  [JndiSessionRegistrarBase] Binding the following Entries in G
lobal JNDI:

     remote/MailerEJB - EJB3.x Default Remote Business Interface
     MailerBean/remote-com.packtpub.ejb.example1.Mailer - EJB3.x Remote Busin
ess Interface
```

Creating a test client

Creating the EJB wasn't a big deal; let's see how to set up a remote client for testing it. Add another Java class to the project by selecting **File | New | Class**. Choose a convenient name and package. Following is our sample client:

```
package com.packtpub.example1.client;

import javax.naming.InitialContext;
import com.packtpub.ejb.Mailer;

public class MailClient {
    public static void main(String[] args) throws Exception
    {
        InitialContext ctx = new InitialContext();
        Mailer mailer = (Mailer) ctx.lookup(«remote/MailerEJB»);
            mailer.sendMail("address@domain.com","subject","text");

    }

}
```

The `InitialContext` constructor is used to look up resources on the network. When you are getting an initial context from outside of the EJB container, you must specify the properties for the initial context. These properties include the `InitialContextFactory` class, the URL of the server, and possibly authentication parameters. These properties can either be created programatically using a `java.util.Properties` object, or can be loaded at runtime from the `jndi.properties` file that can be found in the classpath.

In order to get acquainted with the Eclipse build path, we will show how to provide these properties with a `jndi.properties` file. Create a new folder named `client-config` somewhere in your project. Add a new file named `jndi.properties` in it.

```
java.naming.factory.initial=org.jnp.interfaces.NamingContextFactory
java.naming.provider.url=jnp://localhost:1099
java.naming.factory.url.pkgs=org.jnp.interfaces
```

Eclipse is a sensible tool and recognizes this file as being a configuration file. You can view or edit it either from a graphical interface or from a plain text editor.

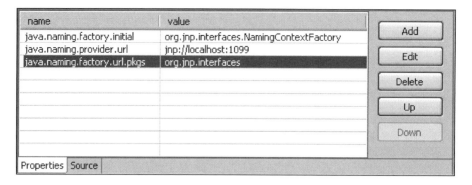

Now we are going to tell Eclipse to append this folder to the classpath. Right-click on your project and select **Properties**. There, select the **Java Build Path** option.

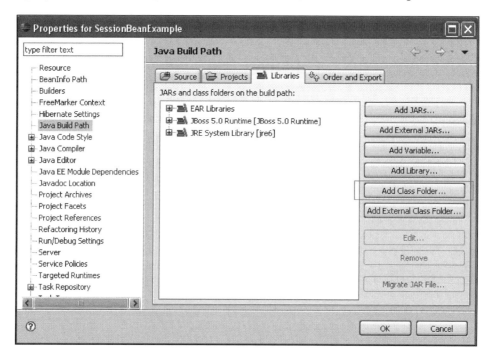

Click on the **Add Class Folder...** button and select the newly created `client-config` directory in the **Class Folder Selection** window.

Now your client is instructed to hunt for classes/files in the `client-config` folder. Running your application is just a matter of right-clicking on your class and selecting **Run As | Java Application**.

Configure your Java mail provider to get it actually working

In order to test this sample EJB, you would need to configure a Java SMTP gateway server. This can be done by setting the `mail.smtp.host` property from your `deploy/mail-service.xml` configuration file.

Adding interceptors to your Bean

EJB 3.0 allows you to define interceptor methods that are called around the business methods and life cycle events of the Bean instances. An interceptor method will always be executed before any of the Bean's business methods are invoked. The great benefit of interceptors is that they are a seamless way to add **aspect-oriented programming** to your business methods.

Interceptors can be bound to your EJB in three different ways:

- **Default interceptors**: These interceptors need to be declared in your `ejb-jar.xml` and are valid across all your EJB deployed.

```
<assembly-descriptor>
    <interceptor-binding>
      <ejb-name>*</ejb-name>
      <interceptor-class>com.packtpub.DefaultInterceptor
        </interceptor-class>
    </interceptor-binding>
    ...
</assembly-descriptor>
    <assembly-descriptor>
        <interceptor-binding>
          <ejb-name>*</ejb-name>
          <interceptor-class>sample.interceptor.
            MyDefaultInterceptor</interceptor-class>
        </interceptor-binding>
        ...
    </assembly-descriptor>
```

- **Class-level interceptors**: This kind of interceptor wraps calls to every method of the enclosing EJB.

```
@Stateless
  @Interceptors(value= com.packtpub.SampleInterceptor.class)
  public class StatelessBean    {       }
```

- **Method-level interceptors**: The method level interceptor intercepts only calls to a single method.

```
@Interceptors(value=com.packtpub.MethodInterceptor.class)
  public void doSomething()   {  ...  }
```

In our example, we will apply an interceptor at method level, which can be used to validate the parameters of the `sendMail` method.

```
public   class MailerBean implements Mailer {

  @Interceptors(value= com.packtpub.ejb.MailInterceptor.class)
  public void sendMail(String aToEmailAddr,
                          String aSubject, String aBody) {   }

}
```

This is the interceptor implementation, which can be added as a new class to your application.

```
package com.packtpub.ejb;

import javax.ejb.EJBException;
import javax.interceptor.*;

public class MailInterceptor {

    @AroundInvoke [1]
    public Object checkMail(InvocationContext ctx) throws Exception
    {
        System.out.println("*** Entering MailInterceptor method " +
                        ctx.getMethod().getName());

        String mailAddress = (String)ctx.getParameters()[0];
        if (mailAddress.indexOf("@")== -1   ||
            mailAddress.indexOf(".") == -1) {
            throw new EJBException("Invalid mail address");
        }

        try
        {
            return ctx.proceed(); [2]
        }
        catch(Exception e)
        {
            throw e;
        }
        finally
        {
            System.out.println("*** Leaving MailInterceptor");
        }
    }
}
```

As you can see, EJB 3.0 interceptors take the form of methods annotated with the `@javax.ejb.AroundInvoke` **[1]** annotation. Our `checkMail` method validates the email address and then, if successful, invokes the method `ctx.proceed()` **[2]**. This method is used to invoke the next interceptor in the chain (if you had defined any) and finally the business method.

Interceptors are particularly useful if you need to perform fine-grained activities such as logging, performance measuring, parameters validation, or any other functionality in your business methods, without modifying the methods' code.

Stateful Session Beans

Stateful Session Beans are called **stateful** because they maintain a conversational state with the client. In other words, they have instance fields that can be initialized and changed by the client with each method invocation. The Bean can use the conversational state as it processes business methods invoked by the client.

Stateful Session Beans are usually developed to act as agents for the client, managing the interaction of other Beans and performing work on behalf of the client application.

Stateful Bean life cycle

Whenever a new client session is started, the default constructor of the SFSB is invoked, resources are injected (if any), and the @PostConstruct callback takes place. At this stage, the newly created Bean is stored in a **cache** and executes the requested business method invoked through the business interface by the client.

If the client remains idle for a certain amount of time, the container **passivates** the bean instance. Passivating a Stateful bean means moving it from the active cache, serializing, and storing it in temporary storage. If the client happens to invoke a passivated bean, it is then reactivated (brought back into memory from temporary storage).

If the client does not invoke a passivated bean instance for a period of time, it is destroyed. The Bean can also be destroyed on demand, by means of the "remove" method.

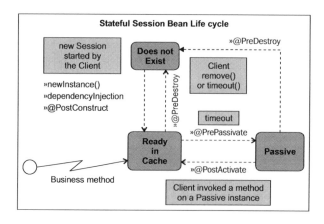

In addition to the @PostConstruct and @PreDestroy life cycle callback methods, SFSB also has the @PrePassivate and @PostActivate callback methods. A @PrePassivate method is invoked **before** a Stateful Bean instance is passivated. This can be used to release resources that cannot be serialized such as database connections or sockets. If needed, you might save some "pointers" to your connections into serializable fields.

The @PostActivate callback is invoked **after** a bean instance is brought back into the memory and is method ready. This callback can be used accordingly to restore the Bean's functionalities such as dropped connections.

Another annotation, which is specific to SFSB, is the @Remove annotation. When a method marked with the @Remove annotation is called, the container will remove the Bean instance from the cache after the method is executed. For example, the following removeBean() method, which has the @Remove annotation, can be used to evict the Bean from memory.

```
@Remove
public void removeBean()
    {
    // The method body can be empty.
    System.out.println("Session terminated");
    }
```

Developing a simple Stateful Session Bean

Do you like gambling? To make this reading lighter, we will dissect Stateful Beans with a tiny game application. Add a new EJB 3 Session Bean named **BlackJack** to your project. From the **File** Menu select **New | Other | EJB | EJB3 Session Bean**.

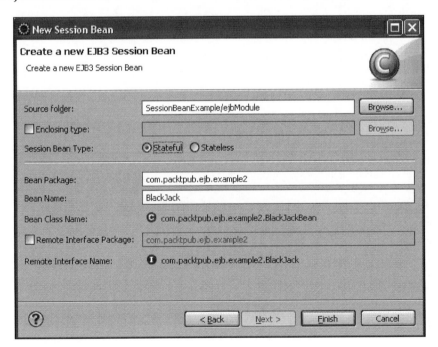

Here is the implememtation class:

```
package com.packtpub.ejb.example2;

import javax.ejb.Remote;

@Remote
public interface BlackJack {
    public int deal();
    public int quit();
}
```

As you can see, it is a pretty simple class. Black Jack fans might be disappointed that we did not consider all aspects of the game; however, this will give you an immediate perception of how an SFSB works.

```
package com.packtpub.ejb.example2;

import java.util.Random;

import javax.ejb.*;
import com.packtpub.ejb.BlackJack;
```

@Stateful [1]

```
public class BlackJackBean implements BlackJack {
    int score;

    public int deal() {     [2]
        Random randomGenerator = new Random();
        int randomInt = (randomGenerator.nextInt(13)) + 1;

        if (randomInt > 10) randomInt = 10; // Q - J - K

        score+=randomInt;

        if (score > 21){
            score = 0;
            throw new BustedException("You Busted!");
        }
        return score;
    }
    @Remove
    public int quit() { [3]
        return score;
    }

}
```

The bean, declared as `Stateful` **[1]**, contains only two methods. The `deal` method **[2]**, used for extracting a random number that is added to the score, and the `quit` method **[3]** that destroys the Bean instance when the game ends. In this class, we use a `BustedException` class that simply extends the `EJBException`.

```java
package com.packtpub.ejb.example2;

import javax.ejb.EJBException;

public class BustedException extends EJBException {

    public BustedException(String string) {
        super(string);
    }

}
```

The client application is a plain Java client, which requests the player to deal or quit.

```java
package com.packtpub.client.example2;

import java.util.Scanner;
import javax.naming.*;
import com.packtpub.ejb.example2.BlackJack;

public class BlackJackClient {

    public static void main(String[] args) throws Exception
    {
        Context ctx = new InitialContext();
        BlackJack b = (BlackJack) ctx.lookup
                    ("BlackJackBean/remote");

        Scanner keyIn = new Scanner(System.in);
        while (true) {
            System.out.print("\nEnter 'd' to deal
                            and 'q' to quit");
            String key = keyIn.next();
            if (key.startsWith("d")) {
                System.out.println("You have got "+b.deal());
            }
            else if (key.startsWith("q")) {
                System.out.println("You quit with "+b.quit());
                break;
            }
            else { System.out.print("\nUnrecognized character");
            }

        }

    }

}
```

Run your application by right-clicking on the class and selecting **Run as | Java Application**. If you want to send keyboard input to an Eclipse application, you need to select the **Console** window, thus making it the active window.

Configuring the EJB container

An EJB container manages the **Enterprise Beans** contained within it. For each Enterprise Bean, the container is responsible for registering the object, creating and destroying object instances, checking security for the object, managing its active state, and coordinating distributed transactions.

The configuration of the EJB container in earlier releases of JBoss was made through the `conf/standardjboss.xml` file. This file is still present in the 5.0 distribution for backward compatibility with EJB 1.x – 2.x specifications. However, if you are focusing on the EJB 3.x release your new configuration file is `ejb3-interceptors-aop.xml`, located in the `deploy` folder of your server.

This file contains a lot of information, but don't be scared. The configuration file is divided into domains; so you have a domain for each EJB component.

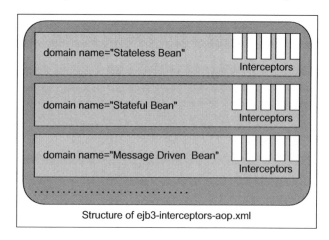

Structure of ejb3-interceptors-aop.xml

Inside each domain, you have a sequence of actions, which are called **interceptors**. An interceptor stack is a set of components in which every call proceeds through the stack from first to last, until finally the target is called. After the target method is executed, the call unwinds through the stack in reverse order.

In order to give the maximum flexibility to interceptors, they have been designed as **stateless** components so they do not save state information. The information about the state of the call is carried on, instead, by means of the **context of the calling thread**.

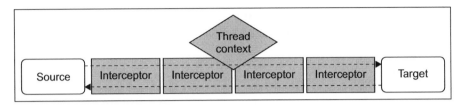

It is very unlikely that you need to replace the interceptor stack with your own implementations; however, this gives you the idea of how interceptors are structured.

Configuring Stateless Session Bean pool size

The EJB container maintains a pool of Stateless Session Beans to avoid creating and destroying instances. You can configure the size of the EJB pool by setting the appropriate value in the relative domain—for example, assume we want to increase the **stateless pool size** from the default (which is 30) to a higher value.

Open `deploy/ejb3-interceptors-aop.xml` and look for the domain "Stateless Bean". Here's an excerpt from it:

```
<domain name="Stateless Bean" extends="Intercepted Bean"
inheritBindings="true">
    <annotation expr="!class(@org.jboss.ejb3.annotation.Pool)">
        @org.jboss.ejb3.annotation.Pool (value="ThreadlocalPool",
                                         maxSize=30, timeout=10000)
    </annotation>
</domain>
```

The `maxSize` attribute determines the upper limit of your SLSB pool. Suppose the default 30 is not enough for you; change the attribute with a consistent value and restart JBoss.

The `timeout` attribute is the time in milliseconds, for which you want to block when waiting for an instance to be ready. This attribute will thus come into play if your requests are overflowing the pool size.

The `value` attribute is concerned with the *pooling mechanism*. The basic configuration of JBoss uses a **Thread Local Pool** (`org.jboss.ejb3.ThreadLocalPool`) to avoid the burden of *Java synchronization*. You can conversely configure JBoss to use an alternative pooling mechanism. For example, JBoss has a **strict pool size** implementation that will allow only a **fixed** number of *concurrent* requests to run at one time. If there are more requests running than the pool's strict size, those requests will block until an instance becomes available.

```
<annotation expr="!class(@org.jboss.annotation.ejb.PoolClass)">
    @org.jboss.annotation.ejb.PoolClass (value=org.jboss.ejb3.
                    StrictMaxPool.class, maxSize=5, timeout=10000)
</annotation>
```

Your pool configuration can be, at any time, inspected from the JMX console. Select the `jboss.j2ee` domain from the left frame and, once you are in the agent view, select the **EJB 3 service** you want to scan.

Here is a dump of attributes for the Stateless Session Beans, which we have been customized to reach the maximum size of 100 units.

Attribute Name	Access	Type	Description	Attribute Value
CreateCount	R	int	MBean Attribute.	0
InvokeStats	R	org.jboss.ejb3.statistics.InvocationStatistics	MBean Attribute.	InvocationStatistics concurrentCalls='0'
CurrentSize	R	int	MBean Attribute.	0
RemoveCount	R	int	MBean Attribute.	0
MaxSize	R	int	MBean Attribute.	100
AvailableCount	R	int	MBean Attribute.	100

- **AvailableCount**: This is a critical runtime attribute that reveals how many EJB instances are available in the pool to service your requests.

- **InvokeStats**: This attribute should also be closely monitored, as it informs you about the number of concurrently executing calls, the elapsed minutes, and the maximum time for single method calls.

For example, if you have the following output in your stats:

InvocationStatistics concurrentCalls='2'

method name='doSomething' count='5' minTime='4594' maxTime='24594' totalTime='89594'

Then you know that your EJB has serviced requests with the doSomething method, has a minimum response time of 4.5 seconds, and a maximum response time of 24.5 seconds. The total time spent calling this method was about 89 seconds for 5 total requests (2 of which were issued concurrently).

How to set the MininumSize of the EJB pool?

The MinimumSize element appears in the conf/standardjboss. xml file. It should determine the minimum number of instances to keep in the pool, although JBoss does not currently seed an InstancePool to the MinimumSize value. If you really need to initialize some EJB at startup (supposing you have a costly start-up for your EJB), you need a bit of coding. If you plan to include a web application along with your EJB, then just create a Startup Servlet that will initialize some EJBs in its init () method.

```
<servlet>
    <servlet-name>EJBInitializationServlet</servlet-
name>
    <servlet-class>sample.EJB.InitializationServlet</
servlet-class>
    <load-on-startup>-1</load-on-startup>
</servlet>
```

Specializing the configuration

The configuration discussed earlier affects **every** stateless EJB deployed in your container. You can, however, restrict the customization to a single component of your application.

The simplest way to configure the pool for a single EJB is applying a @PoolClass annotation at class level:

```
@Stateless
@PoolClass (value=org.jboss.ejb3.StrictMaxPool.class,
            maxSize=5, timeout=10000)
  public class CustomSessionBean implements CustomSession
  {
    . . .
  }
```

If you don't want to embed the configuration in your EJB class, you have got another (not so immediate) option that needs a couple of steps. Firstly, define a new domain in your `ejb3-interceptors-aop.xml` configuration file:

```
<domain name="Custom Pooled Stateless Bean" extends="Stateless Bean"
inheritBindings="true">
    <annotation expr="!class(@org.jboss.annotation.ejb.PoolClass)">
           @org.jboss.annotation.ejb.PoolClass (value=org.jboss.ejb3.
StrictMaxPool.class, maxSize=5, timeout=10000)
    </annotation>
</domain>
```

The next thing you have to do is apply the domain to your EJB within the `jboss.xml` file deployed along with your application.

```
<?xml version="1.0"?>
<jboss
        xmlns="http://java.sun.com/xml/ns/javaee"
        xmlns:xsi="http://www.w3.org/2001/XMLSchema-instance"
        xsi:schemaLocation="http://java.sun.com/xml/ns/javaee
                            http://www.jboss.org/j2ee/schema/
                            jboss_5_0.xsd"
        version="3.0">
    <enterprise-beans>
      <session>
        <ejb-name>CustomSessionBean</ejb-name>
        <aop-domain-name>Custom Pooled Stateless Bean
                                    </aop-domain-name>
      </session>
    </enterprise-beans>
</jboss>
```

This file needs to be placed in the META-INF folder of your deployed archive.

Configuring the Stateful Session Bean cache

A Stateful Session Bean has to maintain state (instance variables' values) across the methods for a client. Once created, an SFSB is stored in a cache. This area of memory stores active EJB instances so that they are immediately available for client requests. So, Stateful Session Beans in cache are bound to a determinate client.

You can configure Stateful Session beans through the domain "Stateful Bean" in the file `ejb3-interceptors-aop.xml`. There you can see the configuration is split in two parts:

- The **Non-clustered cache** configuration that will be used for single node applications
- The **Clustered cache configuration** that will affect applications deployed in a cluster of JBoss instances

```
<domain name="Stateful Bean" extends="Base Stateful Bean"
            inheritBindings="true">
    <!-- NON Clustered cache configuration -->

        @org.jboss.ejb3.annotation.CacheConfig (maxSize=100000,
        idleTimeoutSeconds=300, removalTimeoutSeconds=0)
    </annotation>

    <!-- Clustered cache configuration -->

        @org.jboss.ejb3.annotation.CacheConfig (name="sfsb-cache",
                    maxSize=100000, idleTimeoutSeconds=300,
                    removalTimeoutSeconds=0)
    </annotation>
</domain>
```

The `maxSize` parameter is the upper limit to the cache size.

`idleTimeoutSeconds` defines the maximum length of time a Stateful Session EJB should remain in cache. After this time has elapsed, JBoss removes the bean instance from the cache and starts to passivate it.

`removalTimeoutSeconds` defines how long the Bean remains active before it is completely removed. The default `0` represents infinity, so by default SFSB are not removed from the container.

You can reach the SFSB information from the JMX console by digging into the `jboss.j2ee` domain and then, from the JMX agent view, selecting your Stateful Session Bean service.

In the MBean view, you'll be presented with the following list of attributes:

Attribute Name	Access	Type	Description	Attribute Va
CacheSize	R	int	MBean Attribute.	1
PassivatedCount	R	int	MBean Attribute.	0
CreateCount	R	int	MBean Attribute.	1
InvokeStats	R	InvocationStatistics	MBean Attribute.	InvocationStatistics concurrentCalls='0' method name='doSomething' count='4' minTime
CurrentSize	R	int	MBean Attribute.	1
RemoveCount	R	int	MBean Attribute.	0
MaxSize	R	int	MBean Attribute.	100000
AvailableCount	R	int	MBean Attribute.	-1
TotalSize	R	int	MBean Attribute.	1

The **CacheSize** attribute indicates the current size of the Stateful cache. When a Stateful Bean is passivated, the **CacheSize** is decremented, whereas **PassivatedCount** is increased.

The **CurrentSize** attribute needs a bit more explanation. Each thread local pool holds a pool of active thread instances, just in case the instance will be used again. So, **CurrentSize** indicates how many thread instances have been created. If each thread uses only one instance of Stateful Bean, the **CurrentSize** should match **CreateCount**.

Warning!

At the time of writing SFSB pooling statistics, when using ThreadLocalPool, do not properly collect data for a few attributes such as **MaxSize** and **AvailableCount**. Check in the JBoss bug parade for JIRA EJBTHREE-1703.

How to disable Stateful Bean passivation

Passivation of a Stateful Bean is a trade off between memory and performance. In most cases, it is preferred to swap resources that have been idle for a long time onto a persistent storage; however, there are some situations where you can opt for a different approach. For example, if you have plenty of memory available, maybe you would like to avoid the costly marshalling/unmarshalling of a complex list of objects. You may also find passivation cumbersome, if you have lots of **transient** fields (such as external resources) that somehow need to be re-acquired when the SFSB is restored.

You have got a few options to avoid passivation. The simplest is to set **a removal timeout smaller (but greater then zero) then the idle timeout** in the file `deploy/ejb3-interceptors-aop.xml`.

```
    <domain name="Stateful Bean" extends="Base Stateful Bean"
                inheritBindings="true">
 .  .  .  .  .  .  .  .  .
        <annotation expr="!class(@org.jboss.ejb3.annotation.CacheConfig)
 AND !class(@org.jboss.ejb3.annotation.Clustered)">
            @org.jboss.ejb3.annotation.CacheConfig (maxSize=100000,
                    idleTimeoutSeconds=300, removalTimeoutSeconds=50)
        </annotation>
 .  .  .  .  .  .  .  .
    </domain>
```

This way the Bean is going to be removed before it has even got a chance to be passivated. This approach is a bit aggressive even if it ensures that memory consumption problems are less likely to occur.

Another possible solution is switching from the default SFSB **cache passivation** implementation to a **no-passivation** cache implementation. Here's how to do it: Pick up the `deploy/ejb3-interceptors-aop.xml` file and locate the following line:

```
<domain name="Stateful Bean" extends="Base Stateful Bean"
inheritBindings="true">
<annotation expr="!class(@org.jboss.ejb3.annotation.Cache) AND
!class(@org.jboss.ejb3.annotation.Clustered)">
    @org.jboss.ejb3.annotation.Cache ("SimpleStatefulCache")
</annotation>)
```

Replace the hightlighted line with the following text:

```
@org.jboss.ejb3.annotation.Cache(org.jboss.ejb3.cache.
NoPassivationCache.class)
```

Using this approach you are guaranteed that your SFSB **will not passivate** because they will use a separate cache that doesn't persist objects after an `idleTimeout`.

 Setting NoPassivationCache for a single EJB

You can also set the `NoPassivationCache` strategy at single EJB level by adding the **@Cache(org.jboss.ejb3.cache.NoPassivationCache.class)** annotation at Class level.

Which approach is the most viable? If your application creates many short-living sessions that are not invalidated by the client, then you can choose the first option (removal timeout smaller then idle timeout), which is more aggressive but keeps memory consumption low.

If, on the other hand, your EJB Client fully controls how long the conversation lasts, then choose the **NoPassivationCache** option, which guarantees that your SFSB will not be removed until the client issues a `remove()`.

Summary

We have covered a great deal of topics in this chapter. Let's just recall what we have been doing. First we entered the world of Session Beans, dissecting the two different components that can be used for handling the business logic—Stateless and Stateful Session Beans.

Initially we learned a whole lot of things about EJB development, so in the latter part of this chapter we stopped the "production" wheel for a moment, and illustrated how we can possibly configure the EJB container for best results.

In the next chapter, we will introduce the new Java EE Persistence API (JPA), showing how it greatly simplify the previous EJB Entity Beans' model.

Developing JPA Entities

Ambition is the path to success. Persistence is the vehicle you arrive in. – Bill Bradley (a politician).

The EJB 3.0 specification includes a persistence specification called the **Java Persistence API (JPA)**. It is an API for creating, removing, and querying Java objects called **entities** that can be used within both, a compliant EJB 3.0 container and a standard Java SE 5 environment.

In this chapter, we introduce the **AppStore** application, which will be a central theme of this book. The application includes a persistence layer designed around JPA, a session bean facade, and a frontend delivered with **JavaServer Faces (JSF)** web framework (we will see this in the next chapter).

In this chapter, we will discuss the following topics in more detail:

- The key elements of JPA
- How to create entities starting from database tables
- How to manipulate the entities with a session bean
- Delivering a standalone client for testing the application

Data persistence meets a standard

The arrival of an **Enterprise Java Persistence** standard, based on a "POJO" development model, fills a substantial gap in the Java EE platform. The previous attempt of EJB 2.x specification missed the mark and created the stereotype of EJB entity beans as awkward to develop and too heavy for many applications. Therefore, it never reached the level of widespread adoption or general approval in many sectors of the industry.

Software developers knew what they wanted, but many could not find it in the existing standards, so they decided to look elsewhere. What they found was proprietary persistence frameworks, both in the commercial and open source domains.

In contrast to EJB 2.x entity beans, the EJB 3.0 Java Persistence API is a metadata-driven POJO technology. That is, to save data held in Java objects into a database, our objects are not required to implement an interface, extend a class, or fit into a framework pattern.

Another key feature of JPA is the query language, called the **Java Persistence Query Language** (**JPQL**) that gives you a way to specify the semantics of queries in a portable way, independent of the particular database you are using in an enterprise environment. JPA queries resemble SQL queries in syntax, but operate against entity objects rather than directly with database tables.

Working with JPA

Inspired by **object-relational mapping** (**ORM**) frameworks, such as Hibernate, JPA uses annotations to map objects to a relational database. JPA entities are POJOs that neither extend a class nor implement an interface. You don't even need XML descriptors for your mapping. Actually, the Java Persistence API is made up of annotations and only a few classes and interfaces. For example, we would mark the class Company as entity, as follows:

```
@Entity
public class Company {
public Company () {  }
@Id
String companyName;
}
```

The last code snippet shows the minimal requirements for a class to be persistent, which are:

- It must be identified as an entity using the `@javax.persistence.Entity` annotation

- It must have an identifier attribute with the `@javax.persistence.Id` annotation

- It must have a no-argument constructor

I guess you would learn better from an example, so in the next section we will show how to create and deploy a sample JPA application on JBoss 5.

Creating a sample application

Our sample application will be a small store application, which tracks orders from a list of customers. The application will be developed using MySQL database, which is freely downloadable from `http://dev.mysql.com/downloads/`.

We suggest that you download MySQL 5.x, as well as **MySQL Connector/J**, which is used for **Java Database Connectivity (JDBC)**. Once the download is complete, extract the file `mysql-connector-java.jar` and place it in the `JBOSS_HOME/common/lib`, thus making it available to all your server configurations.

Setting up the database

We will create a database named `appstore`, and then we will add a user named `jboss` assigning it all privileges on the schemas, as shown in the following code snippet:

```
CREATE DATABASE appstore;
USE appstore;
CREATE USER 'jboss'@'localhost' IDENTIFIED BY 'jboss';
GRANT ALL PRIVILEGES ON appstore.* TO 'jboss'@'localhost' WITH GRANT
    OPTION;
```

Our simple schema will be made up of two tables—the **Customer** table that contains the list of all customers and the **Item** table that holds the list of all orders. The two tables are in a 1-n relationship and the **Item** table hosts a **Foreign key** (**customer_id**) that relates to the **id** of the **Customer** table.

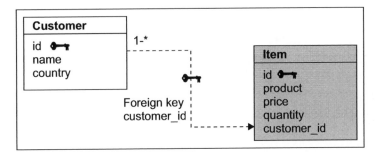

```
CREATE TABLE  appstore.customer (
    `ID` int(10) unsigned NOT NULL auto_increment,
    `NAME` varchar(45) NOT NULL,
    `COUNTRY` varchar(45) NOT NULL,
    PRIMARY KEY  (`ID`)
```

```
) ENGINE=InnoDB;
CREATE TABLE  appstore.item (
    `ID` int(10) unsigned NOT NULL auto_increment,
    `PRODUCT` varchar(45) default NULL,
    `PRICE` int(11) default NULL,
    `QUANTITY` int(11) default NULL,
    `CUSTOMER_ID` int(10) unsigned NOT NULL,
    PRIMARY KEY  (`ID`),
    KEY `FK_orders` (`CUSTOMER_ID`),
    CONSTRAINT `FK_orders` FOREIGN KEY (`CUSTOMER_ID`) REFERENCES
        `customer` (`ID`) ON DELETE CASCADE ON UPDATE CASCADE
) ENGINE=InnoDB;
```

Rolling the EJB project

Once we are done with the data layer, we will create our entities. A preamble is necessary before we begin. Depending on the release of your Eclipse and JBoss Tools, you can model your project in several ways. In this example, we will create our entities using a wizard, so you will not need to write mapping classes manually. However, if you don't have the latest JBoss Tools installation, you still have other options available. For example, you can use Hibernate Tools to automatically generate mapping classes (this will be covered in Chapter 8, *Developing Applications with JBoss and Hibernate*).

Here we go. This project will contain both session beans and entities. Therefore, the simplest way to start is by creating a new EJB project and adding a JPA nature to it.

From the **File** menu, select **New | Other | EJB | EJB Project**, and name it **AppStore**—an application for handling a store. (I have to admit sometimes IT guys don't have much imagination!)

Now we will add JPA capabilities to our project. Right-click on the project and select **Properties**. The property we are interested in is **Project Facets**, which is the collection of capabilities added to our project. Select **Java Persistence**, as indicated in the following screenshot, and click **OK**.

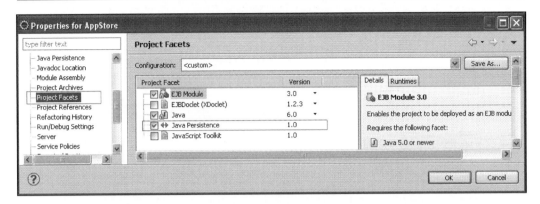

Now your **AppStore** has got some new interesting options. Let's see where you can find them. Move to the root of your project and right-click on **AppStore**. Select **New | Entities From Tables** (see the following screenshot):

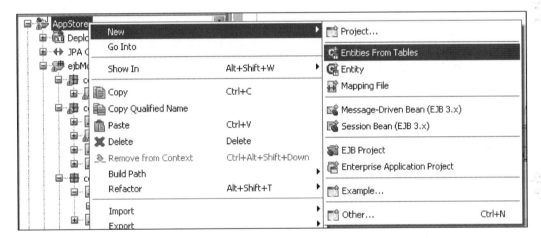

The JPA wizard will start. The process of reverse engineering the database into Java entities can be roughly divided into two steps as follows:

1. **Configuring the database connection**: This step involves the definition of a database connection that needs to be performed just the first time you use the JPA wizard.

2. **Generating entities**: This second step is the actual process of reverse engineering.

These steps are discussed in more detail as follows:

Configuring the database connection

As we don't have any configured connection, you have to create a new one by clicking on the shiny little button at the top-right corner of your wizard, which is shown in the following screenshot:

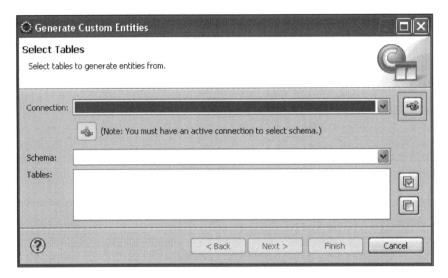

In the next window, you have to select the database that contains your planned entities. Select **MySQL** (or whichever database you are using) from the next wizard and choose an appropriate label for our connection; here we select **MySQL Connection**.

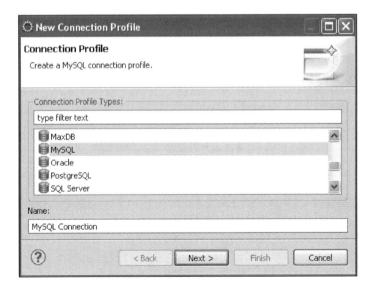

Hit **Next**. A new window will let you specify a driver and connection details. As we do not have any JDBC driver configured yet, you should first click on the little icon (+) in the top-right corner.

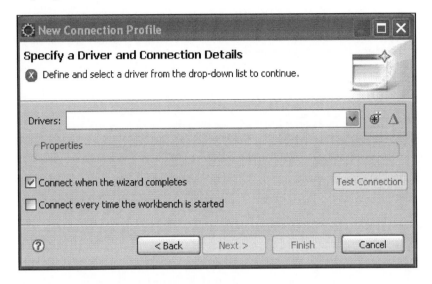

The **New Driver Definition** dialog appears. First, select the driver template from the list of available options; in our case select **MySQL 5.0**. Then in the **Jar List** tab, point to the MySQL connector, which we downloaded earlier.

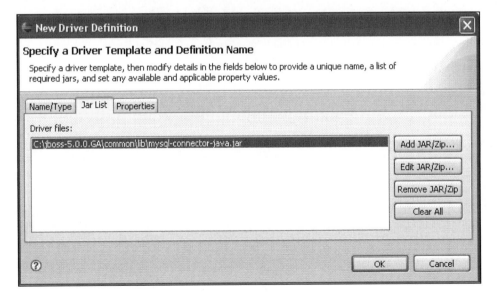

Okay, we are almost done. The last thing you need to select is the JDBC Driver properties in the **New Connection Profile**, which should match with your **appstore** database.

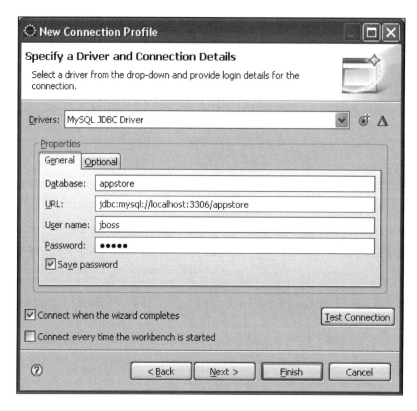

Before clicking **Finish**, we suggest you verify the connection with the **Test Connection** button. If for some reason the test fails, verify the **General Properties** and, of course, that the database is up and running.

Generating entities

Once the connection configuration is complete, it's time to roll your entities. You will be taken back to the first JPA wizard window, where you can now select the **Schema** as **appstore** and the **Tables** as **customer** and **item**:

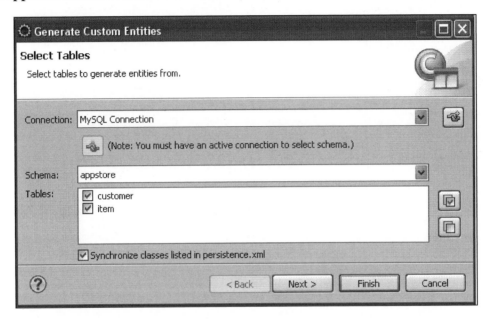

Selecting **Synchronize classes listed in persistence.xml** will insert the entity definition in the main JPA configuration file—`persistence.xml`. This is not a mandatory step; however, Eclipse will complain later if the entities are not synchronized with the configuration file.

Click **Next**. In the subsequent wizard you have to deal with **Table Associations**. As you can see in the following screenshot, the JPA facet correctly recognizes the 1-n association between **customer** and **item**. In terms of entities, this will mean that the `Customer` entity will contain a list of `Item` entities ordered and the `Item` class will contain a reference to the `Customer`.

Click on the association diagram and choose names for the entity fields that will describe the relation.

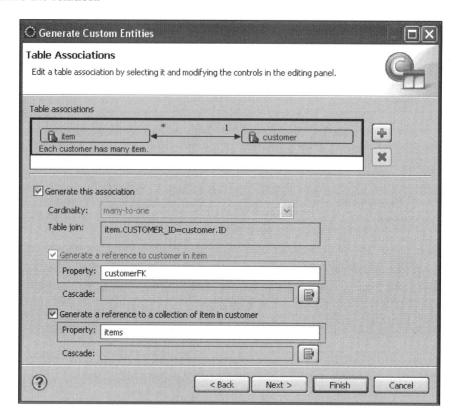

In the last screenshot, **customerFK** will be a reference to the Customer (in the Item class) and **items** will hold the list of items ordered by a single customer. You are just one step away from finishing. Click **Next**. In the next wizard, you have to customize your entities.

The options that override the defaults are framed in the following screenshot:

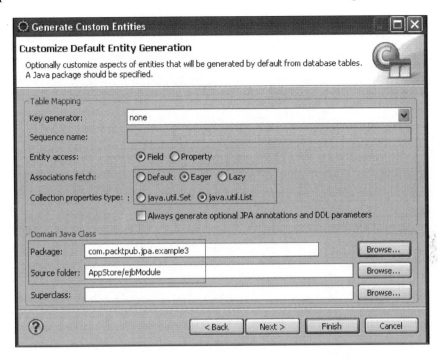

First, we want our entities to use an **Eager** fetching strategy. What does this mean? By default, when we have an association between two entities, the referenced objects are **lazy loaded**, that is, fetching and loading the data from the persistent storage is done only when it is needed. In contrast to lazy loading, eager loading loads the full object tree at once. Lazy loading contributes a lot to improving the performance of an application, by limiting the number of objects that will be needed. However, if you need to traverse the tree of objects from the client side (as in our example), you will need to use the eager fetching strategy.

Then, select the class **java.util.List** as **Collection properties type**, which will be just fine for returning a vector of items and customers.

Lastly, choose the target package for the entities, that is, com.packtpub.jpa. example3. If you want to preview the entities that are going to be generated, have a look at the next windows. Otherwise, you can complete the JPA wizard by clicking on the **Finish** button.

Reverse engineering aftermath

From the **Project Explorer** window, let's explore what the wizard has created for you:

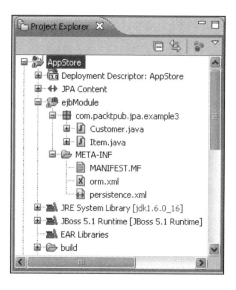

If you have successfully completed all the wizard steps, your entities will be correctly packaged in the com.packtpub.jpa.example3 folder.

Let's have a look at the Customer entity:

```
package com.packtpub.jpa.example3;
import java.io.Serializable;
import javax.persistence.*;
import java.util.List;
import static javax.persistence.FetchType.EAGER;
@Entity   [1]
@Table(name="customer")   [2]
public class Customer implements Serializable {
    private static final long serialVersionUID = 1L;
    @Id   [3]
    @GeneratedValue(strategy=GenerationType.AUTO)
    @Column(name="ID")   [4]
    private int id;
    @Column(name="COUNTRY")
    private String country;
    @Column(name="NAME")
    private String name;
    //bi-directional many-to-one association to Item
```

```
@OneToMany(mappedBy="customerFK", fetch = EAGER)   [5]
private List<Item> items;
public Customer() {
}
public int getId() {
    return this.id;
}
public void setId(int id) {
    this.id = id;
}
public String getCountry() {
    return this.country;
}
public void setCountry(String country) {
    this.country = country;
}
public String getName() {
    return this.name;
}
public void setName(String name) {
    this.name = name;
}
public List<Item> getItems() {
    return this.items;
}
public void setItems(List<Item> items) {
    this.items = items;
}
}
```

The first meaningful annotation is @Entity **[1]** that declares the class as an entity. The @Table **[2]** annotation is used to map the bean class with a database table.

The @Id annotation **[3]** is mandatory; it describes the primary key of the table. Along with @Id, there's the @GeneratedValue annotation. This is used to declare that the database is in charge of generating the value.

Moving along, the @Column **[4]** annotation is used to map the Java field with the corresponding database column. You can leave out this annotation, if the two elements are equal.

The @OneToMany annotation **[5]** defines an association with one-to-many multiplicity. Actually, the Customer class has many orders. The corresponding orders are contained in a List collection.

In the JPA wizard, we have chosen the EAGER attribute to the @OneToMany annotation so that all orders are populated at the same time when we issue a query on the Customer entity.

At this point we have inspected the Customer entity. Let's have a look at the Item entity:

```
package com.packtpub.jpa.example3;
import java.io.Serializable;
import javax.persistence.*;
@Entity
@Table(name="item")
public class Item implements Serializable {
   private static final long serialVersionUID = 1L;
   @Id
   @GeneratedValue(strategy=GenerationType.AUTO)
   @Column(name="ID")
   private int id;
   @Column(name="PRICE")
   private int price;
   @Column(name="PRODUCT")
   private String product;
   @Column(name="QUANTITY")
   private int quantity;
   //bi-directional many-to-one association to Customer
   @ManyToOne   [1]
   @JoinColumn(name="CUSTOMER_ID")   [2]
   private Customer customerFK;
   public Item() {
   }
   public int getId() {
      return this.id;
   }
   public void setId(int id) {
      this.id = id;
   }
   public int getPrice() {
      return this.price;
   }
   public void setPrice(int price) {
      this.price = price;
   }
   public String getProduct() {
      return this.product;
   }
```

```
    public void setProduct(String product) {
        this.product = product;
    }
    public int getQuantity() {
        return this.quantity;
    }
    public void setQuantity(int quantity) {
        this.quantity = quantity;
    }
    public Customer getCustomerFK() {
        return this.customerFK;
    }
    public void setCustomerFK(Customer customerFK) {
        this.customerFK = customerFK;
    }
}
```

As you can see, the Item entity has the corresponding @ManyToOne **[1]** annotation, which naturally complements the @OneToMany relationship. The @JoinColumn **[2]**, which has the same syntax of the @Column annotation, notifies the JPA engine that the customerFK field is mapped through the foreign key of the database customer_id.

Configuring persistence

The entity API looks great and very intuitive, but how does the server know which database is supposed to store/query the entity objects? The persistence.xml file (located in the META-INF folder of your project) is the standard JPA configuration file. Believe it, this is a huge leap towards application server compatibility. By configuring this file, you can easily switch from one persistence provider to another and thus, also from one application server to another.

At the beginning, the persistence.xml file contains just the mapped entities we created. We have to specify the persistence provider and the underlying datasource used.

```
<?xml version="1.0" encoding="UTF-8"?>
<persistence version="1.0" xmlns="http://java.sun.com/xml/ns/
persistence" xmlns:xsi="http://www.w3.org/2001/XMLSchema-instance"
xsi:schemaLocation="http://java.sun.com/xml/ns/persistence http://
java.sun.com/xml/ns/persistence/persistence_1_0.xsd">
    <persistence-unit name="AppStore" transaction-type="JTA">
        <provider>org.hibernate.ejb.HibernatePersistence</provider>
        <jta-data-source>java:/MySqlDS</jta-data-source>
        <class>com.packtpub.jpa.example3.Customer</class>
        <class>com.packtpub.jpa.example3.Item</class>
        <properties>
```

```
        <property name="hibernate.dialect"
            value="org.hibernate.dialect.MySQLDialect"/>
        </properties>
    </persistence-unit>
</persistence>
```

The highlighted attributes need to be added to `persistence.xml`. The attribute name is a mandatory element, which will be used to reference the persistence unit from our Enterprise JavaBeans. Then, we have specified the `provider` factory, which will be used (in our case, it's `HibernatePersistence`). Another key attribute is the `jta-data-source` that needs to point to a datasource component. The last property, `hibernate.dialect`, will specify the O/R dialect class.

The only thing we have missed out is adding a datasource to the JBoss configuration. Beginning with the templates in `docs\examples\jca` folder of JBoss, we will create a MySQL datasource, which points to our **appstore** schema:

```
<?xml version="1.0" encoding="UTF-8"?>
<datasources>
    <local-tx-datasource>
        <jndi-name>MySqlDS</jndi-name>
        <connection-url>jdbc:mysql://localhost:3306/
            appstore</connection-url>
        <driver-class>com.mysql.jdbc.Driver</driver-class>
        <user-name>jboss</user-name>
        <password>jboss</password>
        <exception-sorter-class-name>org.jboss.resource.adapter.
            jdbc.vendor.MySQLExceptionSorter
        </exception-sorter-class-name>
        <metadata>
            <type-mapping>mySQL</type-mapping>
        </metadata>
    </local-tx-datasource>
</datasources>
```

Save this file as `mysql-ds.xml` in the `deploy` folder of your JBoss configuration.

Creating a Session Bean client

With the classes that we just saw, we have completed the entity layer but we have not finished with the EJB project. Actually, if you allow client applications to directly access the entity, then the client requires knowledge of the entity implementation that goes beyond what clients should have. For instance, manipulating an entity requires knowledge of the entity relationships (such as associations and inheritance) that are involved, inappropriately exposing the client to all of the details of the business model.

The best practice advocated by Java EE architects is to provide a business interface to the entity subsystem; the standard interfaces for the persistence entities are Stateless Session Beans.

In our example, we are going to create two interfaces for our EJB clients—one for remote clients and another for local clients. Java SE clients will connect to our session beans through the remote interface, whereas web clients (described in the next chapter) will conveniently use the local interface.

At this stage you should be comfortable with stateless bean. Create a new session EJB 3 from the **File** menu: **New | Other | EJB | EJB 3 Session Bean**. The suggested name for this example is `com.packtpub.ejb.example3.StoreManager`. This will also create the implementing class `com.packtpub.ejb.StoreManagerBean`. Here is its interface contract:

```
package com.packtpub.ejb.example3;

import java.util.List;

import javax.ejb.Local;

import com.packtpub.jpa.example3.Customer;
import com.packtpub.jpa.example3.Item;

public interface StoreManager {
    public void createCustomer(String country,String name);
    public List<Customer> findAllCustomers();
    public Customer findCustomerByName(String name);
    public Customer findCustomerById(int id);

    public void saveOrder(int idCustomer, int price,
            int quantity,String product);
    public List<Item> findAllItems(int customerId);

}
```

We have defined one method `createCustomer` that will be used to add new customers to our store. Then we have added some finder methods: `findAllCustomers`, `findAllCustomerByName`, and `findCustomerById` that can be used to retrieve the single `Customer` or the whole list.

Items ordered can be persisted by means of the `saveOrder` method and queried with the `findAllItems` method.

The interface we just saw will be extended by the `StoreManagerLocal` and `StoreManagerRemote` interfaces, which will provide respectively the local and remote view of the EJB:

```
package com.packtpub.ejb.example3;
import javax.ejb.Local;
@Local
public interface StoreManagerLocal
extends StoreManager {
}
```

And here's the `StoreManagerRemote` interface:

```
package com.packtpub.ejb.example3;
import javax.ejb.Remote;
@Remote
public interface StoreManagerRemote
extends StoreManager{
}
```

The concrete implementation class is contained in the `StoreManagerBean` class:

```
package com.packtpub.ejb.example3;

import java.util.List;

import javax.ejb.Stateless;
import javax.persistence.*;

import org.jboss.ejb3.annotation.LocalBinding;
import org.jboss.ejb3.annotation.RemoteBinding;

import com.packtpub.jpa.example3.*;

@Stateless

@RemoteBinding(jndiBinding="AppStoreEJB/remote")
@LocalBinding(jndiBinding="AppStoreEJB/local")

public  class StoreManagerBean implements StoreManagerLocal,
                                          StoreManagerRemote {
    @PersistenceContext(unitName="AppStore")
    private EntityManager em;

    public void createCustomer(String country,String name) {
        Customer customer = new Customer();
        customer.setCountry(country);
        customer.setName(name);
        em.persist(customer);
    }
    public void saveOrder(int idCustomer, int price,
```

```
                int quantity, String product) {
        Customer customer = findCustomerById(idCustomer);

        Item order = new Item();
        order.setCustomerFK(customer);
        order.setPrice(price);
        order.setQuantity(quantity);
        order.setProduct(product);
        em.persist(order);
    }
    public List<Item> findAllItems(int customerId)
    {

        Query query = em.createQuery("FROM Customer where id=:id");
        query.setParameter("id", customerId);
        Customer customer = (Customer)query.getSingleResult();

        List <Item>customerOrders = customer.getItems();

        return customerOrders;

    }
    public Customer findCustomerByName(String customerName)
    {

        Query query = em.createQuery("FROM Customer
                    where name=:name");
        query.setParameter("name", customerName);
        Customer customer = (Customer)query.getSingleResult();

        return customer;

    }

    public Customer findCustomerById(int id)
    {

        Query query = em.createQuery("FROM Customer where id=:id");
        query.setParameter("id", id);
        Customer customer = (Customer)query.getSingleResult();

        return customer;

    }
    public List<Customer> findAllCustomers() {
        Query query = em.createQuery("FROM Customer");
        List<Customer> customerList = query.getResultList();

        return customerList;

    }
}
```

The @PersistenceContext [1] annotation added to the EntityManager field, injects a container-managed persistence context. You might think of this as an object-oriented connection to the RDBMS. The following diagram illustrates the whole sequence:

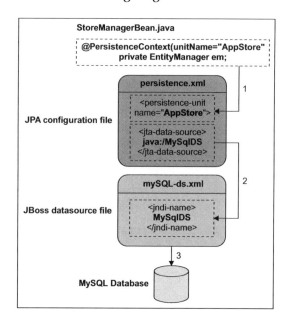

As you can see, the injected resource **AppStore** references the persistence unit defined in persistence.xml. This in turn points to the jta datasource named **MySqlDS.** The datasource (defined in the mySQL-ds.xml configuration file) contains the connection details of the MySQL appstore schema.

The first method, createCustomer, illustrates how you can perform the equivalent of a CREATE SQL statement using JPA. As you can see, it's all about creating object instances [2]. Until you persist [3] your objects, however, all changes are held in memory.

The method saveOrder works quite the same. Moving to the finder methods, we meet the findAllItems method. If you have already worked with Hibernate, this should sound very familiar to you. In fact, JPA also uses a database-independent language, Java Persistence Query Language, to issues queries. It is a rich language that allows you to query any complex object's model (associations, inheritance, abstract classes, and so on) using common built-in database functions. There are functions that deal with strings (LOWER, UPPER, TRIM, CONCAT, LENGTH, and SUBSTR), numbers (ABS, SQRT, and MOD), or collections (COUNT, MIN, MAX, and SUM). Like SQL, you can also sort the results (ORDER BY) or group them (GROUP BY).

In our sample method, we issue a query **[4]**, which is filtered by the `id` parameter **[5]**. The use of parameters here is quite similar to plain `PreparedStatements` bound variables. The EJB contains additional finder methods (`findCustomerById`, `findCustomerByName`, and `findAllCustomers`) that are modeled using the same steps as in `findAllItems`.

At this point, our EJB layer is completed. Here's a screenshot of the **Project Explorer** that depicts the complete **AppStore** project:

It's now time to deploy the EJB project to our application server. Follow the same steps described in the session bean examples, that is, from the JBoss AS perspective right-click on the server node and choose **Add and remove Project**; then in the same window choose **Full Publish** in order to deploy the project. Verify from the server console that your EJB has bound correctly in the JNDI tree:

```
AppStoreEJB/remote - EJB3.x Default Remote Business Interface
AppStoreEJB/local - EJB3.x Default Local Business Interface
```

The next section is about creating the client interface for this application.

Creating a test client for our AppStore

Clients for session beans can be simple J2SE classes or server-side components such as JSP-servlets. We will now create a very simple Java class for interacting with the session remote interface. Add a new Java class to the project from **File | New | Class** and choose a name for it. Here's the com.packtpub.client.example3. TestAppStore class:

```java
package com.packtpub.client.example3;

import java.util.*;

import javax.naming.*;

import com.packtpub.ejb.example3.*;
import com.packtpub.jpa.example3.*;

public class TestAppStore {

    public static void main(String[] args) throws Exception {
        Hashtable hash = new Hashtable();
        hash.put("java.naming.factory.initial","
                org.jnp.interfaces.NamingContextFactory");
        hash.put("java.naming.provider.url","jnp://localhost:1099");
        hash.put("java.naming.factory.url.pkgs","
                org.jnp.interfaces");

        Context ctx = new InitialContext(hash);

        StoreManager storeManager = (StoreManager)ctx.
                                    lookup("AppStoreEJB/remote");

        // Create a Customer [1]
        storeManager.createCustomer("Usa","Clint Eastwood");

        // Retrieve the Customer [2]
        Customer customer = storeManager.findCustomerByName
                            ("Clint Eastwood");

        // Save an order for an Item
        storeManager.saveOrder(customer.getId(), 1000,5, "Bycycle");

        // Find all Items ordered by the Customer [3]
        List<Item> items = storeManager.findAllItems
                            (customer.getId());

        System.out.println("Listing orders for "
                            +customer.getName());
        Iterator <Item> iter = items.iterator();
        while (iter.hasNext()) {
            Item item = iter.next();
```

```
                    System.out.println("---------------");
                    System.out.println("id #" +item.getId());
                    System.out.println("product #" +item.getProduct());
                    System.out.println("qty #" +item.getQuantity());
                    System.out.println("$ #" +item.getPrice());
                }
            }
        }
```

The Java class should be self-explanatory at this stage. We have created a customer from `Usa` [1] who places an order for an item [2]. The list of pending items ordered is queried by the `findCustomerByName` method [3]. That's all folks!

Summary

The aim of the new Java Persistence API is to simplify the development of persistent entities. It meets this objective through a simple POJO-based persistence model that reduces the number of required classes and interfaces.

Mapping database tables with Java objects can be cumbersome, so we have first shown here a quick reverse engineering solution, which is available in the Eclipse development environment. In the latter part of this chapter, we have added a session bean facade to our entities and tested it with a Java standalone client.

In the next chapter, we will further enhance our example application by introducing a web project that controls user interaction.

6
Creating a Web Application

Wonder what was the first message sent through Internet? At 22:30 hours on October 29, 1969, a message was transmitted using ARPANET (the predecessor of the global Internet) on a host-to-host connection. It was meant to transmit "login". However, it transmitted just "lo" and crashed.

This chapter is about developing and configuring web applications using JBoss web container. Most developers have surely gained some experience with web applications. Therefore, we will not cover the basics of web applications; we will rather disclose how easy it can be to create a consistent web layer for your applications, using just the right tools and, of course, the right technique.

We will cover the following topics in more detail:

- What is JSF and how to install it on JBoss AS
- How to create a JSF facade for our pasture application
- How to configure JBoss Web Server

Developing web layout

The basic component of any Java web application is the **servlet**. Born in the middle of the 90s, servlets quickly gained success against their competitors, the CGI scripts. This was because of some innovative features, especially the ability to execute requests concurrently, without the overhead of creating a new process for each request. However, a few things were missing, for example, the **servlet API** did not address any APIs specifically for creating the client GUI. This resulted in multiple ways of creating the presentation tier, generally with tag libraries that differed from job to job and from individual developers.

The second thing that was missing in the servlet specification was a clear distinction between the presentation tier and the backend. A plethora of web frameworks tried to fill this gap; particularly the **Struts** framework effectively realized a clean separation of the **model** (application logic that interacts with a database) from the **view** (HTML pages presented to the client) and the **controller** (instance that passes information between view and model).

However, the limitation of these frameworks was that even if they realized a complete modular abstraction, they still failed as they always exposed the `HttpServletRequest` and `HttpServletSession` objects to their action(s). Their actions, in turn, needed to accept the interface contracts such as `ActionForm`, `ActionMapping`, and so on.

The JavaServer Faces that emerged on the stage a few years later pursued a different approach. Unlike request-driven **Model–View–Controller** (**MVC**) web frameworks, JSF chose a component-based approach that ties the user interface component to a well-defined request processing life cycle. This greatly simplifies the development of web applications.

The JSF specification allows you to have presentation components be POJOs. This creates a cleaner separation from the servlet layer and makes it easier to do testing by not requiring the POJOs to be dependent on the servlet classes.

In the following sections, we will describe how to create a web layout for our application store using the JSF technology. For an exhaustive explanation of the JSF framework, we suggest you to surf the JSF homepage at `http://java.sun.com/javaee/javaserverfaces/`.

Installing JSF on JBoss AS

JBoss AS already ships with the JSF libraries, so the good news is that you don't need to download or install them in the application server. There are different implementations of the JSF libraries. Earlier JBoss releases adopted the **Apache MyFaces** library. JBoss AS 4.2 and 5.x ship with the **Common Development and Distribution License** (**CDDL**) implementation (now called "Project Mojarra") of the JSF 1.2 specification that is available from the java.net open source community.

Switching to another JSF implementation is anyway possible. All you have to do is package your JSF libraries with your web application and configure your `web.xml` to ignore the JBoss built-in implementation:

```
<context-param>
     <param-name>org.jboss.jbossfaces.WAR_BUNDLES_JSF_
IMPL</param-name>
     <param-value>true</param-value>
</context-param>
```

We will start by creating a new JSF project. From the **File** menu, select **New | Other | JBoss Tools Web | JSF | JSF Web project**. The JSF applet wizard will display, requesting the **Project Name**, the **JSF Environment**, and the default starting **Template**.

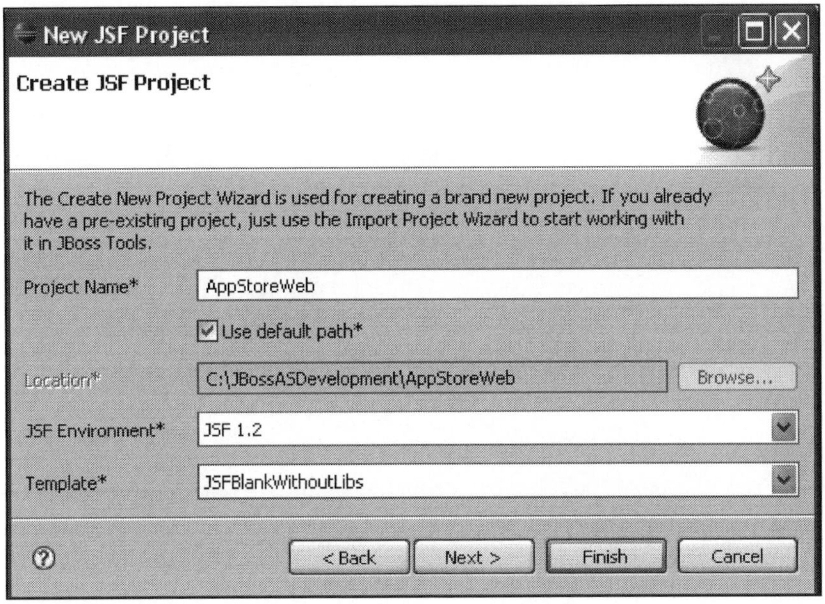

Choose **AppStoreWeb** as the project name, and check that the **JSF Environment** used is **JSF 1.2**. You can leave all other options to the defaults and click **Finish**. Eclipse will now suggest that you switch to the **Web Projects** view that logically assembles all JSF components. (It seems that the current release of the plugin doesn't understand your choice, so you have to manually click on the **Web Projects** tab.)

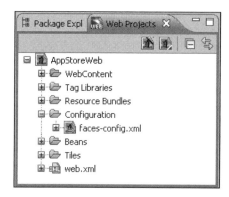

The key configuration file of a JSF application is `faces-config.xml` contained in the `Configuration` folder. Here you declare all **navigation rules** of the application and the **JSF managed beans**. Managed beans are simple POJOs that provide the logic for initializing and controlling JSF components, and for managing data across page requests, user sessions, or the application as a whole.

Adding JSF functionalities also requires adding some information to your `web.xml` file so that all requests ending with a certain suffix are intercepted by the `Faces Servlet`. Let's have a look at the `web.xml` configuration file:

```
<?xml version="1.0"?>
<web-app version="2.5" xmlns="http://java.sun.com/xml/ns/javaee"
  xmlns:xsi="http://www.w3.org/2001/XMLSchema-instance"
  xsi:schemaLocation="http://java.sun.com/xml/ns/javaee
    http://java.sun.com/xml/ns/javaee/web-app_2_5.xsd">
  <display-name>AppStoreWeb</display-name>
  <context-param>
    <param-name>javax.faces.STATE_SAVING_METHOD</param-name>
    <param-value>server</param-value>
  </context-param>
  <context-param>   [1]
    <param-name>com.sun.faces.
      enableRestoreView11Compatibility</param-name>
    <param-value>true</param-value>
  </context-param>
  <listener>
```

```xml
      <listener-class>com.sun.faces.config.
        ConfigureListener</listener-class>
  </listener>
  <!-- Faces Servlet -->
  <servlet>
    <servlet-name>Faces Servlet</servlet-name>
    <servlet-class>javax.faces.webapp.FacesServlet</servlet-class>
    <load-on-startup>1</load-on-startup>
  </servlet>
  <!-- Faces Servlet Mapping -->
  <servlet-mapping>
    <servlet-name>Faces Servlet</servlet-name>
    <url-pattern>*.jsf</url-pattern>
  </servlet-mapping>
  <login-config>
    <auth-method>BASIC</auth-method>
  </login-config>
</web-app>
```

> The `context-param` pointed out here **[1]** is not added by default when you create a JSF application. However, it needs to be added, else you'll stumble into an annoying `ViewExpiredException` when your session expires (JSF 1.2).

Setting up navigation rules

In the first step, we will define the navigation rules for our AppStore. A minimalist approach would require a homepage that displays the orders, along with two additional pages for inserting new customers and new orders respectively.

Let's add the following navigation rule to the `faces-config.xml`:

```xml
<faces-config>
<navigation-rule>
    <from-view-id>/home.jsp</from-view-id>    [1]
    <navigation-case>
      <from-outcome>newCustomer</from-outcome>    [2]
      <to-view-id>/newCustomer.jsp</to-view-id>
    </navigation-case>
  <navigation-case>
      <from-outcome>newOrder</from-outcome>    [3]
      <to-view-id>/newOrder.jsp</to-view-id>
    </navigation-case>
  </navigation-rule>
```

```
<navigation-rule>
  <from-view-id></from-view-id>    [4]
  <navigation-case>
    <from-outcome>home</from-outcome>
    <to-view-id>/home.jsp</to-view-id>
  </navigation-case>
</navigation-rule>
</faces-config>
```

In a navigation rule, you can have one `from-view-id` that is the (optional) starting page, and one or more landing pages that are tagged as `to-view-id`. The `from-outcome` determines the navigation flow. Think about this parameter as a Struts `forward`, that is, instead of embedding the landing page in the JSP/servlet, you'll simply declare a virtual path in your JSF beans.

Therefore, our starting page will be `home.jsp` **[1]** that has two possible links — the `newCustomer.jsp` form **[2]** and the `newOrder.jsp` form **[3]**. At the bottom, there is a navigation rule that is valid across all pages **[4]**. Every page requesting the `home` outcome will be redirected to the homepage of the application.

The above JSP will be created in a minute, so don't worry if Eclipse validator complains about the missing pages. This configuration can also be examined from the **Diagram** tab of your `faces-config.xml`:

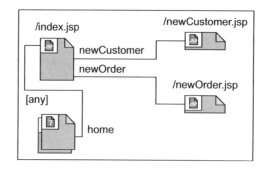

The next piece of code that we will add to the configuration is the JSF managed bean declaration. You need to declare each bean here that will be referenced by JSF pages. Add the following code snippet at the top of your `faces-config.xml` (just before navigation rules):

```
<managed-bean>
  <managed-bean-name>manager</managed-bean-name>    [1]
    <managed-bean-class>
      com.packpub.web.StoreManagerJSFBean
```

```
          </managed-bean-class>    [2]
        <managed-bean-scope>request</managed-bean-scope>    [3]
      </managed-bean>
```

The `<managed-bean-name>` **[1]** element will be used by your JSF page to reference your beans. The `<managed-bean-class>` **[2]** is obviously the corresponding class. The managed beans can then be stored within the request, session, or application scopes, depending on the value of the `<managed-bean-scope>` element **[3]**.

Adding a JSF managed bean

The `StoreManagerJSFBean` class follows the JavaBean patterns, providing `get` and `set` methods for its properties (to make the code more maintainable, we have skipped the `getter`/`setter` methods that simply wrap the fields of the class). We have declared the bean as request bound, so for each user of the application, JSF creates a `StoreManagerJSFBean` instance, which is stored within the `request` scope.

Add to your project a new Java class and name it `com.packtpub.web.` `StoreManagerJSFBean`:

```java
package com.packpub.web;
// skipping imports
public class StoreManagerJSFBean {
    @EJB(mappedName = "AppStoreEJB/local")    [1]
    private StoreManager storeManager;
    private int customerId;
    private int orderQuantity;
    private int orderPrice;
    private String customerName;
    private String customerCountry;
    private String orderProduct;
    List<Order> listOrders;
    List <SelectItem> listCustomers;
    public List<SelectItem> getListCustomers() {
      if (listCustomers == null) {
        listCustomers= new ArrayList();
        findAllCustomers();
      }
      return listCustomers;
    }
    /*
      other getter/setter methods omitted for brevity
    */
    public StoreManagerJSFBean() {  }
```

```
   public void findOrders() {   [2]
     listOrders = storeManager.findAllItems(this.customerId);
   }
public void findAllCustomers() {
        List<Customer> listCustomersEJB =
                storeManager.findAllCustomers();

        for(Customer customer:listCustomersEJB) {
            listCustomers.add(new
                SelectItem(customer.getId(),customer.getName()));
        }
      }
}
  public void saveOrder() {
  storeManager.saveOrder(customerId,this.orderPrice,
    this.orderQuantity,this.orderProduct);
    FacesMessage fm = new FacesMessage("Saved order for
      "+this.orderQuantity+ " of "+this.orderProduct);
    FacesContext.getCurrentInstance().addMessage("Message", fm);
    this.orderPrice=0;
    this.orderQuantity=0;
    this.orderProduct=null;
  }
  public void insertCustomer() {
    storeManager.createCustomer(this.customerCountry,
      this.customerName);
    FacesMessage fm = new FacesMessage(«Created Customer
      «+this.customerName+ « fromf «+this.customerCountry);
    FacesContext.getCurrentInstance().addMessage("Message", fm);
    this.customerName=null;
    this.customerCountry=null;
      // Forces customer reloading
      this.listCustomers=null;
  }
  /* Navigation rules */
  public String home() {   [4]
    return "home";
  }
  public String newOrder() {
    return "newOrder";
  }
  public String newCustomer() {
    return "newCustomer";
  }
}
```

As you can see, the `StoreManagerJSFBean` references the session bean we have created previously (`StoreManager`). Therefore, we must tell the compiler how to solve this dependency. This can be easily solved by choosing **Properties** on the current project, and then choosing **Projects** from the **Java Build Path** option. Add the project **AppStore** to your build path, as shown here:

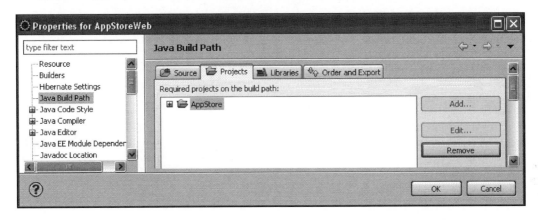

Having fixed the compilation issues, we can now concentrate on the JSF bean. The first thing we want to capture your attention to is how the `StoreManager` EJB is injected **[1]** in the class, skipping completely the lookup/casting/exception handling part.

The `findOrders()` method **[2]** retrieves the list of orders from the `StoreManager` EJB. They will be displayed later in the `dataTable` component.

The `findAllCustomers()` **[3]** is slightly different. It recalls our entity bean's corresponding `findAllCustomers()` method and then populates a `SelectItem` object with the list of customers. `SelectItem` is a JSF object used to render a combobox programmatically. In our case, we will populate it with the `customerId` (as value) and `customerName` (as label).

The remaining EJB wrapper methods, `saveOrder()` and `insertCustomer()`, are quite intuitive; their job is to persist data for `Orders` and `Customers`.

The final piece of code is about navigation rules **[4]** that are coded as simple Java methods returning the outcome view as a string. For example, in order to return to the homepage from any other page, we will add the following button:

```
<h:commandButton action="#{manager.home}" value="Back" />
```

Setting up the view

JSF pages are just behind-the-scenes JSP pages that are engineered by the JSF servlet. Therefore, in order to create your views, add the following pages to your web application: `home.jsp`, `newCustomer.jsp` and `newOrder.jsp`. A new JSP page can be added from the **Web Projects** menu by right-clicking on the `WebContent` folder, then choosing **New | File | JSP Page** and naming it `home.jsp`.

```
<%@ taglib uri="http://java.sun.com/jsf/html" prefix="h"%>   [1]
<%@ taglib uri="http://java.sun.com/jsf/core" prefix="f"%>

<html>
<body>
<f:view>   [2]
  <style type="text/css">   [3]
    @import url("css/appstore.css");
  </style>
  <h:panelGrid columns="1" border="1" styleClass="spring">   [4]
    <f:facet name="header">
    <h:outputText value="Order List"/>
    </f:facet>
    <h:form id="listOrdersForm">   [5]
      <h:outputText value="Select Customer:" />   [6]
      <h:selectOneMenu id="selectCustomer"
        value="#{manager.customerId}" styleClass="buttons">   [7]
        <f:selectItems
          value="#{manager.listCustomers}" />
      </h:selectOneMenu>
      <h:commandButton action="#{manager.findOrders}"
        value="ListOrders" styleClass="buttons"/>   [8]
      <h:dataTable value="#{manager.listOrders}" var="orders"
        border="1" rowClasses="row1, row2" headerClass="header">   [9]
      <h:column>
        <f:facet name="header">
          <h:outputText value="Product" />
        </f:facet>
        <h:outputText value="#{orders.product}" />
      </h:column>
      <h:column>
        <f:facet name="header">
          <h:outputText value="Price" />
        </f:facet>
        <h:outputText value="#{orders.price}" />
      </h:column>
      <h:column>
```

```
            <f:facet name="header">
               <h:outputText value="Quantity" />
            </f:facet>
            <h:outputText value="#{orders.quantity}" />
         </h:column>
      </h:dataTable>
         <h:commandButton action="#{manager.newCustomer}"
           value="Insert Customer" styleClass="buttons" />   [10]
         <h:commandButton action="#{manager.newOrder}"
           value="Insert Order" styleClass="buttons" />   [11]
      </h:form>
   </h:panelGrid>
 </f:view>
 </body>
 </html>
```

JSF contains two tag libraries [1] called JSF core and HTML Basic. The former provides a few general tags and some other tags that let you register validators and event listeners to UI components. The latter contains JSP tags that render HTML UI components such as buttons, text fields, checkboxes, lists, and so on. The standard prefixes of these two tag libraries are h and f, and they are declared at the beginning of home.jsp.

The view tag [2] is the container for all JavaServer Faces component tags used on a page. **Stylesheets [3]** are used here to decorate the UI components. The panelGrid [4] component simplifies the task of constructing a layout table, to hold form fields, labels, and buttons. In this case, it will contain the main input form.

The form element [5] manages an HTML form just the same way as standard form HTML. Rendering simple text on the page can be achieved with an outputText tag [6]. Here, you can use value-binding expressions from your JSF beans.

The selectOneMenu element [7] is used to display an HTML combobox that is bound to a bean collection. Review the findAllCustomers() method of your StoreManagerJSFBean, where the combobox is built dynamically.

The commandButton [8] is applied to render an HTML button. In our case, we have bound the button to the findOrders() method of our JSF bean.

A core JSF tag is the dataTable tag [9] that can be used to render an HTML table using a collection from the backing bean. This component is generally used to display tabular data and it offers a vast choice of built-in options for customizing its header and footer, and for paginating the table.

The last two buttons, **[10]** and **[11]**, plot the route to the newCustomer and newOrder forms.

The form for inserting a new customer is as follows:

```
<%@ taglib uri="http://java.sun.com/jsf/html" prefix="h"%>
<%@ taglib uri="http://java.sun.com/jsf/core" prefix="f"%>

<html>
<body>
<f:view>
    <style type="text/css">
        @import url("css/appstore.css");
    </style>
  <h:form id="newCustomer">
    <h:panelGrid columns="2" border="1" styleClass="spring">
      <f:facet name="header">
        <h:outputText value="Insert new Customer" />
      </f:facet>
      <h:outputText value="Name" />
      <h:inputText value="#{manager.customerName}" />   [1]
      <h:outputText value="Country" />
      <h:inputText value="#{manager.customerCountry}" />
      <h:commandButton action="#{manager.insertCustomer}"   [2]
        value="Insert Customer" />
      <h:commandButton action="#{manager.home}" value="Back" />
    </h:panelGrid>
    <h:messages />
  </h:form>
</f:view>
</body>
</html>
```

The inputText fields **[1]** are used to populate the individual managed bean properties. With the commandButton **[2]**, the insertCustomer() action is recalled, thus inserting a new customer. This is the last JSP needed for our example newOrder.jsp:

```
<%@ taglib uri="http://java.sun.com/jsf/html" prefix="h"%>
<%@ taglib uri="http://java.sun.com/jsf/core" prefix="f"%>

<html>
<body>
<f:view>
  <style type="text/css">
    @import url("css/appstore.css");
  </style>
```

```
<h:form id="newOrder">
  <h:panelGrid columns="2" border="1" styleClass="spring">
    <f:facet name="header">
      <h:outputText value="Insert new Order" />
    </f:facet>
    <h:outputText value="Product" />
    <h:inputText value="#{manager.orderProduct}" />
    <h:outputText value="Quantity" />
    <h:inputText value="#{manager.orderQuantity}" />
    <h:outputText value="Price" />
    <h:inputText value="#{manager.orderPrice}" />
    <h:outputText value="Customer" />
    <h:selectOneMenu id="selectCustomerforOrder"
      value="#{manager.customer}">
    <f:selectItems value="#{manager.listCustomers}" />
    </h:selectOneMenu>
    <h:commandButton action="#{manager.saveOrder}"
      value="Save Order" />
    <h:commandButton action="#{manager.home}" value="Back" />
  </h:panelGrid>
  <h:messages />
</h:form>
</f:view>
</body>
</html>
```

Assembling and deploying the application

So far, you have got two standalone projects, one EJB project and one web project. While you could technically deploy them separately, it is worth combining them in an **Enterprise ARchive (EAR)**. The most obvious reason for deploying the application as an Enterprise ARchive is that the web application will be loaded by a `ClassLoader` in the same hierarchy as the EJB classloader. In short, you don't need to provide the EJB interfaces to the web application, as you would for a standalone application.

Packaging the application can be done entirely by Eclipse, without messing with archive files. From the menu, select **New | Other | Java EE | Enterprise Application project**. The next facet will request the **Project name** and a few details about the configuration. Your archive name will be, by default, the project name plus the extension `.ear`. Verify that both **Target Runtime** and the **Configuration** point correctly to the JBoss 5.0 environment.

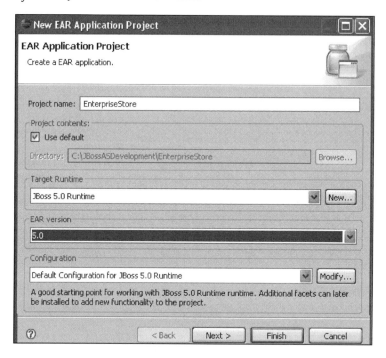

Click **Next**. On the window that follows, you can select the components of your archive application, that is, the **AppStore** application and the **AppStoreWeb** component. Check the option **Generate Deployment Descriptor**.

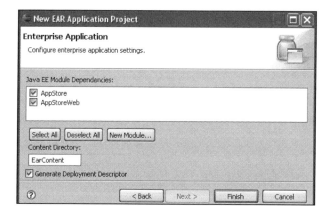

Verify that `META-INF/application.xml` deployment descriptors contain both the modules enlisted below:

```
<application>
  <display-name>EnterpriseStore</display-name>
  <module>
    <web>
      <web-uri>AppStoreWeb.war</web-uri>
      <context-root>AppStoreWeb</context-root>
    </web>
  </module>
  <module>
    <ejb>AppStore.jar</ejb>
  </module>
</application>
```

Okay, now you need only a few more laps to complete the race. Let's deploy the process to JBoss by switching on the **JBoss Server View**. Right-click on the JBoss server and select **Add and remove projects**. Add the **EnterpriseStore** to the configured projects.

Now deploy the application in the usual way. Right-click on the **EnterpriseStore** and select **Full Publish** (at the time of writing, JBoss 5 doesn't support partial deployment of this component).

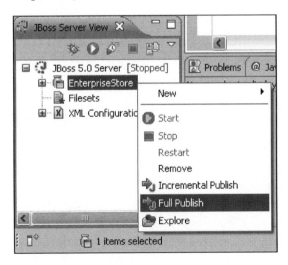

Verify from the console that the application has been deployed correctly.

Running the store

The application gateway will be `home.jsf` page. Point the browser to the location `http://localhost:8080/AppStoreWeb/home.jsf`.

Testing the application is quite simple. First add some customers and then link some orders to the customers. In the `home.jsf` page, check that the orders are correctly listed from the datagrid.

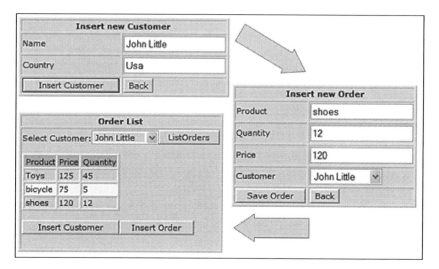

A last trick

Usually web applications ship with a **welcome file list** so that you don't have to remember anything else besides the web context. If you have already tried to add `home.jsf` to the welcome file list (in `web.xml`), you would have noticed that it doesn't work. Actually, Tomcat is a bit stubborn and requires a trick to set a JSF page as a welcome file. First, add the following to your `web.xml`:

```
<welcome-file-list>
    <welcome-file>home.jsf</welcome-file>
</welcome-file-list>
```

Then create an empty `home.jsf` page in your web context root. This will trick Tomcat to detect `home.jsf` as the welcome file and will load `home.jsp` instead.

Configuring JBoss Web Server

Apache Tomcat provides the core functionality of JBoss Web Server. Its embedded engine allows seamless integration with JBoss components, by using the underlying Microkernel system. JBoss Web Server currently uses the **Apache Tomcat 6.0** release and it is ships as **service archive (SAR)** application in the deploy folder. The location of the embedded web server has changed at almost every new release of JBoss. The following table could be a useful reference if you are using different versions of JBoss:

JBoss release	Location of Tomcat
5.0.0 GA	deploy/jbossweb.sar
4.2.2 GA	deploy/jboss-web.deployer
4.0.5 GA	deploy/jbossweb-tomcat55.sar
3.2.X	deploy/jbossweb-tomcat50.sar

The main configuration file is server.xml which, by default, has the following minimal configuration:

```
<Server>
  <Listener className="org.apache.catalina.core.AprLifecycleListener"
    SSLEngine="on" />
  <Listener className="org.apache.catalina.core.JasperListener" />
  <Service name="jboss.web">
    <Connector protocol="HTTP/1.1" port="8080"
      address="${jboss.bind.address}"
      connectionTimeout="20000" redirectPort="8443" />
    <Connector protocol="AJP/1.3" port="8009"
      address="${jboss.bind.address}"
      redirectPort="8443" />
    <Engine name="jboss.web" defaultHost="localhost">
    <Realm className="org.jboss.web.tomcat.security.JBossWebRealm"
      certificatePrincipal="org.jboss.security.
      auth.certs.SubjectDNMapping" allRolesMode="authOnly" />
    <Host name="localhost">
    <Valve className="org.jboss.web.tomcat.service.
      jca.CachedConnectionValve"
      cachedConnectionManagerObjectName="jboss.
      jca:service=CachedConnectionManager"
      transactionManagerObjectName="jboss:
      service=TransactionManager" />
    </Host>
    </Engine>
  </Service>
</Server>
```

Following is a short description for the key elements of the configuration:

Element	Description
Server	The Server is Tomcat itself, that is, an instance of the web application server and is a top-level component.
Service	An Engine is a request-processing component that represents the **Catalina servlet engine**. It examines the HTTP headers to determine the virtual host or context to which requests should be passed.
Connector	This is the gateway to Tomcat Engine. It ensures that requests are received from clients and are assigned to the Engine.
Engine	Engine handles all requests. It examines the HTTP headers to determine the virtual host or context to which requests should be passed.
Host	One virtual host. Each virtual host is differentiated by a fully qualified hostname.
Valve	A component that will be inserted into the request processing pipeline for the associated Catalina container. Each Valve has distinct processing capabilities.
Realm	This contains a set of users and roles.

As you can see, all the elements are organized in a hierarchical structure where the **Server** element acts as top-level container:

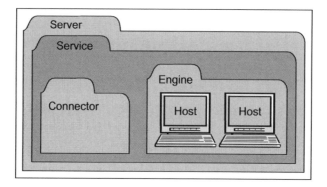

The lowest elements in the configuration are **Valve** and **Realm**, which can be nested into **Engine** or **Host** elements to provide unique processing capabilities and role management.

Customizing connectors

Most of the time when you want to customize your web container, you will have to change some properties of the connector.

```
<Connector protocol="HTTP/1.1" port="8080"
   address="${jboss.bind.address}"
   connectionTimeout="20000" redirectPort="8443" />
```

A complete list of the connector properties can be found on the Jakarta Tomcat site (`http://tomcat.apache.org/`). Here, we'll discuss the most useful connector properties:

- port: The TCP port number on which this connector will create a server socket and await incoming connections. Your operating system will allow only one server application to listen to a particular port number on a particular IP address.

- acceptCount: The maximum queue length for incoming connection requests, when all possible request processing threads are in use. Any requests received when the queue is full will be refused. The default value is 10.

- connectionTimeout: The number of milliseconds the connector will wait after accepting a connection for the request URI line to be presented. The default value is 60000 (that is, 60 seconds).

- address: For servers with more than one IP address, this attribute specifies which address will be used for listening on the specified port. By default, this port will be used on all IP addresses associated with the server.

- enableLookups: Set to true if you want to perform DNS lookups in order to return the actual hostname of the remote client and to false in order to skip the DNS lookup and return the IP address in string form instead (thereby improving performance). By default, DNS lookups are enabled.

- maxHttpHeaderSize: The maximum size of the request and response HTTP header, specified in bytes. If not specified, this attribute is set to 4096 (4 KB).

- maxPostSize: The maximum size in bytes of the POST, which will be handled by the container FORM URL parameter parsing. The limit can be disabled by setting this attribute to a value less than or equal to zero. If not specified, this attribute is set to 2097152 (2 megabytes).

- maxThreads: The maximum number of request processing threads to be created by this connector, which therefore determines the maximum number of simultaneous requests that can be handled. If not specified, this attribute is set to 200.

The new Apache Portable Runtime connector

Apache Portable Runtime (APR) is a core Apache 2.x library designed to provide superior scalability, performance, and better integration with native server technologies.

The mission of the Apache Portable Runtime (APR) project is to create and maintain software libraries that provide a predictable and consistent interface to underlying platform-specific implementations. The primary goal is to provide an API to which software developers may code and be assured of predictable if not identical behaviour regardless of the platform on which their software is built, relieving them of the need to code special-case conditions to work around or take advantage of platform-specific deficiencies or features.

The high-level performance of the new APR connector is made possible by the introduction of **socket pollers** for persistent connections (**keepalive**). This increases the scalability of the server, and by using `sendfile` system calls, static content is delivered faster and with lower CPU utilization.

Once you have set up the APR connector, you are allowed to use the following additional properties in your connector:

- `keepAliveTimeout`: The number of milliseconds the APR connector will wait for another HTTP request, before closing the connection. If not set, this attribute will use the default value set for the `connectionTimeout` attribute.

- `pollTime`: The duration of a poll call; by default it is `2000` (5 ms). If you try to decrease this value, the connector will issue more poll calls, thus reducing latency of the connections. Be aware that this will put slightly more load on the CPU as well.

- `pollerSize`: The number of sockets that the poller kept alive connections can hold at a given time. The default value is `768`, corresponding to 768 keepalive connections.

- `useSendfile`: Enables using kernel `sendfile` for sending certain static files. The default value is `true`.

- `sendfileSize`: The number of sockets that the poller thread dispatches for sending static files asynchronously. The default value is `1024`.

If you want to consult the full documentation of APR, you can visit `http://apr.apache.org/`.

Installing the APR connector

In order to install the APR connector, you need to add some native libraries to your JBoss server. The native libraries can be found at http://www.jboss.org/jbossweb/downloads/jboss-native/.

JBoss Web Downloads

JBoss Web > Downloads > JBoss Web Native Connectors

Name	Description	Size	Released	
JBoss Native 2.0.6 Linux x86	binary tar format	1.6MB	2008-10-30	Download
JBoss Native 2.0.6 Linux x86-64	binary tar format	1.7MB	2008-10-30	Download
JBoss Native 2.0.6 Linux IA64	binary tar format	2.0MB	2008-10-30	Download
JBoss Native 2.0.6 Win32	binary zip format	1.0MB	2008-10-30	Download
JBoss Native 2.0.6 Win64 AMD64/EMT64	binary zip format	1.2MB	2008-10-30	Download
JBoss Native 2.0.6 Win64 IA64	binary zip format	2.0MB	2008-10-30	Download
JBoss Native 2.0.6 HP-UX 9000/800	binary tar format	2.6MB	2008-10-30	Download
JBoss Native 2.0.6 MacOSX x86	binary tar format	1.2MB	2008-10-30	Download
JBoss Native 2.0.6 Solaris9 Sparc	binary tar format	1.9MB	2008-10-30	Download
JBoss Native 2.0.6 Solaris10 x86	binary tar format	1.7MB	2008-10-30	Download
JBoss Native 2.0.6 binaries all platforms	binary tar format	20.3MB	2008-10-30	Download

Download the version that is appropriate for your OS. Once you are ready, you need to simply unzip the content of the archive into your JBOSS_HOME directory.

As an example, Unix users (such as HP users) would need to perform the following steps:

```
cd jboss-5.0.0.GA
tar tvfz jboss-native-2.0.6-hpux-parisc2-ssl.tar.gz
```

Now, restart JBoss and, from the console, verify that the connector is bound to `Http11AprProtocol`.

```
15:50:11,713 INFO  [TransactionManagerService] Setting up property manager MBean
and JMX layer
15:50:13,768 INFO  [TransactionManagerService] Initializing recovery manager
15:50:15,071 INFO  [TransactionManagerService] Recovery manager configured
15:50:15,072 INFO  [TransactionManagerService] Binding TransactionManager JNDI R
eference
15:50:15,322 INFO  [TransactionManagerService] Starting transaction recovery man

15:50:15,048 INFO  [AprLifecycleListener] Loaded Apache Tomcat Native library 1
.16.
15:50:15,055 INFO  [AprLifecycleListener] APR capabilities: IPv6 [true], sendfi
[true], accept filters [false], random [true].

15:50:20,079 INFO  [StandardEngine] Starting Servlet Engine: JBoss Web/2.1.1.GA
15:50:20,594 INFO  [Catalina] Server startup in 1217 ms
15:50:20,804 INFO  [TomcatDeployment] deploy, ctxPath=/jbossws, vfsUrl=jbossws.s
ar/jbossws-management.war
15:50:25,972 INFO  [TomcatDeployment] deploy, ctxPath=/web-console, vfsUrl=manag
ement/console-mgr.sar/web-console.war
15:50:28,885 INFO  [TomcatDeployment] deploy, ctxPath=/invoker, vfsUrl=http-invo
ker.sar/invoker.war
15:50:30,378 INFO  [RARDeployment] Required license terms exist, view vfszip:/u0
1/app/oracle/nms/jb/jboss-5.0.0.GA/server/default/deploy/jboss-local-jdbc.rar/ME
TA-INF/ra.xml
15:50:30,593 INFO  [RARDeployment] Required license terms exist, view vfszip:/u0
```

A word of caution!

At the time of writing, the APR library still has some open issues that prevent it from loading correctly on some platforms, particularly on the 32-bit Windows.

Please consult the JBoss Issue Tracker (`https://jira.jboss.org/jira/secure/IssueNavigator.jspa?`) to verify that there are no open issues for your platform.

Configuring contexts

Every request issued to a web server can basically be split into three sections. The first one is made up of the **hostname** and **logical port** where the web server is running. By default, the embedded web server is started on port 8080.

The second piece of information is the **web context**. This is a virtual path to a web application and by default corresponds to the name of the web application archive deployed. So, for example, if you have deployed your application with the name `webapp.war`, then your default web context will be `webapp`.

The last element is the individual resource that we are trying to access such as a JavaServer Page, a servlet, or an HTML page.

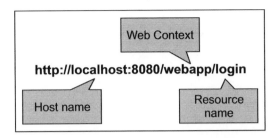

However, the default web context provided by Tomcat can be overridden. In standalone Tomcat installations, you can customize the `context` configuration by nesting its element inside the `Engine` configuration. However, in JBoss-embedded Tomcat, you need to use a JBoss-specific configuration file descriptor named `jboss-web.xml`. This file is located in the `WEB-INF` folder of your web application and can be used to add JBoss-specific information. Consider, for example, if you place the following `jboss-web.xml` file under the `WEB-INF` folder of your `webapp.war`:

```
<jboss-web>
  <context-root>/newWebContext</context-root>
</jboss-web>
```

Then the new location for your resource will be `http://localhost/newWebContext/home.jsp`.

Configuring virtual hosts

By default, web applications are accessible through the localhost hostname. However, it is sometimes desirable to add **virtual hosts** to the basic configuration. What are virtual hosts? Simply put, virtual hosts refers to the practice of maintaining more than one server on a machine, as differentiated by their apparent hostname or IP address.

Many businesses utilize virtual hosts for internal purposes, where there is a technology or administrative reason to keep several separate websites, such as a customer extranet website, employee extranet, and intranets for different departments.

If you want to add a virtual host to your configuration, you first have to declare your virtual host in a `Host` section, as shown in the following code snippet:

```
<Host name="myvirtualhost" autoDeploy="false"
  deployOnStartup="false" deployXML="false" />
```

The `name` element defines your virtual host. The other attributes are set to `false`, so as to avoid conflicts between the Tomcat deployer and the JBoss deployer.

The second step needs to be performed in the **deployment** stage, adding the virtual host information into the JBoss-specific deployment descriptor, `jboss-web.xml`.

```
<jboss-web>
  <virtual-host>myvirtualhost</virtual-host>
</jboss-web>
```

If you have deployed an application named `webapp.war` that is targeted on the host `myvirtualhost`, then you can invoke it like this:

`http://myvirtualhost:8080/webapp.`

You can further expand your virtual host configuration by adding `Alias` for each virtual host, as follows:

```
<Host name="myvirtualhost1" autoDeploy="false"
  deployOnStartup="false" deployXML="false">
  <Alias>myvirtualhost2</Alias>
</Host>
```

`Alias` can be quite useful if you need to define multiple domain names for a single virtual host.

> When creating a virtual host, it's assumed that your network administrator has registered the virtual host **domain name** on the DNS. If you want to perform a quick and dirty test, simply add an entry for your virtual host in the `hosts` filename of your OS.
>
> `127.0.0.1 myvirtualhost`
>
> On a Windows machine, the `hosts` file is located at `Windows\system32\drivers\etc`, on a Unix/Linux box it's in filesystem `/etc`.

Configuring HTTP logs

JBoss Web Server, as it ships, doesn't track incoming requests. However, if you want to enable detailed logs of the requests, you can uncomment two valves that are present in the main configuration file, `server.xml`. The first one is the `AccessLogValve` that is responsible for tracking all incoming requests.

```
<Valve className="org.apache.catalina.valves.AccessLogValve"
  prefix="localhost_access_log." suffix=".log"
  pattern=»common» directory=»${jboss.server.log.dir}»
  resolveHosts="false" />
```

The `prefix` parameter defines the prefix added to the start of each log file's name (by default it is `localhost_access_log`). The `suffix` parameter is clearly the suffix added to the end of each log file's name. The `pattern` is the formatting layout identifying the various information fields from the request and response to be logged. Finally, `resolveHosts` is set to `true`, if you want to convert the IP address of the remote host into the corresponding hostname through a DNS lookup. Here, it is set to `false` to skip this lookup and report the remote IP address instead. Values for the `pattern` attribute are made up of literal text strings and pattern identifiers. These patterns are introduced by the `%` character and cause replacement of the variable with the corresponding value. Here are a few useful patterns. For an exhaustive description of all code take a look at `http://tomcat.apache.org/tomcat-5.5-doc/config/valve.html`.

Useful patterns for logging

`%a` — remote IP address

`%A` — local IP address

`%b` — bytes sent, excluding HTTP headers, or `'-'` if zero

`%q` — query string (prepended with a `'?'` if it exists)

`%r` — first line of the request (method and request URI)

`%s` — HTTP status code of the response

`%S` — user session ID

`%t` — date and time, in Common Log Format

`%u` — remote user that was authenticated (if any), else `'-'`

`%U` — requested URL path

`%D` — time taken to process the request, in milliseconds

`%T` — time taken to process the request, in seconds

`%I` — current request thread name (can compare later with stacktraces)

The second valve is the `RequestDumperValve` that performs a dump of the request, both on the console appender and on the file appender of JBoss.

```
<Valve className="org.apache.catalina.valves.RequestDumperValve" />
```

By default, this valve is commented. Uncommenting it will produce a dump of the HTTP request, for every request:

```
=============================================
REQUEST URI=/jmx-console/filterView.jsp
authType=null
characterEncoding=null
```

```
contentLength=-1
contentType=null
contextPath=/jmx-console
header=referer=http://10.2.20.245:8080/jmx-console/
header=user-agent=Mozilla/4.0
header=host=10.2.20.245:8080
header=connection=Keep-Alive
header=cookie=JSESSIONID=736DBB892CCB331E2E972BA9E4711396
method=GET
remoteAddr=10.2.20.245
remoteHost=10.2.20.245
remoteUser=null
requestedSessionId=736DBB892CCB331E2E972BA9E4711396
serverName=10.2.20.245
serverPort=8080
servletPath=/filterView.jsp
isSecure=false
--------------------------------------------------------------------------
-------------------
```

Tuning advice

If you want to tune your configuration, then the connector parameters we have described are the right place to investigate. Let's see a few useful tips to improve the performance of your web server.

Disable DNS lookup

Setting enableLookups to true forces the web engine to retrieve the fully qualified hostname of every HTTP client that connects to your site. This adds latency to every request, as performing a DNS lookup on every request is an expensive operation. It's always recommended to turn off DNS lookups on production sites. Remember that you can always look up the names later with any network software/command-line utility.

Choose the right HTTP connector

As we have seen in the previous section, you have three different options about the protocol of the connector. There is no clear winner; all of them have some advantages. The new APR is the most advanced tuning solution, and it is clearly the best solution when your configuration is using the **Keep-Alive** extension that allows persistent connections causing multiple long-lived HTTP session requests to be sent over the same TCP connection.

APR is also a perfect choice if your application needs to be secured using **SSL** – APR uses the fast **OpenSSL** libraries. On the other hand, the earlier HTTP connector has the advantage of major stability, which could be a good match if your web container doesn't expect a high volume of requests.

The Java **non-blocking I/O (NIO)** protocol is a compromise between the two solutions, having better performances than the older HTTP connector, but not as good as the APR. On the other hand, this connector has the advantage of being a pure Java solution.

The following table presents these statements in a matrix:

Requirement	Preference order		
High traffic – KeepAlive on	APR	NIO	HTTP 1.1
High traffic – KeepAlive off	HTTP 1.1	APR	NIO
Low traffic	HTTP 1.1	APR	NIO
Stability	HTTP 1.1	APR	NIO
Secure connections	APR	NIO	HTTP 1.1

Set the correct size for your thread pool

Setting an appropriate value for the thread pool plays an essential role in the web server's processing throughput capacity. Every single request directed into JBoss Web Server goes through the web thread pool.

If this pool has very few active request-processing objects and if the traffic increases dramatically, then a delay in request processing results due to pool component instantiation. If the pool is too large (that is, the number of ready threads is too high), then the CPU cycles and memory may become overused.

You can control the number of threads allocated through the maxThreads attribute that, by default, allows a maximum of 200 threads.

This setting can be optimal for medium-load web servers. However, when your servers are performing heavy-duty work, let's say 1000 requests per second, then you need to increase the maxThreads value. A good starting point for high-volume sites could be around 400 maxThreads. However, the best criterion to set this to the optimal value is to try many different settings, and then test them with simulated traffic loads while watching response times and memory utilization.

Monitoring your thread pool

The JMX console is an indispensable tool for monitoring your thread. The thread pool information can be reached from the **jboss.web** domain. From the agent view, select the MBean `name=http-localhost-8080,type=ThreadPool` (or whatever your hostname is). The most interesting attributes are located in the lower part of the screen.

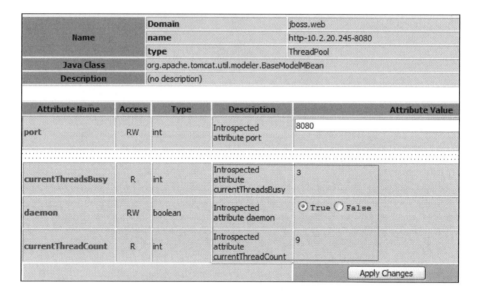

The `currentThreadsBusy` attribute accounts for the total number of threads that are handling HTTP requests. The attribute `currentThreadCount` states how many worker threads have been created up to that moment.

On the other hand, if you need low-level information about the request such as bytes sent/received, processing time, error count, max time, and request count, then you need to switch to the MBean `name=http-localhost-8080,type=GlobalRequestPr ocessor` that is available in the same **jboss.web** domain.

Summary

In this chapter, we have completed our Enterprise application (AppStore) by adding a web layer designed using JSF.

JavaServer Faces has gained a lot of popularity in the last few years and, as you have learned here, it does not require any extra effort to deploy a JSF-based application on JBoss AS. If you are interested in improving the collaboration between EJB applications and JSF views, we strongly suggest you to have a look at the JBoss Seam project (`http://www.jboss.com/products/seam/`), which is a key component of the JBoss Enterprise application platform.

In the next chapter, we will cover the **JBoss Messaging system**, thus completing the EJB picture with message-driven bean components.

7
Developing Applications with JBoss Messaging Service

The medium is the message. – Marshall McLuhan

Messaging is a method of communication between software components or applications. The **Java Message Service (JMS)** is a Java API designed by Sun that allows applications to create, send, receive, and read messages (refer to `http://java.sun.com/products/jms/docs.html`).

Messaging differs from other standard protocols, such as **Remote Method Invocation (RMI)** and **Hypertext Transfer Protocol (HTTP)**, in two ways. Firstly, the conversation is mediated by a messaging server, so it's not a two-way conversation between peers. Secondly, the sender and receiver need to know only the message format and the destination to be used. This is in contrast to tightly coupled technologies such as RMI, which requires an application to know a remote application's methods.

In this chapter, we will cover:

- A brief introduction to message-oriented systems
- The new **JBoss Messaging** system that replaces the earlier **JBossMQ**
- Setting up some proof-of-concept programming examples

Short introduction to JMS

JMS defines a vendor-neutral (but Java-specific) set of programming interfaces for interacting with asynchronous messaging systems. Messaging enables distributed communication, which is *loosely coupled*. A component sends a message to a destination, which in turn is retrieved by the recipient with the mediation of the JMS server. In JMS, there are two types of destinations, **topics** and **queues**, and they have different semantics.

In the **point-to-point** model, messages are sent from producers to consumers through queues. A given queue may have multiple receivers, but only one receiver may consume each message. The first receiver to fetch the message will get it, while everyone else will not.

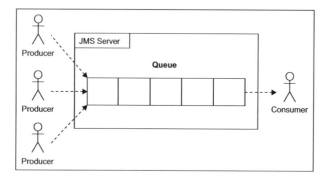

On the other hand, a message sent to a topic may be received by multiple parties. Messages published on a specific topic are sent to all message consumers who have registered (subscribed) to receive messages on that topic. A subscription can be durable or non-durable. A **non-durable** subscriber can receive only those messages that are published while it is *active*. Also, non-durable subscription does not guarantee the delivery of the message or may deliver the same message more than once. On the other hand, a **durable subscription** guarantees that the consumer receives the message only once.

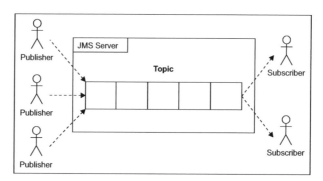

Even though JMS is inherently **asynchronous**, the JMS specification allows messages to be consumed in either of the following two ways:

- **Synchronous**: A subscriber or a receiver explicitly fetches the message from the destination by calling the `receive()` method of any `MessageConsumer` instance. The `receive()` method can block until a message arrives, or can time-out if a message does not arrive within a specified time limit.

- **Asynchronous**: With the asynchronous mode, the client must implement the `javax.jms.MessageListener` interface and overwrite the method `onMessage()`. Whenever a message arrives at the destination, the JMS provider delivers the message by calling the listener's `onMessage()` method that acts on the contents of the message.

A JMS message consists of a header, properties, and a body. The message headers provide a fixed set of metadata fields describing the message, using information such as where the message is going and when it was received. The properties are a set of key-value pairs used for application-specific purposes, usually to help filter messages quickly when they have been received. Finally, the body contains the data that is being sent in the message.

The JMS API supports two delivery modes for messages. If the JMS provider fails, these modes specify whether the messages are lost. The two modes are as described:

- **PERSISTENT**: This is the default mode. It instructs the JMS provider to take extra care, to ensure that a message is not lost in transit in case of a JMS provider failure. A message sent with this delivery mode is logged to stable storage when it is sent.

- **NON_PERSISTENT**: This delivery mode does not require the JMS provider to store the message or guarantee that it is not lost if the provider fails.

The building blocks of JMS

The basic building blocks of any JMS application are as follows:

- Administered objects (connection factories and destinations):

    A `ConnectionFactory` object encapsulates a set of connection configuration parameters that have been defined by an administrator. A client uses it to create a connection with a JMS provider. A `ConnectionFactory` object hides provider-specific details from JMS clients and abstracts administrative information into objects in the Java programming language.

A **destination** is the component that a client uses to specify the target of messages it produces and the source of messages it consumes. In the **point-to-point** (**PTP**) messaging domain, destinations are called queues, whereas in the publish/subscribe messaging domain, destinations are called topics.

- Connections:

  A **connection** encapsulates a virtual connection with a JMS provider. A connection could represent an open TCP/IP socket between a client and a service provider. A connection is used to create one or more sessions.

- Sessions:

  A **session** is a single-threaded context for producing and consuming messages. Sessions are used to create message producers, message consumers, and messages. Sessions serialize the execution of message listeners and provide a transactional context to group a set of sent and received messages into an atomic unit of work.

- Message producers:

  A **message producer** is an object created by a session and is used for sending messages to a destination. The PTP form of a message producer implements the QueueSender interface. The publish/subscribe form implements the TopicPublisher interface.

- Message consumers:

  A **message consumer** is an object created by a session and is used for receiving messages sent to a destination. A message consumer allows a JMS client to register interest in a destination with a JMS provider. The JMS provider manages the delivery of messages from a destination to the registered consumers of the destination. The PTP form of message consumer implements the QueueReceiver interface, whereas the publish/subscribe form implements the TopicSubscriber interface.

- Messages:

  The Message is an object that contains the data being transferred between JMS clients. In developer terms, it is defined as an interface that defines the message header and the acknowledge method used for all messages.

The new JBoss Messaging system

JBoss Messaging is the new Enterprise messaging system from JBoss. It is a complete rewrite of JBossMQ, the earlier legacy JMS provider, which is currently in bug-fix mode only. JBoss Messaging implements a high performance and robust messaging core, which is designed to support the largest and most heavily utilized **service-oriented architectures (SOAs)**, **enterprise service buses (ESBs)**, and other integration needs ranging from the simplest to the highest-demand networks.

Compared to JBossMQ, JBoss Messaging offers improved performance in both, single node and clustered environments. To whet your appetite, we have set up a raw benchmark for comparing JMS Messaging against the earlier JBossMQ implementation. The benchmark was executed on a Pentium 4 Dual Core (Windows XP) running JDK 1.6.

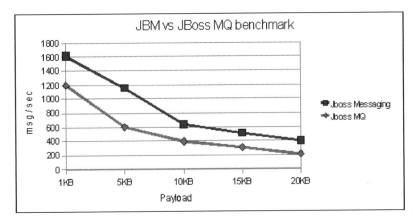

In this benchmark, we are sending 5,000 progressively larger text messages. The consumer of the queue is a message-driven bean with default configuration. The database persistence model is the default HSQLDB.

As you can see from the graph, the **Jboss MQ** implementation has a throughput of around **1200** messages/second with small payloads, while **Jboss Messaging** goes up to **1600** messages/second. As the payload increases, both providers drop the messages/second throughput progressively.

This benchmark does not have any official value because it is limited to a single typology of messages (queues) with minimal hardware configuration. However, we believe that the performance improvement achieved by switching to JBoss Messaging can be estimated around 30 to 40 percent.

Configuring connection factories

New JMS connections are created by `ConnectionFactory` that encapsulates the connections parameters. A `ConnectionFactory` is bound in the JNDI naming service and can be looked up by both local and remote clients, provided they supply the correct environment parameters.

The configuration for connection factories is located in the file `deploy\messaging\connection-factories-service.xml`. JBoss ships with both, non-clusterable and clusterable connection factories. The non-clusterable connection factories are bound to the following JNDI contexts: `/ConnectionFactory`, `/XAConnectionFactory`, `java:/ConnectionFactory`, and `java:/XAConnectionFactory`. You can use this implementation if you don't need load balancing or failover of messages. On the other hand, clusterable factories are available at the following JNDI contexts: `/ClusteredConnectionFactory`, `/ClusteredXAConnectionFactory`, `java:/ClusteredConnectionFactory`, and `java:/ClusteredXAConnectionFactory`.

Why do we have a redundant list of factories?

The answer is that the factories bound in the `java:` namespace are reserved for local JMS clients (running in the same JVM of the server), whereas the factories bound in the global namespace can be accessed remotely too.

However, you are not restricted to default factories. If you need to customize the JMS connections, you can set up your own connection factory. Here's an example of it:

```
<mbean
    code="org.jboss.jms.server.connectionfactory.ConnectionFactory"
    name="jboss.messaging.connectionfactory:
    service=MyConnectionFactory"
    xmbean-dd="xmdesc/ConnectionFactory-xmbean.xml">
    <constructor>
      <arg type="java.lang.String" value="MyClientID"/>   [1]
    </constructor>
    <depends optional-attribute-
      name="ServerPeer">jboss.messaging:service=ServerPeer</depends>
    <depends optional-attribute-
      name="Connector">jboss.messaging:service=Connector,
      transport=bisocket</depends>
    <depends>jboss.messaging:service=PostOffice</depends>
    <attribute name="PrefetchSize">150</attribute>   [2]
    <attribute name="DupsOKBatchSize">5000</attribute>   [3]
    <attribute name="SupportsFailover">false</attribute>   [4]
    <attribute name="SupportsLoadBalancing">false</attribute>
```

```
    <attribute name="SlowConsumers">false</attribute>   [5]
    <attribute name="JNDIBindings">   [6]
      <bindings>
        <binding>/packpub/CF</binding>
        <binding>java:/packpub/CF</binding>
      </bindings>
    </attribute>
  </mbean>
```

The above example would create a connection factory with preconfigured client ID MyClientID [1], bound to the JNDI context in two places: /packpub/CF and java:/packpub/CF [6].

The connection factory overrides the default value for PrefetchSize [2]. What is the meaning of this attribute? You should know that each message consumer maintains a local buffer of messages from which it consumes messages. The server typically sends messages as fast as it can to the consumer and, when the consumer is full, it sends a "stop" message to the server to indicate it is full. When it clears enough space, it sends a "start" message to the server to continue sending messages. The PrefetchSize parameter determines the size of this buffer; larger values give better throughput.

The setting DupsOKBatchSize [3] works with the JMS acknowledge mode of DUPS_OK_ACKNOWLEDGE. It determines how many acknowledgments it will buffer locally before sending.

We have set failover and load balancing attributes [4] to false, so we don't plan to use this factory in a clustered environment. The attribute SlowConsumers [5] can be used if some of your consumers are slow at consuming messages. By setting this property to true, you can make sure that the connection will not buffer any messages. This can prevent faster consumers from "capturing" all messages, thus distributing the load of messages equally.

Save the above configuration file using the xxx-service.xml name pattern (for example, myconnection-service.xml) in the deploy/messaging folder of your server configuration.

08:58:57,879 INFO [ConnectionFactory] Connector bisocket://localhost has leasing enabled, lease period 10000 milliseconds

08:58:57,879 INFO [ConnectionFactory] org.jboss.jms.server.connectionfactory.Co nnectionFactory@1ac281e started

Configuring JMS destinations

JBoss Messaging system configuration can be found in the `deploy/messaging` folder. By default, JBoss ships with a default set of preconfigured destinations, which will be deployed during the server startup. The file that contains the configuration for these destinations is `destinations-service.xml`.

You can create new destinations at any time, so let's see a few basic examples. The following `sample-destinations-service.xml` can be used to set up a queue named `exampleQueue` and a topic `exampleTopic` in the `jboss.messaging.destination` domain.

```
<server>
  <mbean code="org.jboss.jms.server.destination.QueueService"
  name="jboss.messaging.destination:
  service=Queue,name=exampleQueue»
  xmbean-dd=»xmdesc/Queue-xmbean.xml»>
    <depends optional-attribute-
      name=»ServerPeer»>jboss.messaging:service=ServerPeer</depends>
  </mbean>
  <mbean code="org.jboss.jms.server.destination.TopicService"
    name=»jboss.messaging.destination:
    service=Topic,name=exampleTopic"
    xmbean-dd="xmdesc/Topic-xmbean.xml">
    <depends optional-attribute-
      name="ServerPeer">jboss.messaging:service=ServerPeer</depends>
  </mbean>
</server>
```

Deploy the JMS destinations by copying the `sample-destinations-service.xml` in the `deploy` folder of your JBoss server. You don't need to restart the server, as your topics and queues will be immediately available.

Inspecting destination attributes

In the previous example, we have shown how to set up two JMS destinations using a minimal configuration. However, JMS destinations have many other configurable parameters that can be modified or inspected from the JMX console.

Launch the JMX console and point to the domain (**jboss.messaging.destination**) where we have just added the two destinations.

Advanced message configuration

The previous queue and topic contain the minimal set of attributes for configuring a JMS destination. If you are eager to learn all possible configuration elements, here's a more complex example:

```
<mbean code="org.jboss.jms.server.destination.QueueService"
   name="jboss.messaging.destination:service=Queue,name=exampleQueue2"
   xmbean-dd="xmdesc/Queue-xmbean.xml">
   <depends optional-attribute-
      name="ServerPeer">jboss.messaging:service=ServerPeer</depends>
   <attribute name="DLQ">
      jboss.messaging.destination:service=Queue,name=PrivateDLQ
   </attribute>
   <attribute name="ExpiryQueue">
      jboss.messaging.destination:service=Queue,name=PrivateExpiryQueue
   </attribute>
   <attribute name="RedeliveryDelay">1500</attribute>
   <attribute name="MaxDeliveryAttempts">5</attribute>
   <attribute name="FullSize">50000</attribute>
```

```
<attribute name="PageSize">5000</attribute>
<attribute name="DownCacheSize">2500</attribute>
<attribute name="MaxSize">75000</attribute>
<attribute name="SecurityConfig">
  <security>
    <role name="guest" read="true" write="true"/>
    <role name="publisher" read="true" write="true"
      create="false"/>
  </security>
</attribute>
</mbean>
```

An explanation for the individual attributes is summarized in the following table. Please consult the JBoss Messaging documentation (`http://www.jboss.org/jbossmessaging/docs/index.html`) for a detailed description of these parameters.

Attribute	Description
name	The name of the queue.
JNDIName	The JNDI name where the queue is bound.
DLQ	The dead letter queue used for this queue. This is a special destination where messages are sent when the server has attempted to deliver them unsuccessfully more than a certain number of times.
ExpiryQueue	The expiry queue used for this queue. An expiry queue is a special destination where messages are sent when they have expired.
RedeliveryDelay	The redelivery delay to be used for this queue.
MaxDeliveryAttempts	The maximum number of times delivery of a message will be attempted before sending the message to the DLQ, if configured. If set to -1 (the default), the value from the ServerPeer config is used.
SecurityConfig	Allows you to determine which roles are allowed to read, write, and create on the destination.
FullSize	This is the maximum number of messages held by the queue or topic subscriptions in memory at any given time. The actual queue or subscription can hold many more messages than this, but these are paged to and from storage as necessary, when messages are added or consumed.

Attribute	Description
PageSize	When loading messages from the queue or subscription, this is the maximum number of messages to preload in one operation.
DownCacheSize	When paging messages to storage from the queue, they first go into a down cache before being written to storage. This enables the write to occur as a single operation, thus aiding performance. This setting determines the maximum number of messages that the down cache will hold before they are flushed to storage.
MaxSize	A maximum size (in number of messages) can be specified for a queue. Any messages that arrive beyond this point will be dropped. The default is -1, which is unbounded.

Configuring JBM for heavy duty

Pageable channels is a new feature available in JBoss Messaging. It performs automatic paging of messages to storage and allows the use of very large queues (too large to fit in memory at once).

JBoss Messaging will keep in memory as many messages as the FullSize parameter (default 75,000). When the number of messages to be delivered exceeds the FullSize value, the messages are moved to a temporary destination named DownCache. The DownCache is not persisted at every new message, but as a single batch when the DownCacheSize attribute value is reached (default 2,000). This avoids the burden of continuous input/output operations.

Scheduled delivery

Scheduled delivery is a useful feature of JBoss Messaging that allows you to configure the delivery of the message to a future date. Scheduling the delivery can be done programmatically by setting the property JMS_JBOSS_SCHEDULED_DELIVERY_ PROP_NAME to a consistent value (in milliseconds). A message can be scheduled in one hour from now as follows:

```
long now = System.currentTimeMillis();
Message msg = sess.createMessage();
msg.setLongProperty(JBossMessage.JMS_JBOSS_SCHEDULED_DELIVERY_PROP_NA
              ME, now + 1000 * 60 * 60 * 1);
prod.send(msg);
```

Developing JMS applications

In the following sections, we will introduce the core components used in the Enterprise to leverage JMS programming. Our first round will be with message-driven beans that are part of the Java EE specification. Next, we will add a JBoss-specific component named message-driven POJO to our list of deliverables.

Message-driven beans

Message-driven beans (**MDBs**) are stateless, server-side, transaction-aware components, for processing asynchronous JMS messages.

One of the most important aspects of message-driven beans is that they can consume and process messages concurrently. This capability provides a significant advantage over traditional JMS clients, which must be custom-built to manage resources, transactions, and security in a multi-threaded environment. The message-driven bean containers manage concurrency automatically so that the bean developer can focus on the business logic of processing the messages. The MDB can receive hundreds of JMS messages from various applications and process all of them at the same time, as numerous instances of the MDB can execute concurrently in the container.

A message-driven bean is classified as an Enterprise bean, just like a session or an entity bean, but there are some important differences. First, the message-driven bean does not have component interfaces. This is because the message-driven bean is not accessible through the Java RMI API and responds only to asynchronous messages.

Just as the entity and session beans have well-defined life cycles, so does the MDB bean. The MDB instance's life cycle has two states: **Does not Exist** and **Method ready Pool**.

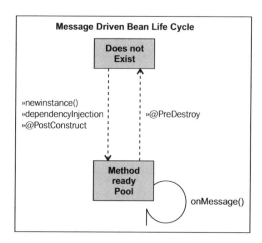

When a message is received, the EJB container checks to see if any MDB instance is available in the pool. If a bean is available in the free pool, JBoss uses that instance. After an MDB instance's onMessage() method returns, the request is complete and the instance is placed back in the free pool. This results in the best response time, as the request is served without waiting for a new instance to be created.

If no bean instances are handy, the container checks if there is room for more MDBs in the pool, by comparing the MDB's MaxSize attribute with the pool size.

If MaxSize value has still not been reached, a new MDB is initialized. The creation sequence, as pointed out in the previous diagram, is just the same as stateless bean. On the other hand, failure to create a new instance will imply that the request will be blocked until an active MDB completes a method call or the transaction times out.

Configuring message-driven beans

You can control the pool size of MDBs from the deploy\ejb3-interceptors-aop. xml file, in a similar manner to that explained for session beans. Locate the domain Message Driven Bean:

```
<domain name="Message Driven Bean" extends="Intercepted Bean"
   inheritBindings="true">
   <annotation expr="!class(@org.jboss.ejb3.annotation.Pool)">
      @org.jboss.ejb3.annotation.Pool (value="StrictMaxPool",
         maxSize=15, timeout=10000)
   </annotation>
</domain>
```

By default, message-driven beans use the StrictMaxPool strategy, allowing for a maxSize of 15 elements in the pool.

Creating a sample application

We will now create a sample application that sends messages over a queue. Have you deployed the sample destinations (sample-destinations-service.xml) that we illustrated before? If not, it's now time to do it.

The consumer of this queue will be a message-driven bean written using EJB 3.0 specifications. Let's first create a new EJB project. From the **File** menu, select **New | Other | EJB | EJB project**. Choose a name for your project (for example, **JMSExample**) and make sure you have selected the JBoss 5 runtime and configuration. Also the EJB module version needs to be 3.0.

Once your project is ready, let's add a new message-driven bean from the same path: **New | Other | EJB | EJB 3 Message Driven Bean**. The job of this component will be invoking a stored procedure on an external system; we will call it **com.packtpub.jms.MDBProcessor**.

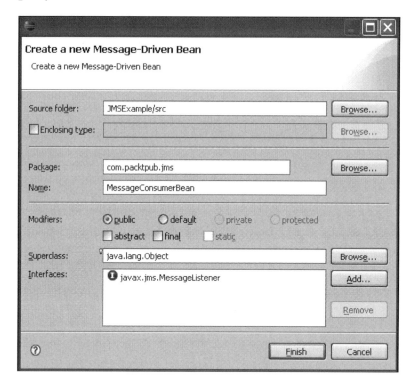

Click **Finish**. Eclipse will create the MDBProcessor class, bearing the annotation @MessageDriven. The core properties of the MDB will be nested into the @MessageDriven annotation marked as @ActivationConfigProperty.

```
@MessageDriven(name = "MessageMDBSample", activationConfig = {
    @ActivationConfigProperty(propertyName = "destinationType",
    propertyValue = "javax.jms.Queue"),   [1]
    @ActivationConfigProperty(propertyName = "destination",
    propertyValue = "queue/exampleQueue})   [2]
```

Here we have connected the bean to a queue destination **[1]**, whose JNDI name is queue/exampleQueue **[2]**. Let's have a look at the complete code:

```
package com.packtpub.jms;
import java.sql.CallableStatement;
import java.sql.Connection;
import java.sql.SQLException;
```

```
import javax.annotation.Resource;
import javax.ejb.MessageDriven;
import javax.ejb.ActivationConfigProperty;
import javax.jms.Message;
import javax.jms.MessageListener;
import javax.jms.TextMessage;
import javax.sql.DataSource;
import java.sql.Types;

@MessageDriven(activationConfig =
{
  @ActivationConfigProperty(propertyName="destinationType",
    propertyValue="javax.jms.Queue"),
  @ActivationConfigProperty(propertyName="destination",
    propertyValue="queue/exampleQueue")
})
public class MDBProcessor implements MessageListener {
  @Resource(mappedName = «java:/MySqlDS»)    [1]
  private DataSource datasource;
  public void onMessage(Message msg)    [2]
  {
    Connection connection = null;
    TextMessage text = (TextMessage)msg;
    try {
      connection = datasource.getConnection();
      String sql = "{ ? = call hello (?) }";
      CallableStatement cs = connection.prepareCall(sql);
      cs.registerOutParameter(1, Types.VARCHAR);
      cs.setString(2,text.getText());
      cs.execute();
      String retMess = cs.getString(1);
      System.out.println(retMess);
    }
    catch (Exception e1) {
      e1.printStackTrace();
    }
    finally {
      try {
        connection.close();
      }
      catch (SQLException e1) {
        e1.printStackTrace();
      }
    }
  }
}
```

In our MDB, we inject a datasource as a resource **[1]** that will be necessary for setting up a database connection with MySQL. The datasource has already been defined in Chapter 5, *Developing JPA Entities*, so you should not need any further configuration.

Warning:

As per Java EE specification, a resource is accessible through JNDI, using the name parameter. However, JBoss requires the mappedName element.

Once a new message is posted to exampleQueue, the container recalls the onMessage() method **[2]** of our MDB. The job of the onMessage() method will be recalling a stored procedure named hello on the MySQL database. This procedure actually returns a greeting message built with the parameter, which is passed to the procedure.

Here is a sample MySQL stored procedure that can be used for testing this example (just add this DDL from your MySQL client):

```
CREATE FUNCTION hello (s CHAR(20))
RETURNS CHAR(50) DETERMINISTIC
RETURN CONCAT('Hello, ',s,'!');
```

Why not just output System.out.println from the MDB?

The last example does not produce anything more than a System.out, so you may wonder why we are adding extra steps to yield the same result. Although the reader can easily turn the example into a Hello World one, we do believe that with a small effort the reader can enjoy projects that are closer to real-world programming.

For example, the MDB processor that gets injected into a datasource can be used as a template if you need to manage your storage with plain JDBC from your Enterprise Java Bean.

The MDB is complete. You can deploy it just like other projects. Right-click on the label **JBoss 5.0 Server** in the **JBoss Server View**. Select **Add and remove projects**. Once your project is added, you can deploy it by clicking on the project label and selecting **Full publish**.

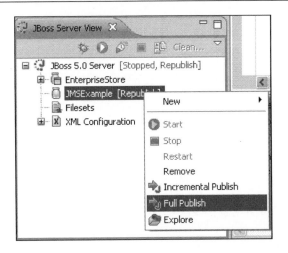

Deployment should take just a minute. If you take a look at the deploy folder of your JBoss server, you should notice a file named JMSExample.jar that contains the compiled MDB processor.

Now we need to create a message producer. A standard Java class is what you need. Add a new class from the menu and name it com.packtpub.jms.QueueSender.

```
package com.packtpub.jms;
import java.util.Properties;
import javax.jms.*;
import javax.naming.*;
public class QueueSender {
  public static void main(String[] args) throws Exception {
    new QueueSender().example();
  }
  public void example() throws Exception
  {
    String destinationName = "queue/exampleQueue";
    Context ic = null;
    ConnectionFactory cf = null;
    Connection connection =  null;
    try {
      ic = getInitialContext();   [1]
      cf = (ConnectionFactory)ic.lookup("/ConnectionFactory");   [2]
      Queue queue = (Queue)ic.lookup(destinationName);
      connection = cf.createConnection();
      Session session = connection.createSession(false,
        Session.AUTO_ACKNOWLEDGE);   [3]
      MessageProducer sender = session.createProducer(queue);
```

```
      TextMessage message = session.createTextMessage("Frank");
      sender.send(message); [4]

      System.out.println("The message was successfully sent to the "
        + queue.getQueueName() + " queue");
    }
  catch(Exception ne){
    ne.printStackTrace();
  }
  finally{
    if(ic != null) {
      try {
        ic.close();
      }
      catch(Exception ignore){ }
    }
  closeConnection(connection);
  }
}
public static Context getInitialContext( )
throws javax.naming.NamingException {
  Properties p = new Properties( );
  p.put(Context.INITIAL_CONTEXT_FACTORY,
    "org.jnp.interfaces.NamingContextFactory");
  p.put(Context.URL_PKG_PREFIXES,
    " org.jboss.naming:org.jnp.interfaces");
  p.put(Context.PROVIDER_URL, "jnp://localhost:1099");
  return new javax.naming.InitialContext(p);
}
private void closeConnection(Connection con){
  try {
    if (con != null) {
      con.close();
    }
  }
  catch(JMSException jmse) {
    System.out.println("Could not close connection " + con +"
      exception was " +jmse);
  }
  }
}
```

We will not detail the steps in the client, which is a standard JMS queue sender. Just recap all that you need to provide. First, you need to provide the environment details of your JMS server **[1]**. In this case, we are creating the `InitialContext` with a set of properties, just to show you an alternative to placing the file `jndi.properties` in the classpath. The `ConnectionFactory` will then be looked up in the JNDI tree **[2]**. The `Factory` is used to set up a `javax.jms.Connection` object and this one in turn is used to start a new JMS session **[3]**. A `MessageProducer` is then created to actually send **[4]** a `TextMessage` to the queue.

I guess you are impatient to test your latest creation. Reach the option **Run As | Java Application**, either from the **Package Explorer** or the **Editor**, and test your messaging application. Successful output should produce the following:

```
C:\WINDOWS\system32\cmd.exe                                        _ □ ×
MDBExample.jar/>
10:28:46,940 INFO  [Ejb3DependenciesDeployer] Encountered deployment AbstractVFS
DeploymentContext@21850977{vfsfile:/C:/jboss-5.1.0.GA-1.6/server/default/deploy/
MDBExample.jar/>
10:28:46,971 INFO  [JBossASKernel] Created KernelDeployment for: MDBExample.jar
10:28:46,986 INFO  [JBossASKernel] installing bean: jboss.j2ee:jar=MDBExample.ja
r,name=MDBProcessor,service=EJB3
10:28:46,986 INFO  [JBossASKernel]    with dependencies:
10:28:46,986 INFO  [JBossASKernel]    and demands:
10:28:46,986 INFO  [JBossASKernel]       jboss.ejb:service=EJBTimerService
10:28:46,986 INFO  [JBossASKernel]    and supplies:
10:28:46,986 INFO  [JBossASKernel]       jndi:null
10:28:46,986 INFO  [JBossASKernel]       Class:javax.jms.MessageListener
10:28:46,986 INFO  [JBossASKernel] Added bean<jboss.j2ee:jar=MDBExample.jar,name
=MDBProcessor,service=EJB3> to KernelDeployment of: MDBExample.jar
10:28:47,065 INFO  [EJBContainer] STARTED EJB: com.packtpub.jms.example1.MDBProc
essor ejbName: MDBProcessor
10:29:00,571 WARN  [InterceptorsFactory] EJBTHREE-1246: Do not use InterceptorsF
actory with a ManagedObjectAdvisor, InterceptorRegistry should be used via the b
ean container
10:29:00,571 WARN  [InterceptorsFactory] EJBTHREE-1246: Do not use InterceptorsF
actory with a ManagedObjectAdvisor, InterceptorRegistry should be used via the b
ean container
10:29:00,571 INFO  [STDOUT] Frank
```

You surely have noticed some boring EJB 3 warnings that appear in the server logs. This message is related to EJB life cycle callbacks and can be issued by the container under some circumstances related to the EJB 3 interceptor's running mode (AOP and container managed interception). This stuff is generally useless for the bean developer and you can get rid of it by adding the `@SuppressWarning` annotation before the `onMessage()` method:

```
@SuppressWarnings(value={"all"})
public void onMessage(Message msg) {}
```

Creating MDB singletons

Sometimes it is appropriate to have exactly one instance of a class; this is called a **singleton**. Making an MDB singleton with EJB 3.0 is trivial; you can just add the `maxSession` property to your annotations. In the container's language, `maxSession` is intended as the maximum number of instances to be created.

```
@ActivationConfigProperty(propertyName = "maxSession",
   propertyValue = "1")
```

If you want this behavior across all your MDBs, then you have to modify the `deploy\ejb3-interceptors-aop.xml` file by adding the following property to your MDB domain:

```
<annotation
  expr="!class(@org.jboss.annotation.ejb.DefaultActivationSpecs)">
  @org.jboss.annotation.ejb.DefaultActivationSpecs
    ({@javax.ejb.ActivationConfigProperty(propertyName =
      "maxSession", propertyValue = "1")})
</annotation>
```

Message-driven POJOs

Message-driven POJOs are not part of Java EE specification, but rather a specific element of the JBoss suite. The term message-driven POJO is not new in the Java Enterprise system. You can find some queries about it in the **Spring** context. However, JBoss MDP is different from Spring implementation because it is a plain POJO implementation and is not constrained by any framework contract.

You can think about JBoss MDP as a half-blood relative of session beans and message-driven beans. They are semantically similar to session beans because they expose the business contract of the POJO, so they are a typed component. In spite of this, they also have some peculiarities of MDBs because they are driven by a JMS transport (queue or topic). Therefore, they inherit all the characteristics of JMS messaging.

MDB or message-driven POJOs?

Choosing the right interface for your JMS-driven application depends on the characteristics of your project. For example, if your priority is to have loosely coupled and portable interfaces, then you should stick to MDB. On the other hand, if you need to expose a business contract to your JMS client, then message-driven POJOs are a safe bet. Message-driven POJOs also carry another advantage versus MDB—they are just POJOs. You just define Java methods, expose them through a producer interface, and your invocations are turned into JMS messages underneath.

As a practical example, we will rebuild our MDB processor using a message-driven POJO. Message-driven POJOs are unknown to Eclipse IDE, so you have to resort again to a simple Java class. Go to **New | Class** and name it `com.packpub.jms.POJOProcessor`. The implementation of the MDP follows here:

```
package com.packtpub.jms;
import java.sql.CallableStatement;
import java.sql.Connection;
import java.sql.SQLException;
import org.jboss.ejb3.annotation.Consumer;
import org.jboss.ejb3.annotation.CurrentMessage;
import javax.annotation.Resource;
import javax.ejb.*;
import javax.jms.*;
import javax.sql.DataSource;
import java.sql.Types;
@Consumer(activationConfig = {    [1]
  @ActivationConfigProperty(
    propertyName = «destinationType»,
    propertyValue = «javax.jms.Queue»),
  @ActivationConfigProperty(
    propertyName = "destination",
    propertyValue = "queue/pojoQueue") })    [2]
public class POJOProcessor implements POJOProcessorItf {    [3]
  @Resource(mappedName = "java:/MySqlDS")
  private DataSource datasource;
  public void callProcedure(String param) {
    Connection connection = null;
    try {
      connection = datasource.getConnection();
      String sql = "{ ? = call hello (?) }";
      CallableStatement cs = connection.prepareCall(sql);
      cs.registerOutParameter(1, Types.VARCHAR);
      cs.setString(2,param);
      cs.execute();
      String retMess = cs.getString(1);
      System.out.println(retMess);
    }
    catch (Exception e1) {
      e1.printStackTrace();
    }
    finally {
      try {
        connection.close();
```

```
      }
      catch (SQLException e1) {
        e1.printStackTrace();
      }
    }
  }
}
```

The first difference with a plain MDB is that a POJO message bean is tagged by an @Consumer **[1]** annotation. Actually, the MDP class will consume the messages that are produced by the business interface **[3]**. The bean is targeted at a destination named pojoQueue **[2]** (you have to provide this destination by adding a new entry in the destinations-service.xml file).

The implemented interface, named com.packtpub.jms.POJOProcessorItf follows:

```
package com.packtpub.jms;
import org.jboss.ejb3.annotation.Producer;
@Producer    [1]
public interface POJOProcessorItf {
  public void callProcedure(String param);
}
```

As we just said, the @Producer annotation **[1]** acts as a **producer** of messages that will be **consumed** by the implementation classes. A message-driven POJO doesn't require anything else. Just pack your compiled bean class and the interface in an archive, and deploy it to JBoss:

```
JMSExample.jar
+---com
|   +---packtpub
|      +---jms
|         +---POJOProcessor.class
|            +---POJOProcessorItf.class
+---META-INF
```

Now the only missing thing is a client invoking our callProcedure method. For this purpose, add another Java class named com.packtpub.jms.POJOClient.

```
import java.util.Properties;
import javax.naming.Context;
import org.jboss.ejb3.mdb.ProducerConfig;
import org.jboss.ejb3.mdb.ProducerManager;
import org.jboss.ejb3.mdb.ProducerObject;
import com.packtpub.jms.POJOProcessorItf;
```

```
public class POJOClient {
  public static void main(String[] args) throws Exception
  {
    Context ctx = getInitialContext();
    POJOProcessorItf proc =
      (POJOProcessorItf)
      ctx.lookup(POJOProcessorItf.class.getName());   [1]
        ProducerManager manager = ((ProducerObject)
          proc).getProducerManager();   [2]
        manager.connect();   [3]
    try
    {
      proc.callProcedure("John");   [4]
    }
    catch (Exception exc)
    {
      exc.printStackTrace();
    }
    finally {
      ProducerConfig.close(proc);   [5]
    }
  }
}
```

When you deploy an MDP, a proxy object named with the producer's classname **[1]** will be bound in the JNDI context. However, we don't directly deal with the proxy, but with the class `org.jboss.ejb3.mdb.ProducerManager` that manages the JMS connection for this proxy **[2]**. The `ProducerManager` starts a JMS connection with the proxy **[3]** and, through the typed interface, invokes the method `callProcedure` **[4]**. When all operations are complete, the connection with the proxy is closed **[5]**.

In the MDP business interface, you expose the business contract just like a session bean. However, the transport protocol will be JMS and not RMI. Sometimes you might need to recover the message properties, as you may need the message ID or any other property of the message. In this case, you can simply inject the message with the `@CurrentMessage` annotation. Your message details will also be available in the MDP implementation class.

```
public class POJOProcessor implements POJOProcessorItf
{
  @CurrentMessage
  private Message currentMessage;
}
```

Advanced JBoss Messaging

If you have read up to this point, you should have a clear picture about the basic concepts of JBoss Messaging. In the next section, we will raise the bar by moving on to more cutting-edge concepts, such as JBoss Messaging bridge, the persistence service, and securing JMS destinations.

JBoss Messaging bridge

JBM bridge is an advanced feature for routing messages from one destination (queue or topic) to another. Typically, JBM bridge is used for sending messages across different message servers. For example, you could post a queue message on server X, which is routed to server Y, where it is consumed by a message-driven bean.

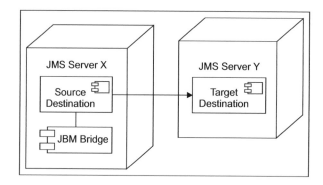

 The source and target servers do not have to be in the same cluster. This makes bridging suitable for reliably sending messages from one cluster to another — for instance, across a WAN and where the connection may be unreliable. Clustering is discussed in detail in Chapter 11, *Clustering JBoss AS*.

Configuring the messaging bridge requires a configuration file in the form of an MBean service. In the first example, we will provide a simple bridge configuration that routes messages from one queue to another, using the default JMS provider.

```
<mbean code="org.jboss.jms.server.bridge.BridgeService"
    name="jboss.messaging:service=Bridge,name=BridgeExample"
    xmbean-dd="xmdesc/Bridge-xmbean.xml">
    <depends optional-attribute-name="SourceProviderLoader">
        jboss.messaging:service=JMSProviderLoader,
        name=JMSProvider</depends>
    <depends optional-attribute-name="TargetProviderLoader">
```

```
        jboss.messaging:service=JMSProviderLoader,
        name=JMSProvider</depends>
   <attribute [1]
      name="SourceDestinationLookup">/queue/exampleQueue</attribute>
   <attribute [2]
      name="TargetDestinationLookup">/queue/exampleQueue2</attribute>
   <attribute name="MaxBatchSize">5</attribute>    [3]
   <attribute name="MaxBatchTime">-1</attribute>     [4]
</mbean>
```

The source **[1]** and target **[2]** destination attributes specify that all messages sent to the `exampleQueue` will be routed to the `remoteQueue`, which is located at the `TargetProvider`.

You must also provide a consistent value for `MaxBatchSize` **[3]**, that is, the number of messages to batch before sending them. The messaging server can be instructed to send messages after an elapsed time, defined by `MaxBatchTime` **[4]**. Setting this value to `-1` forces waiting until `MaxBatchSize` has been reached.

Save the above bridge configuration file as `jbm-bridge-service.xml` in the `deploy/messaging`. In the console log, you should read the following message:

12:14:02,950 INFO [BridgeService] Stopped bridge BridgeService

12:14:03,200 INFO [BridgeService] Started bridge BridgeService. Source: /queue/ exampleQueue Target: /queue/exampleQueue2

Adding a remote JMS provider

The sample bridge is a good starting point for learning; however, its real usefulness appears when you use it for communicating between remote JMS providers.

The JMS provider is also defined as an MBean and uses the same file naming convention. So, let's add the following `jbm-remote-service.xml` to your `messaging` folder:

```
<mbean code="org.jboss.jms.jndi.JMSProviderLoader"
   name="jboss.messaging:service=JMSProviderLoader,
   name=MyRemoteJMSProvider,server=localhost">
   <attribute name="ProviderName">
      RemoteXAConnectionFactory</attribute>    [1]
   <attribute name="ProviderAdapterClass">
      org.jboss.jms.jndi.JNDIProviderAdapter</attribute>
   <attribute name="FactoryRef">XAConnectionFactory</attribute>
   <attribute name="QueueFactoryRef">XAConnectionFactory</attribute>
   <attribute name="TopicFactoryRef">XAConnectionFactory</attribute>
   <attribute name="Properties">   [2]
```

```
    java.naming.factory.initial=org.jnp.interfaces.
      NamingContextFactory
    java.naming.factory.url.pkgs=org.jboss.naming:org.jnp.interfaces
    java.naming.provider.url=remoteserver:1099
  </attribute>
</mbean>
```

Basically, in the JMS provider configuration file, you have to provide all relevant information to reach the JMS server. The upper part of the file **[1]** contains the Factory configuration of the remote server. The attribute named Properties **[2]** handles the NamingContext details of the remote server. You have to substitute the sample IP address remoteserver with the IP address of your remote server.

Now, you have to adapt the bridge configuration so that the new remote provider is used. For example, if the remote provider will route messages to the local JMS provider, all you have to change in your jbm-bridge-service.xml is highlighted as follows:

```
<mbean code="org.jboss.jms.server.bridge.BridgeService"
    name="jboss.messaging:service=Bridge,name=BridgeExample"
    xmbean-dd="xmdesc/Bridge-xmbean.xml">
    <depends optional-attribute-name="SourceProviderLoader">
      jboss.messaging:service=JMSProviderLoader,
      name=MyRemoteJMSProvider,server=remoteserver</depends>
    <depends optional-attribute-name="TargetProviderLoader">
      jboss.messaging:service=JMSProviderLoader,
      name=JMSProvider</depends>
</mbean>
```

Connecting your MDB to a remote provider

Message-driven beans by default consume messages from the built-in JMS provider. However, you can consume messages from any provider that has been deployed. For example, if you want to use the newly defined provider RemoteJMSProvider, all you have to do is adding a couple of ActivationConfigProperty items to your MDB.

```
@MessageDriven(activationConfig =
{
  @ActivationConfigProperty(propertyName="destinationTy
    pe", propertyValue="javax.jms.Queue"),
  @ActivationConfigProperty(propertyName=»destination»,
    propertyValue=»queue/remoteQueue»),
  @ActivationConfigProperty(propertyName=»providerAdapt
    erJNDI», propertyValue=»java:/MyRemoteJMSProvider «)
})
```

Configuring the persistence service

The persistence manager handles all details about JMS storage. By default, the persistence service is configured to run on Hypersonic database and its datasource (identified by the naming context `DefaultDS`). The configuration of "persistent" services is grouped in a `xxx-persistence-service.xml` file, where `xxx` corresponds to the database name. We will show how to change the default database to MySQL.

The first thing we will need is a datasource and a database schema, where JBM tables will be created. In order to avoid extra hops, we will use the MySQL datasource that we have used previously in our examples. In a production environment, we strongly advise you to use a dedicated resource for the messaging store.

The next thing we need is a `mysql-persistence-service.xml` file template. JMS templates are stored in the `docs\examples\jms` folder of your JBoss server. There you will find a list of persistence configuration file for most common databases.

Copy the file `mysql-persistence.xml` in the folder `deploy\messaging` of your server and, at the same time, take care to delete the file `hsqldb-persistence.xml`. Now open the MySQL persistence file and configure it to use MySQL datasource. Here is a reduced version of it:

```
<mbean
    code="org.jboss.messaging.core.jmx.JDBCPersistenceManagerService"
    name="jboss.messaging:service=PersistenceManager" xmbean-
    dd="xmdesc/JDBCPersistenceManager-xmbean.xml">
    <depends>jboss.jca:service=DataSourceBinding,name=MySqlDS</depends>
    <depends optional-attribute-name="TransactionManager">
      jboss:service=TransactionManager</depends>
    <attribute name="DataSource">java:/MySqlDS</attribute>
</mbean>
<mbean code="org.jboss.messaging.core.jmx.MessagingPostOfficeService"
    name="jboss.messaging:service=PostOffice" xmbean-
    dd="xmdesc/MessagingPostOffice-xmbean.xml">
    <depends optional-attribute-
      name="ServerPeer">jboss.messaging:service=ServerPeer</depends>
    <depends>jboss.jca:service=DataSourceBinding,name=MySqlDS</depends>
    <depends optional-attribute-name="TransactionManager">
      jboss:service=TransactionManager</depends>
    <attribute name="PostOfficeName">JMS post office</attribute>
    <attribute name="DataSource">java:/MySqlDS</attribute>
    <attribute name="Clustered">false</attribute>   [1]
    <attribute name="GroupName">
      ${jboss.messaging.groupname:MessagingPostOffice}</attribute>
    <attribute name="FailoverOnNodeLeave">false</attribute>
    <!-- [2] COMMENT OUT THIS
```

```
      <depends optional-attribute-name="ChannelFactoryName">
        jboss.jgroups:service=ChannelFactory</depends>
          <attribute name="ControlChannelName">jbm-control</attribute>
          <attribute name="DataChannelName">jbm-data</attribute>
          <attribute name="ChannelPartitionName">
            ${jboss.partition.name:DefaultPartition}-JMS</attribute>
      -->
</mbean>
<mbean code="org.jboss.jms.server.plugin.JDBCJMSUserManagerService"
    name="jboss.messaging:service=JMSUserManager" xmbean-
    dd="xmdesc/JMSUserManager-xmbean.xml">
    <depends>jboss.jca:service=DataSourceBinding,name=MySqlDS</depends>
    <depends optional-attribute-name="TransactionManager">
      jboss:service=TransactionManager</depends>
    <attribute name="DataSource">java:/MySqlDS</attribute>
</mbean>
```

Apart from configuring the datasource name, if you are not running a clusterable solution, make sure that the attribute `Clustered` is set to `false` **[1]**. You should also comment dependencies on the `ChannelFactory` service **[2]**, which is not available in a single node environment.

Securing destinations

By default, every message that is sent can be accessed by all message consumers connected to the destination. You can restrict access to the JMS destination by configuring the `JMSUserManager` component and then plugging JBM users into **JBoss security framework (JBossSX)**.

By default, the `JMSUserManager` is set up to run with Hypersonic database and its configuration file `deploy\messaging\hsqldb-persistence-service.xml`, should be already familiar to you.

In the previous section, we have shown how to migrate the persistence service to another database provider, namely MySQL database. Therefore, by now, your database should contain all the tables necessary for storing users and role credentials, along with some sample data.

In order to secure your messages, you need to plug your configuration into JBoss security framework so that you can use it to authenticate message senders/ consumers. The configuration of JBoss security framework is discussed in detail in Chapter 13, *JBoss AS Security*. In short, you need to declare a new security domain in the `conf/login-config.xml` file. This file contains all security policies for accessing JBoss components. Add an application policy named `JMSRealm` to the `login-config.xml` file.

```
<application-policy name="JMSRealm">
  <authentication>
    <login-module
      code="org.jboss.security.auth.spi.DatabaseServerLoginModule"
      flag="required">
    <module-option name="dsJndiName">java:/MySqlDS</module-option>
    <module-option name="principalsQuery">
    SELECT passwd from jbm_user WHERE user_id=?
    </module-option>
    <module-option name="rolesQuery">
    SELECT role_id,'Roles' FROM jbm_role WHERE user_id=?
    </module-option>
    </login-module>
  </authentication>
<application-policy>
```

Okay, the configuration is almost complete. The last step is to add the JMSRealm to the configuration of **JBM security store** that can be found in the deploy\messaging\ messaging-jboss-beans.xml file. There, you should add a property named securityDomain **[1]** with the value JMSRealm.

```
<bean name="SecurityStore"
  class="org.jboss.jms.server.jbosssx.JBossASSecurityMetadataStore">
  <property name="defaultSecurityConfig">
  <![CDATA[
    <security>
      <role name="guest" read="true" write="true" create="true"/>
    </security>
  ]]>
  </property>
  <property name="securityDomain">JMSRealm</property>   [1]
</bean>
```

Well done. In order to test the JMS authentication, we will create a topic that is secured against the role publisher.

```
<mbean code="org.jboss.jms.server.destination.TopicService"
  name=»jboss.messaging.destination:service=Topic,name=secureTopic
  xmbean-dd="xmdesc/Topic-xmbean.xml">
  <depends optional-attribute-
    name="ServerPeer">jboss.messaging:service=ServerPeer</depends>
  <depends>jboss.messaging:service=PostOffice</depends>
  <attribute name="SecurityConfig">
    <security>
      <role name="publisher" read="true" write="true"/>
    </security>
  </attribute>
</mbean>
```

This role is added by the persistence service at table creation. It has a user named dynsub associated:

```
INSERT INTO JBM_USER (USER_ID, PASSWD) VALUES ('dynsub', 'dynsub');
INSERT INTO JBM_ROLE (ROLE_ID, USER_ID) VALUES
  ('publisher','dynsub');
```

What are the "read" and "write" properties?

The read access property specifies that the user with role publisher is able to consume messages from the destination. The corresponding write property assigns rights to send messages to that topic. There is one more property, create, that is configurable and is specific to topic destinations and can grant the rights to establish a durable subscription.

In the following code excerpt, we create a topic publisher and a subscriber to the topic secureTopic:

```
public void example() throws Exception
{
  String destinationName = "topic/secureTopic";
  Context ic = null;
  ConnectionFactory cf = null;
  Connection connection =  null;
  try
  {
    ic = getInitialContext();
    cf = (ConnectionFactory)ic.lookup("/ConnectionFactory");
    Topic topic = (Topic)ic.lookup(destinationName);
    connection = cf.createConnection("dynsub","dynsub");   [1]
    Session session = connection.createSession(false,
      Session.AUTO_ACKNOWLEDGE);
    MessageProducer publisher = session.createProducer(topic);
    MessageConsumer subscriber = session.createConsumer(topic);
    subscriber.setMessageListener(this);
    /* Need to implement MessageListener and the
      onMessage method
    */
    connection.start();
    TextMessage message = session.createTextMessage("Hello!");
    publisher.send(message);
  }
}
```

As you can see, accessing a secured destination requires using a constructor with the correct credentials **[1]**. We will not dwell upon the rest of the code that takes care to create a `MessageProducer` and a `MessageConsumer` for this topic and eventually send a JMS text message through this channel.

MDB access control

Message-driven beans can also be configured to authenticate a destination by adding the additional `user` and `password` properties to your MDB annotation.

```
@MessageDriven(activationConfig =
{
  @ActivationConfigProperty(propertyName="destinationType",
    propertyValue="javax.jms.Queue"),
  @ActivationConfigProperty(propertyName="destination",
    propertyValue="queue/secureTopic"),
  @ActivationConfigProperty
    (propertyName=»user», propertyValue=»dynsub»),
  @ActivationConfigProperty
    (propertyName="password", propertyValue="dynsub")
})
public  class MessageConsumerBean implements MessageListener {
}
```

Just be careful to use the property `user` (and not `username`). This is a common pitfall that leads to a `JMSSecurityException` because the username will be considered null.

Summary

We have completed our journey through JBoss Messaging. The new JMS provider is designed to provide a high performance, robust messaging core for the Enterprise.

We have learned how to configure the building blocks of JBoss Messaging system and we have used this environment to develop some components, such as message-driven beans and message-driven POJOs.

Moving on, we have discussed some advanced features, such as the bridge system, the persistence service, and the JMS user manager. You have just learned a good deal about JBoss Messaging, so pat yourself on the back!

Our next chapter will be devoted to the Hibernate framework, which is the default persistence engine of JBoss AS.

Developing Applications with JBoss and Hibernate

Hibernation is a state of regulated hypothermia undergone by some animals to conserve energy during the winter. – Wikipedia

In this chapter, we will introduce Hibernate, which is the *de facto* standard object-relational mapping framework for Java applications. The Hibernate galaxy is quite large and needs a book of its own to be fully explored. Our mission will be to take over one sector of this galaxy, especially where Hibernate applications are managed by JBoss AS.

In this chapter, we will cover the following topics:

- A short introduction to Hibernate
- Setting up our proof of concept for the Hibernate project
- Reverse engineering a database schema into Hibernate POJOs and mapping files
- Deploying the application to JBoss AS
- Comparing the Hibernate technology with EJB 3 persistence (JPA)

Introducing Hibernate

Hibernate provides a bridge between the database and the application by persisting application objects in the database, rather than requiring the developer to write and maintain lots of code to store and retrieve objects.

The main configuration file, `hibernate.cfg.xml`, specifies how Hibernate obtains database connections, either from a JNDI DataSource or from a JDBC connection pool. Additionally, the configuration file defines the persistent classes, which are backed by mapping definition files.

This is a sample `hibernate.cfg.xml` configuration file that is used to handle connections to a MySQL database, mapping the `com.sample.MySample` class.

```
<hibernate-configuration>
  <session-factory>
    <property name="connection.username">user</property>
    <property name="connection.password">password</property>
    <property name="connection.url">
      jdbc:mysql://localhost/database
    </property>
    <property name="connection.driver_class">
      com.mysql.jdbc.Driver
    </property>
    <property name="dialect">
      org.hibernate.dialect.MySQLDialect
    </property>
    <mapping resource="com/sample/MyClass.hbm.xml"/>
  </session-factory>
</hibernate-configuration>
```

From our point of view, it is important to know that Hibernate applications can coexist in both the **managed** environment and the **non-managed** environment. An application server is a typical example of a managed environment that provides services to hosting applications, such as connection pooling and transaction.

On the other hand, a non-managed application refers to standalone applications, such as Swing Java clients that typically lack any built-in service.

In this chapter, we will focus on managed environment applications, installed on JBoss Application Server. You will not need to download any library to your JBoss installation. As a matter of fact, JBoss persistence layer is designed around Hibernate API, so it already contains all the core libraries.

Creating a Hibernate application

You can choose different strategies for building a Hibernate application. For example, you could start building Java classes and map files from scratch, and then let Hibernate generate the database schema accordingly. You can also start from a database schema and reverse engineer it into Java classes and Hibernate mapping files. We will choose the latter option, which is also the fastest. Here's an overview of our application.

In this example, we will design an employee agenda divided into departments. The persistence model will be developed with Hibernate, using the reverse engineering facet of JBoss tools. We will then need an interface for recording our employees and departments, and to query them as well.

The web interface will be developed using a simple **Model-View-Controller (MVC)** pattern and basic JSP 2.0 and servlet features.

The overall architecture of this system resembles the AppStore application that has been used to introduce JPA. As a matter of fact, this example can be used to compare the two persistence models and to decide which option best suits your project needs. We have added a short section at the end of this example to stress a few important points about this choice.

Setting up the database schema

As our first step, we are going to create the necessary tables for our example. Launch a MySQL client and issue the following DDL:

```
CREATE schema hibernate;
GRANT ALL PRIVILEGES ON hibernate.* TO  'jboss'@'localhost' WITH GRANT
OPTION;
CREATE TABLE `hibernate`.`department` (
  `department_id` INTEGER UNSIGNED NOT NULL AUTO_INCREMENT,
  `department_name` VARCHAR(45) NOT NULL,
  PRIMARY KEY (`department_id`)
)
ENGINE = InnoDB;
CREATE TABLE `hibernate`.`employee` (
  `employee_id` INTEGER UNSIGNED NOT NULL AUTO_INCREMENT,
  `employee_name` VARCHAR(45) NOT NULL,
  `employee_salary` INTEGER UNSIGNED NOT NULL,
  `employee_department_id` INTEGER UNSIGNED NOT NULL,
  PRIMARY KEY (`employee_id`),
  CONSTRAINT `FK_employee_1` FOREIGN KEY `FK_employee_1` (`employee_
department_id`)
    REFERENCES `department` (`department_id`)
    ON DELETE CASCADE
    ON UPDATE CASCADE
)
ENGINE = InnoDB;
```

With the first **Data Definition Language** (DDL) command, we have created a schema named Hibernate that will be used to store our tables. Then, we have assigned the necessary privileges on the Hibernate schema to the user jboss (created in Chapter 5, *Developing JPA Entities*).

Finally, we created a table named `department` that contains the list of company units, and another table named `employee` that contains the list of workers. The `employee` table references the `department` with a foreign key constraint.

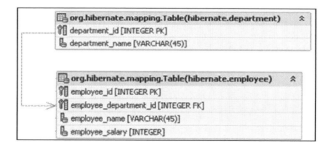

A new Eclipse project

Now start Eclipse. You don't have a specific project for Hibernate applications, so a utility project (that simply packs the classes in an archive) will be enough. You can reach this option from the menu by going to **New | Other | Java EE | Utility Project**.

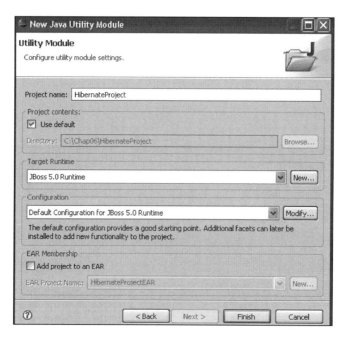

Name the project **HibernateProject** and target it to **JBoss AS 5.0 Runtime**. You can leave the default JBoss AS configuration and hit **Finish**.

Now, we are going to unleash the full potential of **Hibernate tools**. Select from the menu **New | Other | Hibernate | Hibernate Configuration File**. The Hibernate configuration contains all of the details for wiring your application to the database. You will be asked for the name and the parent folder of the configuration file. Accept the default `hibernate.cfg.xml` at the root of your project.

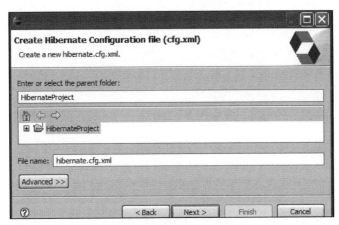

Next, insert the details of your Hibernate configuration. Choose a name for your session factory, which will contain your MySQL connection facets. Remember to check the flag **Create a console configuration,** so that the wizard will complete the console configuration as the next step.

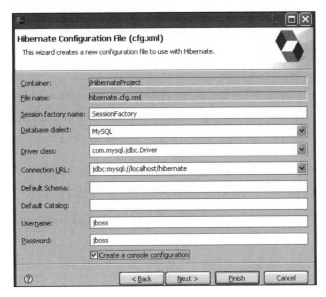

A **console configuration** describes how the Hibernate plugin should interact with Hibernate and what configuration files (including the classpath) are needed to load the POJOs, JDBC drivers, and so on. This step is required to make use of query prototyping, reverse engineering, and code generation.

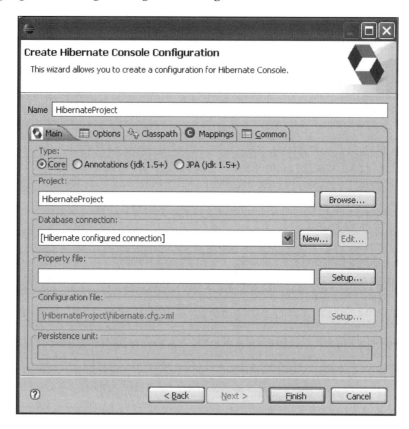

The console wizard will look at the current selection in the IDE and will try to autodetect the settings, which you can approve or modify to suit your needs. For example, you don't need to enter the **Configuration file** or the **Property file** if you have just one in your project; Eclipse will select it automatically.

One important selection is the **Type** option that lets you choose between the **Core** hibernate configuration (Java classes backed by mapping files), **Annotations,** or even **JPA** annotations. We will leave the selected **Core** option.

Before clicking **Finish**, select **MySQL (InnoDB)** as **Database dialect** in the **Options** tab. No other changes are required.

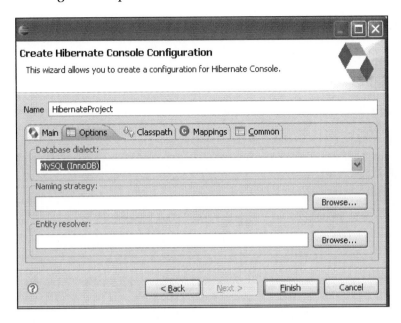

Now verify that you have successfully linked to Hibernate by switching to **Hibernate Configuration**. This view will be composed by a tree of three objects: **Configuration**, **Session Factory**, and **Database**. Choose **Database** and verify that it expands correctly to show the database tables of your schema.

If you fail to browse the database schema, check that you have correctly set up your Hibernate configuration.

Reversing your schema into Java classes

The next move will be reversing our database schema into Java classes and mapping files. This powerful feature is available from the menu: **File | New | Hibernate | Hibernate Reverse Engineering file**. You can place this file in a convenient location for your project and choose a name for it. The default name proposed is `hibernate.reveng.xml`, which looks rather the tile of another fiction movie from G. Lucas.

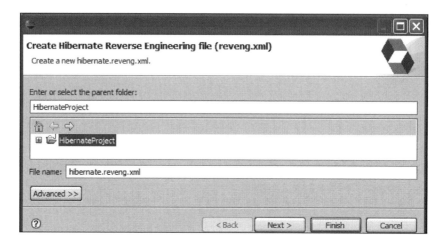

On the next page, select your **Console configuration** and choose the tables that will be included in your reverse engineering process. (Hint: You have to hit **Refresh** first to show the database schema and then click **Include....**)

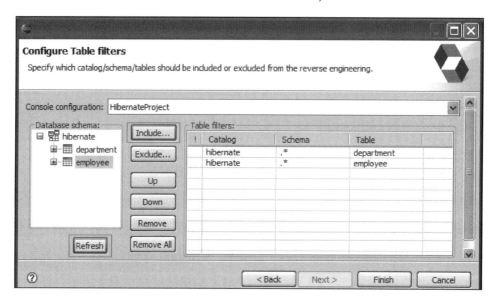

What Eclipse has just created for you is a file named `hibernate.reveng.xml` that should resemble the following code snippet:

```
<hibernate-reverse-engineering>
    <table-filter match-catalog="hibernate" match-name="department"/>
    <table-filter match-catalog="hibernate" match-name="employee"/>
</hibernate-reverse-engineering>
```

If you are smart at noticing variations, you might have discovered a new icon in your toolbar. This is your gateway to the reverse engineering process. (Notice: this icon is visible only in the Hibernate Perspective, you will not be able to find it anywhere else.)

Click on Hibernate's down arrow icon and select **Hibernate Code Generation Configurations**. In the next dialog, you will first have to create a new **Hibernate Code Generation Configuration** that will contain all the details of your reverse engineering process. Click on the **New** button located in the left corner of the wizard.

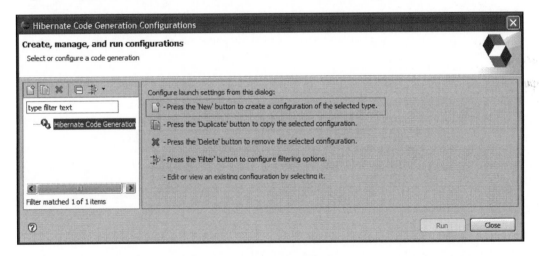

Now, select your brand new configuration and carefully choose the following options. First, wire the **Console configuration** to your project (HibernateProject). Then, choose an output directory for your generated files. We would suggest you to point to your `src` folder. (Be aware that existing files will be overwritten, that's why I just said you have to be *careful!*)

Just below, you will find the checkbox **Reverse engineer from JDBC Connection**. If enabled, the tools will reverse engineer the available database using the connection information in the selected Hibernate Console configuration. Check this option and enter the package name for the generated classes, which will be **com.packtpub. hibernate**. Leave the other text fields to the defaults and move to the tab **Exporters**.

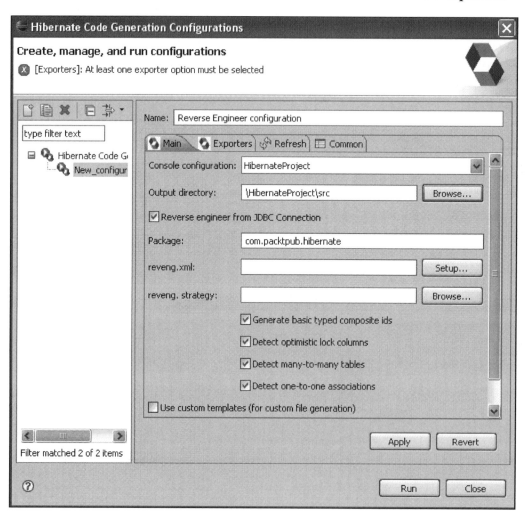

The **Exporters** tab menu is used to specify which type of code should be generated. Each selection represents an Exporter that is responsible for generating the code, hence the name.

In the upper area of the dialog, you will notice an interesting checkbox named **Generate EJB 3 annotations**. We will return to this useful option later. At the moment, what we need is just to check the **Domain code** and **Hibernate XML Mappings** options, which will generate the Java POJOs and mapping files respectively.

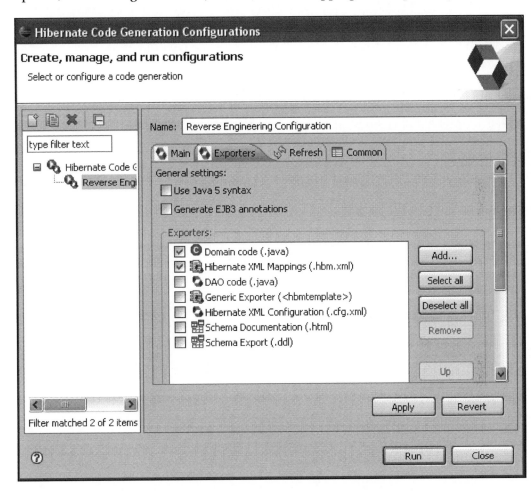

It took a bit of time to complete all of these steps; however, now your Java classes and configuration files are handy and waiting to be packaged.

Adding Hibernate configuration to your project

The advantage of embedding the Hibernate application in JBoss AS is that you can expose **Hibernate SessionFactory** through a JNDI tree and modify its configuration at runtime.

This is indeed a great configuration advantage; before the new release of JBoss AS, you had to delegate to an MBean the creation of the Hibernate SessionFactory and its exposure through JNDI.

For example, if you wanted to configure a SessionFactory at the naming context hibernate/SessionFactory, you would have to package your Hibernate application with a file named xxx-service.xml in the META-INF folder. Here's a sample of it:

```
<server>
  <mbean code="org.jboss.hibernate.jmx.Hibernate"
    name="jboss.har:service=Hibernate">
  <attribute name="DatasourceName">java:/ MySqlDS</attribute>
  <attribute name="Dialect">
    org.hibernate.dialect.MySQLDialect
  </attribute>
  <attribute name="SessionFactoryName">
    java:/hibernate/SessionFactory
  </attribute>
  <attribute name="CacheProviderClass">
    org.hibernate.cache.HashtableCacheProvider
  </attribute>
  </mbean>
</server>
```

This configuration is still valid for pre 5.0 releases of JBoss AS. With the introduction of the new **Virtual Deployment Framework (VDF)**, you now have to provide your **SessionFactory** configuration using the Hibernate XML schema. For example, if you want to link your SessionFactory to your MySQL database, you have to add the following service-hibernate.xml. (Be aware, the suffix is -hibernate.xml and not –service.xml.)

```
<hibernate-configuration xmlns="urn:jboss:hibernate-deployer:1.0">
  <session-factory name="java:/hibernate/SessionFactory"
    bean="jboss.test.har:service=Hibernate,
    testcase=TimersUnitTestCase">
    <property name="datasourceName">java:/MySqlDS</property>
      <property name="dialect">
        org.hibernate.dialect.MySQLDialect
```

```
      </property>
    <depends>jboss:service=Naming</depends>
      <depends>jboss:service=TransactionManager</depends>
    </session-factory>
  </hibernate-configuration>
```

The preceding configuration file needs to be stored in the META-INF folder of your **Hibernate archive (HAR)** file. The structure of the updated project from the **Package Explorer** is as shown in the following snapshot:

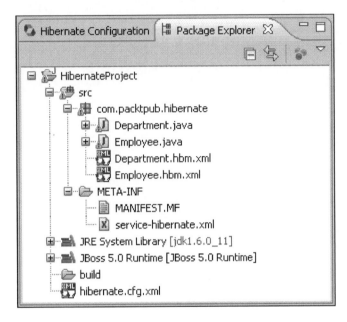

Adding a web client to your project

There are several ways to test our Hibernate application. The simplest of all is adding a web application, which is packaged in an Enterprise application along with the Hibernate application. Create a new dynamic web project named HibernateWeb.

The first step, before adding servlets and JSPs is linking the HibernateProject libraries to your web application, otherwise, you will not be able to reference the Hibernate POJOs. Right-click on your project and select **Properties**. Reach the **Java Build Path** option and select the tab **Projects**. From there add **HibernateProject**.

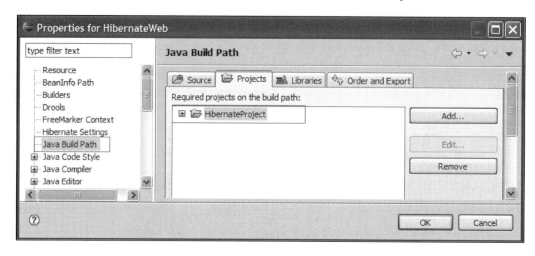

Let's move on. This project will contain a main servlet that acts as a controller, and a few JPSs for the client view. We will start by adding `com.packtpub.hibernateWeb.HibernateServlet` to our project.

In the following snippet, you can see the core section of the servlet. Here, we will not detail the Controller logic, which is straightforward if you have some rudiments of the MVC pattern; rather we want to highlight the most interesting part of it, which is how to query and persist Hibernate objects.

```java
public class HibernateServlet extends HttpServlet {
  private SessionFactory getSessionFactory() {
    return (SessionFactory)getServletContext().
    getAttribute("sessionFactory");
  }
  public void init() { [1]
    if (getSessionFactory() != null) {
      return;
    }
    InitialContext ctx;
    try {
      ctx = new InitialContext();
      factory = (SessionFactory)ctx.
        lookup("java:/hibernate/SessionFactory");
      getServletContext().setAttribute("sessionFactory", factory);
    }
```

```
    catch (NamingException e) {
      e.printStackTrace();
    }
  }
  private String saveEmployee(HttpServletRequest request) {
    Session hsession=null;
    String name=request.getParameter("name");
    String salary=request.getParameter("salary");
    String departmentId=request.getParameter("departmentId");
    try {
      hsession = getSessionFactory().openSession();
      hsession.beginTransaction();
      Query query = hsession.createQuery("from Department d where
        d.departmentId = :departmentId"); [2]
      query.setInteger("departmentId", new Integer(departmentId));
      Department dep = (Department) query.uniqueResult();
      Employee emp = new Employee();
      emp.setDepartment(dep);
      emp.setEmployeeName(name);
      emp.setEmployeeSalary(Integer.parseInt(salary));
      hsession.save(emp); [3]
      hsession.getTransaction().commit();
    }
    catch (Exception e) {
      // TODO Auto-generated catch block e.printStackTrace();
      hsession.getTransaction().rollback();
    }
    finally {
      if (hsession.isOpen())
        hsession.close();
    }
    return employeeList(request);
  }
  private String employeeList(HttpServletRequest request) {
    Session hsession=null;
    Department dep;
    try {
      hsession = getSessionFactory().openSession();
      Query query = hsession.createQuery("select p from Employee p
        join fetch p.department c");   [4]
      List <Employee>list = query.list();
      request.setAttribute("employee", list);
    }
    catch (Exception e) {
      e.printStackTrace();
```

```
        }
        finally {
          if (hsession.isOpen())
            hsession.close();
        }
        return "/listEmployees.jsp";
      }
      private String saveDepartment(HttpServletRequest request) {
        String depName=request.getParameter("depName");
        Session hsession=null;
        Department dep;
        try {
          hsession = getSessionFactory().openSession();
          hsession.beginTransaction();
          dep = new Department();
          dep.setDepartmentName(depName);
          hsession.save(dep); [5]
          hsession.getTransaction().commit();
        }
        catch (Exception e) {
          // TODO Auto-generated catch block
          e.printStackTrace();
          hsession.getTransaction().rollback();
        }
        finally {
          if (hsession.isOpen())
            hsession.close();
        }
        return employeeList(request);
      }
    }
```

As you can see from the preceding code, we recover the SessionFactory from the JNDI tree in the init() **[1]** method of the servlet. Instances of SessionFactory are thread-safe and typically shared throughout an application, so we store it in the ServletContext and share it among all servlet instances.

The SessionFactory is subsequently used to start a Hibernate session, which is not thread-safe and should only be used for a single transaction or unit of work in an application.

In order to store our Employee, in the saveEmployee method, we first retrieve the corresponding Department from our schema **[2]**, and finally the Employee is saved **[3]** and the transaction is committed.

The list of employees is fetched by the `employeeList` method. Notice we are using a `join fetch` statement to retrieve all the employees **[4]**, which will be routed to the `listEmployees.jsp` view. Why? The answer is that with the default fetch mode (Lazy), once the Hibernate session is closed, the client will not be able to navigate through the `department` field of the `Employee`. The common solution to this issue is switching to the EAGER fetch mode that reads the related fields (in our case department) in memory, as soon as we query the `Employee` table.

You have more than one option to achieve this. One possible solution, if you don't want to change the default fetch mode for the `Employee` table, is to build an *ad hoc* query that forces Hibernate to read also those fields that are in relation with the `Employee` table.

```
"select p from Employee p join fetch p.department c"
```

If you prefer to use the XML class files to configure the fetch mode, you can also change the `lazy="true"` attribute in the employee-department relationship.

The last method, `saveDepartment` **[5]** takes care to persist a new `Department` in the corresponding table. We complete our excursus on the web tier with the `listEmployees.jsp` that is used to display a tabular view of the employees:

```
<%@ taglib uri="http://java.sun.com/jsp/jstl/core" prefix="c" %>
<html>
<script language="JavaScript">
function doSubmit(url)  {
  document.module.action = url;
  document.module.submit();
}
</script>
<body>
<table border="1">
  <tr>
    <th>Name</th>
    <th>Salary</th> <TH>department</th>
  </tr>
  <c:forEach items="${employee}" var="emp">
  <tr>
    <td> <c:out value="${emp.employeeName}"/> </td>
    <td> <c:out value="${emp.employeeSalary}"/></td>
    <td> <c:out value="${emp.department.departmentName}"/></td>
  </tr>
  </c:forEach>
</table>
<form name="module" method="POST">
```

```
    <input type="button" value ="New Employee"
      onClick="doSubmit('actionServlet?op=newEmployee')">
    <input type="button" value ="New Department"
      onClick="doSubmit('actionServlet?op=newDepartment')">
  </form>
  </body>
  </html>
```

This page uses JSP 2.0 **Expression Language (EL)** to iterate through the list of employees, as highlighted in the last code snippet. We have also highlighted the taglib directive, at the beginning of the page. This directive will be used to resolve the JSTL core set of libraries that ships with JBoss AS in the server/xxx/deploy/ jbossweb.sar/jstl.jar library. (Eclipse does not contain references to this library when you create a web project; you have to add jstl.jar to your build path, otherwise Eclipse will mark it as an error. However, that's only a visual annoyance because the JBoss web container has got everything it needs to run JSTL.)

The complete web application is available on the Packtpub website (http://www.packtpub.com) and includes two additional JSPs for entering the employee (newEmployee.jsp) and department (newDepartment.jsp) data, plus one placeholder index.jsp that merely forwards to the **HibernateServlet**.

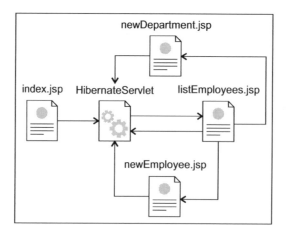

Packaging and deploying the application

Your enterprise application is complete. We need to package it in an EAR archive so that the web application will be able to interact with the Hibernate POJOs. Create a new **Enterprise Application** project from the Java EE folder. You will be prompted to select the projects that will be included as modules. Select both the **HibernateProject** and the web application **HibernateWeb**.

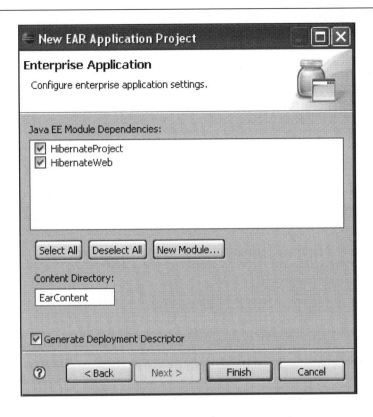

If you have ever worked with JBoss AS and Hibernate, then you might argue that right now something is missing. You're indeed right. Before release 5.0 of the JBoss Application Server, Hibernate classes and mapping files had to be packaged in a JBoss AS custom `.har` archive. The suffix was determinant, as JBoss AS was able to classify the package as a Hibernate resource.

As HAR archives are not Java EE standard components, you have to declare it in a JBoss AS-specific configuration file named `jboss-app.xml` that sits in the META-INF folder of our EAR.

```
<!DOCTYPE jboss-app PUBLIC "-//JBoss//DTD J2EE Application 1.5//EN"
    "http://www.jboss.org/j2ee/dtd/jboss-app_5_0.dtd">
<jboss-app>
  <module>
    <har>HibernateApplication.har</har>
  </module>
</jboss-app>
```

While this approach is still advisable if you want to grant backward compatibility to your applications, with release 5.0 of the Application Server you now have a handy quicker solution. As the new VFS of JBoss AS is able to detect the nature of your application by scanning deployment descriptors, it's enough to pack your Hibernate application in a plain **Java ARchive (JAR)**. JBoss AS will discover the `.hbm.xml` mapping files and look for the corresponding Java classes. If successful, the package will be deployed as a Hibernate application straightaway.

The corollary of this theorem is that you can leave out, as well, the JBoss AS configuration file `jboss-app.xml`, which is not necessary any more. The only update required is to your `application.xml`, where your Hibernate application is declared as a Java module in order to make it available to other enterprise modules.

```
<application>
  <module>
    <web>
      <web-uri>HibernateWeb.war</web-uri>
      <context-root>HibernateWeb</context-root>
    </web>
  </module>
  <module>
    <java>HibernateProject.jar</java>
  </module>
</application>
```

This is how your Enterprise ARchive should look like before deploying it:

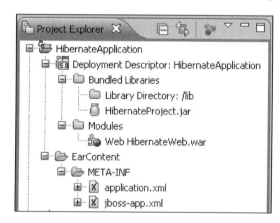

Now deploy your application in the usual way, by adding the project to JBoss AS projects and then choosing **Full Publish**. The application server will then produce a few log pages; if the binding of classes is successful, you will find the following among your logs:

16:46:18,949 INFO [HbmBinder] Mapping class: com.packtpub.hibernate. Employee ->employee

16:46:19,261 INFO [HbmBinder] Mapping class: com.packtpub.hibernate. Department -> department

16:46:19,277 INFO [HbmBinder] Mapping collection: com.packtpub.hibernate. Departm

ent.employees -> employee

In order to test your application, simply recall your JSP default page, using the HibernateWeb context. In our example:

```
http://localhost:8080/HibernateWeb/
```

Using the wizard to generate EJB 3

Hibernate tool capabilities are not limited to Hibernate programming. By using the reverse engineering option, you can also generate EJB 3.0 classes in a matter of seconds. Recall the **Reverse Engineering Configuration**:

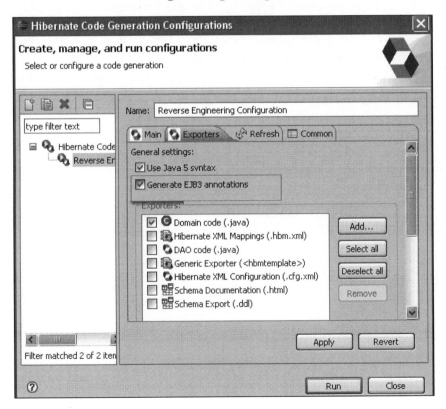

If you Check the **Generate EJB 3 annotations** checkbox along with **Domain code**, then the outcome of your reverse engineering process would be simple Java classes with entity annotations. That's a huge saving of time, especially if your database schema is rather complex. You can still adjust your entity beans to your needs once they are generated.

Hibernate and EJB: Friends or opponents?

In Chapter 4, we introduced the EJB programming model, so at this stage, you might wonder when it's more appropriate to use EJB from your projects and when it's better to stay on the Hibernate framework.

The premise of this debate is that EJB and Hibernate are not fully comparable because they are semantically different. EJBs live in a container, which provides services, such as transactions, concurrent access control, security, instance pooling, and others. On the other hand, Hibernate is classified as an **object-relational mapping tool** and it is independent from a server container.

So, if comparing EJB and Hibernate is technically a mistake, you can actually compare the **Java Persistence API** and Hibernate, which are, in some ways, two *antagonist* technologies. The most important factor, which is in favor of JPA, is that it is a standard. Using industry-standard components allows the business comparatively more flexibility when it's necessary to change its business model, to reorchestrate itself, and to collaborate dynamically.

Technically speaking, it is also important to stress that an EJB-centric approach is the appropriate implementation technology for two types of applications:

- Applications that use distributed transactions initiated by remote clients
- Applications that are heavily message-oriented and need message-driven beans

On the other hand, Hibernate framework has reached a vast community of developers and it offers the benefit of peacefully coexisting in various deployment environments, from application servers to standalone applications.

At the end of the day, the choice between the two technologies might be to preserve your well-tested applications backed by Hibernate Persistence and to definitely consider switching to JPA when you are designing a new project from the ground up. What about using them together instead?

Using Hibernate with EJB

A plausible scenario is that some time ago, you designed the persistence layer of your application with Hibernate. Now you need to expose some functionalities of your application through RMI or Web Services.

The good news is that persistent classes that are mapped using Hibernate `*.hbm.xml` files are supported by JBoss AS EJB 3 implementation. The **EJB 3 deployer** will search the archive for any `.hbm.xml` files and add them to the definition of the underlying Hibernate `SessionFactory`. Let's see how you can leverage Hibernate objects from the EJB environment.

Injecting key Hibernate objects

If you have been through the Hibernate web application carefully, you might advocate that it is not a pure MVC application, as we are accessing the persistence layer from within the servlet.

This approach can be useful for a learner who wants an easy-to-catch example of Hibernate. However, you can create a clean separation of roles between the controller and the model tier, also by introducing an EJB as intermediary.

From inside your Hibernate project, add another Stateless Session Bean named `com.packtpub.hibernate.HibernateDAOBean` implementing a local interface `com.packtpub.hibernate.HibernateDAOLocal`.

Following is a code snippet of the bean implementing the `saveEmployee` method:

```
@Stateless
@LocalBinding(jndiBinding="HibernateDAO/local")
public class HibernateDAOBean implements HibernateDAO {
  @PersistenceUnit(unitName="hibernateUnit") [1]
    SessionFactory factory;
  public void saveEmployee(String name,String salary,String
    departmentId) {
    Session hsession=null;
    try {
      hsession = factory.openSession();
      Query query = hsession.createQuery("from Department d where
        d.departmentId = :departmentId");
      query.setInteger("departmentId", new Integer(departmentId));
      Department dep = (Department) query.uniqueResult();
      Employee emp = new Employee();
      emp.setDepartment(dep);
      emp.setEmployeeName(name);
      emp.setEmployeeSalary(Integer.parseInt(salary));
```

```
        hsession.save(emp);
    }
    catch (Exception e) {
      // TODO Auto-generated catch block
      e.printStackTrace();
      throw new EJBException(e.getMessage());
    }
    finally {
      if (hsession.isOpen())
        hsession.close();
    }
}
```

The most interesting point in this example is that you have injected the Hibernate SessionFactory in your bean by means of the persistence unit named hibernateUnit. Therefore, you have to equip your application with a JPA persistence.xml file:

```
<?xml version="1.0" encoding="UTF-8"?>
<persistence version="1.0" xmlns="http://java.sun.com/xml/ns/
persistence" xmlns:xsi="http://www.w3.org/2001/XMLSchema-instance"
xsi:schemaLocation="http://java.sun.com/xml/ns/persistence http://
java.sun.com/xml/ns/persistence/persistence_1_0.xsd">
  <persistence-unit name="hibernateUnit" transaction-type="JTA">
  <provider>org.hibernate.ejb.HibernatePersistence</provider>
    <jta-data-source>java:/MySqlDS</jta-data-source>
    <properties>
      <property name="hibernate.dialect"
        value="org.hibernate.dialect.MySQLDialect"/>
    </properties>
  </persistence-unit>
</persistence>
```

We leave as exercise to the reader to complete the EJB with all other methods. On the web tier, you will do a clear cut of all the persistence stuff, just taking care to invoke the EJB with the parameters collected from the request. Look how simple and effective your servlet method saveEmployee has become:

```
@EJB(mappedName = "HibernateDAO/local")
HibernateDAO hibernateDAO;
  private String saveEmployee(HttpServletRequest request) {
    Session hsession=null;
    String name=request.getParameter("name");
    String salary=request.getParameter("salary");
    String departmentId=request.getParameter("departmentId");
    try {
```

```
      hibernateDAO.saveEmployee(name,salary,departmentId);
   }
   catch (Exception e) {
      e.printStackTrace();
   }
   return employeeList(request);
}
```

A snapshot of the complete Hibernate EJB-driven project follows here:

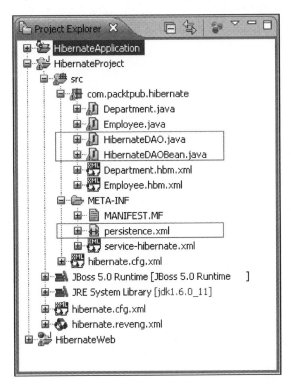

As you can see, using Hibernate API works much the same way as the EntityManager interface. This example reveals another difference with our former web application. Here the EJB must not attempt to manage the life cycle of the Hibernate session; this is done internally by the EJB container, which is in charge of committing or rolling back the transaction, following the EJB container's policies.

Summary

Hibernate is a flexible framework that can be used in any Java application environment. In our excursus, we have showed how to develop a sample application that is geared toward a managed environment. In the last two sections of the chapter, we have compared the Hibernate framework with the JPA persistence standard, showing how the two technologies can be coupled in a single application.

In the next chapter, we will learn JBoss AS JMX infrastructure, which was the backbone of earlier releases of JBoss. Even if it's not the main kernel component anymore, the JMX API is still the glue around many JBoss AS services.

9
Managing JBoss AS

"Hic sunt leones" (Translation: Here live lions).

Formerly used in ancient Roman age maps to denote dangerous or unexplored territories, where wild beasts lived.

At the beginning of this book, we discussed the kernel structure of the application server that has been designed around the **Microcontainer** project. However, **Java Management Extension (JMX)** still plays a vital role in the application server infrastructure and as proof of it, some key services such as the naming service and **Java Message Service (JMS)** are still built on top of the Java Management Extension.

In this chapter, we will dive headlong into the vast and varied JMX ocean, highlighting the following topics:

- An introduction to the JMX framework
- Some detailed examples of standard resources used to manage JMX and how they can complement standard Java EE applications
- The new service POJO
- Monitoring MBeans components

Introducing Java Management Extension

JMX is a standard for managing and monitoring all varieties of software and hardware components from Java. Further, JMX aims to provide integration with the large number of existing management standards. Those resources are represented by objects called **MBeans** (managed beans) that are the management interfaces to the services registered with the JBoss AS.

JMX is based on a three-level architecture:

- The **distributed services level** is the mechanism by which administration applications interact with agents and their managed objects. The interaction can happen through **connectors** or **adapters**. A connector provides full remote access to the **MBeanServer** API using various communication protocols, such as RMI, IIOP, or JMS. On the other hand, the adaptor adapts the API to another protocol, such as SNMP or to a web-based interface.

- The **agent level**, or MBeanServer, is the core of JMX. It is an intermediary between the MBean and the applications.

- The **probe level** contains the probes (called MBeans) instrumenting the resources. These resources are Java classes that can be dynamically loaded and instantiated.

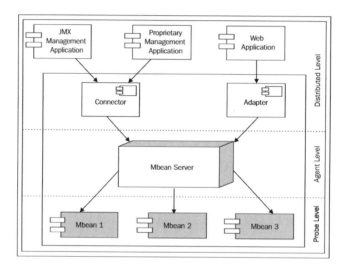

As a developer, you are mostly interested in learning about the probe level (also called the instrumentation level), where MBeans live.

JMX defines four types of MBeans to support different instrumentation needs. They are as follows:

- **Standard MBeans**: These use a simple JavaBean style naming convention and a statically defined management interface. This is currently the most common type of MBean used by JBoss.

- **Dynamic MBeans**: These must implement the `javax.management.DynamicMBean` interface, and they expose their management interface at runtime when the component is instantiated for the greatest flexibility. JBoss makes use of dynamic MBeans in circumstances where the components to be managed are not known until runtime.

- **Open MBeans**: These are an extension of dynamic MBeans. Open MBeans rely on basic data types for universal manageability and are self-describing for user friendliness.

- **Model MBeans**: These are also an extension of dynamic MBeans. Model MBeans must implement the `javax.management.modelmbean.ModelMBean` interface. Model MBeans simplify the instrumentation of resources by providing default behavior. JBoss **XMBeans** are an implementation of model MBeans.

In this chapter, we will cover the standard MBeans as they are the common service implementation for most JBoss JMX services, as well as the preferred solution adopted by the community of developers. We will start with a basic example to let you familiarize yourself with this technology at once, and then we will illustrate some advanced features of MBeans such as service dependency, notifications, and monitoring.

Developing MBeans

As we have mentioned, MBeans are typed components composed by an implementation class and a management interface that is exposed to external applications. As per JMX specifications, standard MBeans do not require implementing any server-specific interface. However, if you want to fully use the JBoss MBeans capabilities, you are strongly encouraged to write MBeans using **JBoss service pattern**.

Writing JBoss-style MBeans requires implementing the `ServiceMBean` interface and extending the `ServiceMBeanSupport` base class that provides a set of life cycle operations. The notifications inform an MBean service when it can create, start, stop, and destroy itself.

For example, if you are writing an MBean that needs a JNDI naming service using JBoss service pattern, it's sufficient to establish a dependency between the two services. When the JNDI life cycle interface signals that the service is started, you can safely start up your service too. The same procedure ranges from difficult to impossible to do with vanilla JMX MBeans, if the only life cycle event is the MBean constructor.

A simple MBean

The first example will be a standard MBean that collects a key-value attribute pair and stores them in the AS system properties.

For packaging our MBeans, we will keep using the Java EE utility project, which is just what we need to settle our classes in an archive.

Some of you might have noticed the option **JBoss Tools | New MBeans stubs**. Honestly speaking, choosing this option doesn't add any great value to your project as it only lets you define the class name and its interface through a wizard. However, I think it is worth informing you about this choice as some new options will be added to the future releases of JBoss Tools.

Create a new utility project **MBeanExample** and add a com.packtpub.jmx.example1.SimpleServiceMBean interface. This will be our JMX contract that implements the ServiceMBean interface:

```
package com.packtpub.jmx.example1;
import org.jboss.system.ServiceMBean;
public interface SimpleServiceMBean extends ServiceMBean {
  public String getProperty(String property);
  public void setProperty(String key, String value);
}
```

 Make sure that the MBean interface adheres to the naming standard where the word "MBean" is appended at the end of any service name.

The interface simply exposes getter and setter methods for storing and retrieving a system property, where com.packtpub.jmx.example1.SimpleService is the implementing class:

```
package com.packtpub.jmx.example1;
import org.jboss.system.ServiceMBeanSupport;
public class SimpleService extends ServiceMBeanSupport
  implements SimpleServiceMBean {
  protected void startService() [1]
  {
    log.info("MBean SimpleService started ");
  }
  protected void stopService() throws Exception [2]
  {
    log.info("MBean SimpleService stopped ");
  }
  public String getProperty(String property) {
    String value = System.getProperty(property);
    log.info("MBean SimpleService returning: "+value);
    return value;
  }
  public void setProperty(String key, String value) {
    System.setProperty(key, value);
  }
}
```

This class extends `ServiceMBeanSupport`, which is an abstract base class. JBoss services can extend it to write JBoss-compliant services. This class overrides the `startService` [1] and `stopService` [2] called by the application server when the `SimpleService` is started (`startService`) or when it's stopped (`stopService`). The `getProperty` and `setProperty` methods are conceivably used to store and read a system property.

> Be aware that this example is only for the purpose of learning MBeans, in a production environment, you would not expose the server properties, at least not without an appropriate security authorization!

Before packaging our MBean, we need to add an MBean configuration file. This is a standalone XML descriptor with a naming pattern that matches `*-service.xml`. In the last section of this chapter, we will illustrate how we can skip this step by using POJO MBeans that can be configured entirely through annotations. Anyway, writing an MBeans configuration file allows your components backward compatibility with earlier releases of JBoss too.

In our example, we will add the following `simple-service.xml` under the `META-INF` folder of your project:

```xml
<server>
  <mbean code="com.packtpub.jmx.example1.SimpleService"
      name="com.packtpub.jmx.example1:service=SimpleService">
  </mbean>
</server>
```

The MBean element specifies that you are declaring an MBean service. The `code` attribute gives the fully qualified name of the MBean implementation class. The required `name` attribute provides the JMX `ObjectName` of the MBean.

The latter attribute is composed of a mandatory element, the domain name, followed by a list a properties as depicted by the following diagram:

jboss. system:	service= Logging ,	type=Log4jService
domain	*Property*	*Property*

The following is a screenshot of the **Project Explorer** before deploying the application to JBoss:

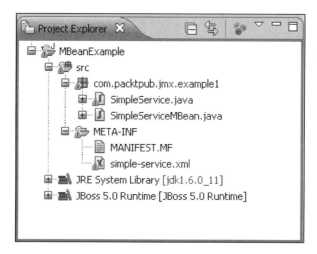

Add the project to JBoss 5 and select **Full Publish** from JBoss Perspective. The outcome of this action will be a file named `MBeanExample.jar` in the `deploy` folder of JBoss.

What happened to SAR extension?

As you can see, your MBeans are flawlessly deployed on JBoss 5 as JAR archives. Using earlier releases of JBoss, you had to package the archive in an SAR file, otherwise the JMX deployer would not recognize the application as an MBean.

If you are curious to know some inner details, the magic trick is performed by the new **JBoss 5 Virtual Deployment Framework (VDF)**. The deployment recognition phase is now split into two rounds. The first one, which is based on the structure of the deployment unit, recognizes the MBeans deployment descriptors in the META-INF folder and proceeds immediately to the second round, which is about parsing the files, class loading, and installation. That being said, using SAR archives is still worthwhile if you need backward compatibility of your MBean applications.

Testing your MBean from the JMX console

The JMX console has been already introduced to you in Chapter 3, so you should already know that it is a web application used to inspect MBeans' attributes and invoke service operations. Launch it the usual way:

```
http://localhost:8080/jmx-console
```

Now look for the domain **com.packtpub.jmx.example1**. In the **Agent View**, you will find a single service available:

Follow the link that will take you to the **MBean View**. This is your playground for testing the MBean. Find the **setProperty** operation, which should be located in the lower area of your view and enter one dummy property name and value:

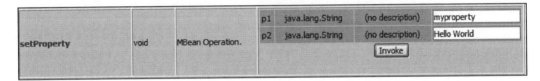

Then you can check the value of your property by clicking **getProperty**, which accepts as input the key property:

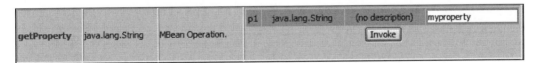

Testing your application programmatically

The same test can be performed using the JMX API. This approach will teach you to create your JMX interfaces for interacting with the agents and their managed components. Just add a web project to your workspace named JMX Web Client. Take care (as usual) to include the libraries from the MBean project in the build path for your web project so that your servlets will compile correctly from Eclipse.

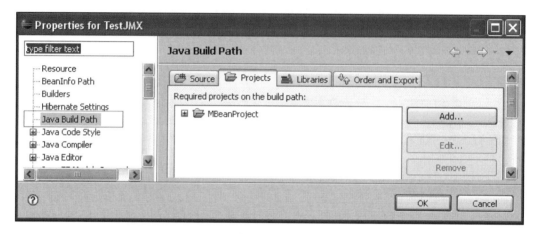

The following servlet needs to be added to your web project:

```
package com.packtpub.jmxweb.example1
import java.io.*;
import javax.management.MBeanServer;
import javax.servlet.ServletException;
import javax.servlet.http.*;
import org.jboss.mx.util.MBeanProxyExt;
import org.jboss.mx.util.MBeanServerLocator;
import com.packtpub.jmx.example1.SimpleServiceMBean;
public class TestJMXServlet extends HttpServlet {
  protected void doGet(HttpServletRequest request,
    HttpServletResponse response) throws ServletException,
    IOException {
    response.setContentType(«text/html»);
    PrintWriter out = response.getWriter();
    SimpleServiceMBean service = null;
    String property= request.getParameter(«property»);
    String value= request.getParameter(«value»);
    try {
      MBeanServer server = MBeanServerLocator.locate();
```

```
    service = (SimpleServiceMBean) MBeanProxyExt.
      create(SimpleServiceMBean.class,"com.packtpub.jmx.
      example1:service=SimpleService",server);
    service.setProperty(property,value);
    out.println("Set property "+property + "=" + value);
    }
  catch (Exception e) {
    e.printStackTrace ();
    }
  }
}
}
```

In this sample code, we are creating an instance of the service through the
`MBeanProxyExt` class that is a factory for producing MBeans proxies. The factory
returns an instance of the `SimpleServiceMBean` that exposes the `setProperty`
and `getProperty` methods in its interface.

What if you need a standalone client? JBoss AS supplies an RMI interface for
connecting to the JMX MBeanServer. This interface is `org.jboss.jmx.adaptor.`
`rmi.RMIAdaptor`. The `RMIAdaptor` interface is bound to JNDI in the default location
of `jmx/invoker/RMIAdaptor`, as well as `jmx/rmi/RMIAdaptor` for backwards
compatibility with older clients.

In the following example, you can see a standalone JMX client that uses the
`RMIAdaptor` to query the `MBeanInfo` for the `SimpleServiceMBean`. As it is a plain
Java class that uses reflection to invoke the MBeans operations, you can place it
anywhere in any project or in a Java project of its own:

```
package com.packtpub.jmxclient.example1;
import java.util.Hashtable;
import javax.management.ObjectName;
import javax.naming.Context;
import javax.naming.InitialContext;
import org.jboss.jmx.adaptor.rmi.RMIAdaptor;
public class SimpleServiceTest {
  public static void main(String args[]) {
    try {
      Hashtable hash = new Hashtable();
      hash.put(«java.naming.factory.initial»,
        «org.jnp.interfaces.NamingContextFactory»);
      hash.put(«java.naming.provider.url»,
        «jnp://localhost:1099»);
      hash.put(«java.naming.factory.url.pkgs»,
        «org.jnp.interfaces»);
      Context ic = new InitialContext(hash);
```

```
    RMIAdaptor server = (RMIAdaptor)
      ic.lookup(«jmx/rmi/RMIAdaptor»);
    // Get the InitialValues attribute
    ObjectName name = new ObjectName(«com.packtpub.jmx.
      example1:service=SimpleService»);
     // Invoke the setProperty(string1,string2) op
     String[] sig = {«java.lang.String»,»java.lang.String»};
     Object[] opArgs = {«name»,»frank»};
     Object result = server.invoke(name, «setProperty»,
       opArgs, sig);
  }
  catch (Exception e) {
    e.printStackTrace ();
  }
 }
}
```

As you can see, this client doesn't use any JBoss-specific class to access the MBean and can be considered a valid alternative if you need to write a portable solution for accessing your Mbeans.

MBeans dependency

Our second example will serve two different purposes. First, we will illustrate how you can define an MBean as *dependent* on other services. This MBean will invoke a stored procedure defined on our database, so the dependency will be on the DataSourceBinding service that is responsible for binding a DataSource in the JNDI tree.

The second purpose of this example is to show how you can configure your MBean to run as a startup class. Add a new interface to your project, and name it com.packtpub.jmx.example2.StartupServiceMBean. The interface will contain the methods for getting and setting the JNDI value of the DataSource and another method clearSessions that can be used to launch the stored procedure on demand too.

```
package com.packtpub.jmx.example2;
import org.jboss.system.ServiceMBean;
public interface StartupServiceMBean extends ServiceMBean {
  public String getJndi();
  public void setJndi(String jndi);
  public void clearSessions();
}
```

The implementation class, `com.packtpub.jmx.example2.StartupService`, is as follows:

```
package com.packtpub.jmx.example2;
import java.sql.CallableStatement;
import java.sql.Connection;
import java.sql.SQLException;
import javax.naming.InitialContext;
import javax.sql.DataSource;
import org.jboss.system.ServiceMBeanSupport;
public class StartupService extends ServiceMBeanSupport
implements
StartupServiceMBean {
  public StartupService() { }
  private String jndi = null;
  @Override
  protected void startService()  [1]
  {
    log.info("[StartupService ] MBean Startup started ");
    clearSessions();
    log.info("[StartupService ] MBean Session Cleaning complete");
  }
  @Override
  protected void stopService() throws Exception
  {
    log.info("[StartupService ] Stopping Startup Mbean");
  }
  @Override
  public String getJndi() {
    return jndi;
  }
  @Override
  public void setJndi(String jndi) {
    this.jndi = jndi;
  }
  public void clearSessions() {
    Connection conn = null;
    CallableStatement cs1 = null;
    try {
      InitialContext ctx = new InitialContext();
      DataSource ds = (DataSource)ctx.lookup(jndi);
      conn = ds.getConnection();
      cs1 =  conn.prepareCall("{call ClearSessions}");
      cs1.execute();
```

```
        }
        catch (Exception exc) {
          exc.printStackTrace();
        }
        finally {
          try {
            cs1.close();
            conn.close();
          }
          catch (SQLException e) {
            e.printStackTrace();
          }
        }
      }
    }
  }
```

As you can see, turning your MBean into a startup class is only a matter of overriding the startService **[1]** method and inserting your logic there. In our example, the MBean will issue a CallableStatement that does some database cleanup. This can be useful if you persist your session data on a table and you need to start your application with a clean state.

As you might guess, the getter and setter methods will be used to inject the JNDI attribute into the class that corresponds to the DataSource JNDI.

Now, let's register our example in the -service.xml descriptor, specifying a dependency of the component with the DataSourceBinding service for the DataSource bound in the JNDI tree as MySqlDS. (For further information on how to configure and install this DataSource, refer Chapter 5, *Developing JPA Entities*.)

```
<mbean code="com.packtpub.jmx.example2.StartupService"
  name="com.packtpub.jmx.example2:service=StartupService">
  <attribute name="Jndi">java:/MySqlDS</attribute>
  <depends>jboss.jca:name=MySqlDS,
    service=DataSourceBinding</depends>
</mbean>
```

Your second example is completed. To get it working, you need a stored procedure in your database named ClearSessions—this is a sample procedure that deletes all data found in the table SESSION_DATA:

```
CREATE TABLE 'hibernate`.`SESSION_DATA` (
  `SESSION_ID` INTEGER UNSIGNED,
  PRIMARY KEY (`SESSION_ID`)
)
ENGINE = InnoDB;
```

And here's the `ClearSessions` procedure definition:

```
DELIMITER $$
CREATE PROCEDURE `ClearSessions`()
BEGIN
DELETE FROM SESSION_DATA;
COMMIT;
END $$
```

You can insert some proof-of-concept data in this table to make sure that your example worked correctly. Redeploy your JMX project. In your console, you should immediately notice the MBean-started logs.

09:08:03,299 [StartupService] MBean Startup started

09:08:03,694 [StartupService] MBean Session Cleaning complete

Sending MBeans notifications

In general, MBeans have attributes/operations and they can optionally emit and consume notifications. Notifications provide a convenient way for an MBean to be informed about various events that occur inside the `MBeanServer` and its registered MBeans.

For example, an MBean can be dedicated to monitoring the system memory and emit notifications when the level falls below a certain threshold.

JBoss provides a built-in helper class, `org.jboss.system.ServiceMBeanSupport` that can be subclassed to implement services that conform to the `ServiceMBean` interface. This class provides an excellent base for writing standard MBeans that act as notification broadcasters.

However, if you need to specify at runtime the set of MBeans/notifications that the service wants to subscribe/receive, you'll find it indispensable to extend the abstract class `org.jboss.system.ListenerServiceMBeanSupport` that acts as JBoss service and in addition, as notification listener.

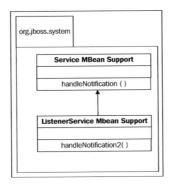

Let's see a concrete example. Create a new class named com.packtpub. jmx.example3.SampleNotificationListener. This class will extend the ListenerServiceMBeanSupport class and implement its MBean interface, SampleNotificationListenerMBean.

```
package com.packtpub.jmx.example3;
import EDU.oswego.cs.dl.util.concurrent.SynchronizedLong;
import javax.management.Notification;
import javax.management.ObjectName;
import org.jboss.logging.DynamicLogger;
import org.jboss.logging.Logger;
import org.jboss.system.ListenerServiceMBeanSupport;
public class SampleNotificationListener extends
  ListenerServiceMBeanSupport
  implements SampleNotificationListenerMBean
{
  public SampleNotificationListener() {    }
  public void startService()
  throws Exception
  {
    super.subscribe(true);   [1]
  }
  public void stopService()
  throws Exception
  {
    super.unsubscribe();   [2]
  }
  public void handleNotification2(Notification notification,
    Object handback)
  {
    log.info("Got notification: " + notification + ", handback: " +
      handback);  [3]
  }
}
```

The MBean interface doesn't expose any method but needs to extend the ListenerServiceMBean contract that contains the JMX subscription list.

```
package com.packtpub.jmx.example3;
import javax.management.ObjectName;
import org.jboss.system.ListenerServiceMBean;
public interface SampleNotificationListenerMBean
  extends ListenerServiceMBean { }
```

As you can see, turning an MBean into a notification listener only requires activating subscriptions in the `startService` method **[1]** and switching them off in the corresponding `stopService` **[2]**. Your notifications will be handled in the `handleNotification2()` method **[3]** as soon as they are emitted.

Be aware that your implementation class is also able to override the `handleNotification()` method. Be careful, don't override this method, which is the implementation provided by the `JBossNotificationBroadcasterSupport` class to handle the notification synchronously.

Receiving heartbeat notifications

Before deploying your `SampleNotificationListener`, you need to specify what kind of notification you're interested to receive. For impatient readers, note that JBoss has already got some services emitting notifications. For example, the useful `TimerService` can be used to send notifications at *predetermined* time intervals. As this MBean is already bundled in JBoss, you simply need to add the following MBean descriptor in your project in order to activate it. (You can also deploy it as a standalone `-service.xml` file.)

```
<server>
  <mbean code="org.jboss.monitor.services.TimerService"
    name="jboss.monitor:name=Heartbeat,type=TimerService">
    <attribute
      name="NotificationType">jboss.monitor.heartbeat</attribute>
    <attribute name="NotificationMessage">JBoss is alive!</attribute>
    <attribute name="TimerPeriod">5sec</attribute>
    <depends optional-attribute-name="TimerMBean">
      <mbean code="javax.management.timer.Timer"
        name=»jboss.monitor:name=Heartbeat,type=Timer»></mbean>
    </depends>
  </mbean>
</server>
```

This descriptor will trigger a notification every five seconds to all subscribers of the `TimerService`. All we need now is to subscribe to our `TimerService` from our `SampleNotificationListener`:

```
<mbean code="com.packtpub.jmx.example3.SampleNotificationListener"
  name="com.packtpub.jmx.example3:service=NotificationListener">
    <attribute name="SubscriptionList">
      <subscription-list>
        <mbean
          name="jboss.monitor:name=Heartbeat,type=Timer"></mbean>
      </subscription-list>
    </attribute>
</mbean>
```

Now redeploy your JMX project and watch on the JBoss console to see if every step was executed correctly. You should see the **JBoss is alive!** message popping up on the console.

Sending your own notifications

In the previous example, we were listening passively for notifications coming from an external channel. However, you can be in charge of sending notifications from your own MBeans as well.

This will not be a big effort for us. Recall our SimpleServiceExample where we set a system property. Let's add a notification that warns us about a system property being changed:

```
public void setProperty(String key, String value) {
   System.setProperty(key, value);

   Notification notification = new  Notification("SimpleService",
      this, getNextNotificationSequenceNumber(), "Warning: Changed
      system property: "+key);
   sendNotification(notification);
}
```

Now update your subscription list so that the SampleNotificationListener will be tuned in to the SimpleService MBean:

```
<mbean code="com.packtpub.jmx.example3.SampleNotificationListener"
   name="com.packtpub.jmx.example3:service=NotificationListener">
     <attribute name="SubscriptionList">
       <subscription-list>
         <mbean
           name="com.packtpub.jmx.example1:service=SimpleService">
         </mbean>
       </subscription-list>
     </attribute>
</mbean>
```

Redeploy your MBean application and try setting some properties from your SimpleService. You should be able to intercept the notification emitted in the handleNotification2 method.

Got Notification: Warning: Changed system property: myproperty

Service POJOs

Service POJOs are the new generation of JBoss services. While you can keep programming MBeans in the standard way (building an MBean interface, an implementation class, and XML descriptors), you can simplify the process of developing MBeans with service POJOs. Actually, service POJOs are plain Java classes with some annotations that denote the special nature of the component.

The way you define them is very similar to defining Stateless or Stateful Session Beans. One very important difference is that there will only be one instance of the service bean, that is, it is not pooled—the bean instance is a singleton. The singleton bean contains shared state, so data set by one client is accessible by other clients.

Let's see a concrete example. We will create a `CurrencyConverter` service that converts a sum of money from Euros into other currencies. A service like this is an ideal example of a singleton service that can be shared across other components of your applications.

Add an interface named `com.packtpub.jmx.example4.CurrencyConverter` to your project.

This interface will contain the life cycle methods of your `servicePOJO`, the `getter`/`setter` methods, and the management methods:

```
package com.packtpub.jmx.example4;
public interface CurrencyConverter {
    public String getCurrency();
    public void setCurrency(String currency);
    // The management method
    public double convert (double amount);
    // Life cycle method
    public void create () throws Exception;
    public void destroy () throws Exception;
}
```

The implementation class follows here:

```
package com.packtpub.jmx.example4;
import java.util.HashMap;
import javax.ejb.Local;
import org.jboss.ejb3.annotation.LocalBinding;
import org.jboss.ejb3.annotation.Service;
import org.jboss.ejb3.annotation.Management;
@Service(objectName = "servicePOJO:service=CurrencyConverter")
@Management(CurrencyConverter.class)
```

```
public class CurrencyConverterService implements CurrencyConverter {
  private String currency;
  private HashMap<String, Double> mapCurrency = new HashMap();
  public double convert(double amount) {
    double currVal = new Double(mapCurrency.get(currency));
    return (currVal * amount);
  }
  // Lifecycle methods
  public void create() throws Exception {
    System.out.println("CurrencyConverterMBean - Creating");
    mapCurrency.put("USD", new Double(1.40));
    mapCurrency.put("YEN", new Double(135));
    mapCurrency.put("GBG", new Double(0.85));
  }
  public String getCurrency() {
    return currency;
  }
  public void setCurrency(String currency) {
    this.currency = currency;
  }
  public void destroy() {
    System.out.println("CurrencyConverterMBean - Destroying");
  }
}
```

Like standard MBeans, POJO services need to define an `ObjectName`—the `@Service` annotation is used for this purpose. It defines the object name for this MBean using the same pattern we have already learned: `domain:property=value`.

The other mandatory annotation is `@Management`. When JBoss finds this annotation, it will look for the corresponding interface in order to set up an MBean with the defined attributes and operations.

For the sake of simplicity, the list of currencies is stored in a `HashMap`, which is loaded in the `create()` life cycle method. Implementing life cycle methods is not mandatory, you can just choose among the following ones that are needed by your service:

- `create()`: Called by the server when the service is created, as well as when all dependent services are created. Here the service is registered among services yet not fully functional.

- `start()`: Called by the server after `create()`, when all the initialization process is completed. At this point, the service is ready to serve requests (and so are all the services it depends on).

- `stop()`: Called by the server when the service is stopped. At this point the service (and all the services that depend on it) is no longer fully operational.

- `destroy()`: Called by the server when the service is removed from the MBean server.

Your ServicePOJO is now ready to be deployed. As you can see in the following screenshot, the structure of a service POJO is not different from a plain Java library:

That being said, deploy your **ServicePOJO** as standalone JAR archive or as part of the MBean project and verify from your JMX console that your service has been correctly registered under the **ServicePOJO** domain:

Creating a web test client

A sample scenario for your service POJO is an Enterprise application that requires a currency conversion for international orders. Again we will use our JMX Web Client project that we have set up for the `SimpleService` MBean.

Now add a simple **JavaServer Pages (JSP)** technology to your project, which will be in charge of contacting the **CurrencyPOJO** service and invoke the `convert()` method:

```
<%@ page
  import="javax.management.*,com.packtpub.jmx.example4.*,
    org.jboss.mx.util.*"%>
<%
  CurrencyConverter cal = null;
  try {
    int amount = 250;
    MBeanServer server = MBeanServerLocator.locate();
    cal = (CurrencyConverter) MBeanProxyExt.create(
      CurrencyConverter.class,
      "servicePOJO:service=CurrencyConverter", server);
```

```
      cal.setCurrency("USD");
      out.println(amount + " EURO equal to " + cal.convert(amount) + "
        " + cal.getCurrency());
    }
    catch (Exception e) {
      e.printStackTrace();
    }
  %>
```

The code is self-explanatory—we are creating a proxy for CurrencyConverter using the MBeanProxyExt factory. Then the convert method is recalled to exchange some USD amount into Euros.

Before testing, pack your web application and the MBean project in an **Enterprise ARchive (EAR)**. The following screenshot is a view of your application from the **Project Explorer**:

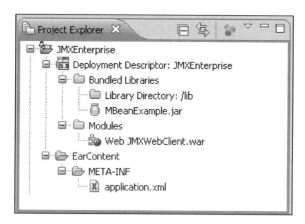

Packaging your application requires a little patch to your META-INF/application. xml. As a matter of fact, Eclipse by itself doesn't mention Java libraries in this configuration file, so you have do add the MBeanExample.jar archive manually:

```
<application>
  <module>
    <web>
      <web-uri>JMXWebClient.war</web-uri>
      <context-root>JMXWebClient</context-root>
    </web>
  </module>
  <module>
    <java>MBeanExample.jar</java>
  </module>
</application>
```

Exposing your service as an EJB

Sometimes you might find it useful to expose your service POJO with a **local** or **remote** interface. Using this approach you don't deal with the `MBeanProxyExt` interface from your client anymore, rather you can *inject* your service reference into your Enterprise components, just the same way you would do with an ordinary EJB.

Morphing your service into an EJB requires just two small additions to your service. Depending on whether you need a local or remote interface (or both of them), you need to add the `@Local` or `@Remote` annotation:

```
import javax.ejb.Local;
import org.jboss.ejb3.annotation.LocalBinding;
import org.jboss.ejb3.annotation.Service;
import org.jboss.ejb3.annotation.Management;
@Service(objectName = "sampleJMX:service=CurrencyConverter")
@Management(CurrencyConverter.class)
@Local(CurrencyConverter.class) [1]
@LocalBinding(jndiBinding = «service/CurrencyConverter») [2]
public class CurrencyConverterService implements CurrencyConverter {
}
```

Here we are exposing the service through the `CurrencyConverter` interface that has been marked as local interface **[1]** and bound to the JNDI naming context `service/CurrencyConverter` **[2]** (the same annotations you would normally use in an EJB 3 session bean).

You can safely inject your POJO service into either a web component or another EJB. As we have already set up a web application, the simplest test would be to add a servlet that interacts without POJO service:

```
public class ServletConverter extends HttpServlet {
  @EJB(mappedName="service/CurrencyConverter")
  CurrencyConverter currLocal;
  protected void doGet(HttpServletRequest request,
    HttpServletResponse response) throws ServletException,
    IOException {
      response.setContentType("text/html");
      PrintWriter out = response.getWriter();
      int amount = 300;
      currLocal.setCurrency("GBG");
      out.println(amount +" EURO equal to " +currLocal.convert(250)+
      " " +currLocal.getCurrency());
    }
}
```

This should produce the same output as your JSP. The concrete difference is that our web application is now dealing with a singleton EJB.

Service POJO dependency

MBean dependency can be applied to a service POJO in much the same way as we have shown with standard MBeans. The annotation used to specify a dependency is @Depends. Here we are stating that our CurrencyConverterService will not start until our DataSourceBinding service is available.

```
@Depends ("jboss.jca:name=MySqlDS,service=DataSourceBinding")
public class CurrencyConverterService implements CurrencyConverter
{
}
```

This annotation can also be used for injecting a service in our POJO:

```
@Depends ("servicePOJO:service=AnotherService")
public AnotherService service;
```

This way, our POJO service will wait for AnotherService to be available. When this service is started, it is injected into the instance field service and thus it is accessible to our service.

JBoss AS Administration Console

The most significant change introduced by release 5.1.0 of the application server is the new administration console that is also known as **Embedded Jopr** project. For those who are new to the **Jopr** project, this is a sophisticated management platform for the JBoss middleware stack and is based on project RHQ.

Embedded Jopr is based on the same set of libraries as the Jopr project. However, there's a clear distinction between them; Jopr is a **distributed management solution** with agents on the managed resources and a central server. On the other hand, Embedded Jopr is supposed to run **within a JBoss AS instance** and thus it is intended to replace the JMX console.

In Chapter 3, *Customizing JBoss AS Services*, we had a bird's eye view of the new administration console. So by now you should already have some rudiments of it. The following section will be a useful administration reference for the most common management tasks.

Managing applications

A very common need of every software administrator is the management of deployed applications. If we are running the application server locally, this task is generally easy and can also be carried out by the Eclipse IDE. However, handling remotely deployed applications can be awkward if the only instrument available is the JMX console.

The administration manages Java EE applications in the following squared section:

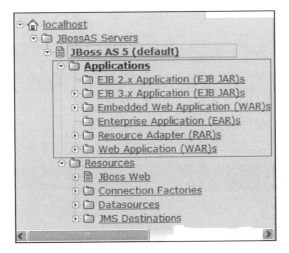

Deploying/undeploying applications

In order to deploy or undeploy an application, first choose the appropriate application type you need to manage, for example, a web application, and then focus on the central frame. There you can see the list of deployed applications for your selected type.

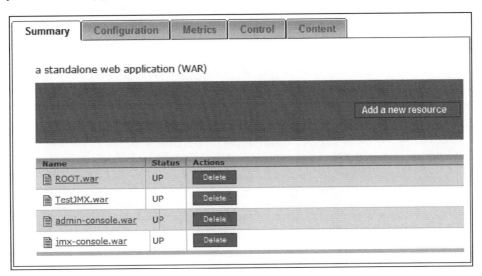

If you need to undeploy an application, just hit the **Delete Actions** button. Conversely, if you need to deploy a new application, click the **Add a new resource** button. The deployment of a new resource merely requires browsing the filesystem to locate the application and choosing whether to deploy it in the exploded format or not.

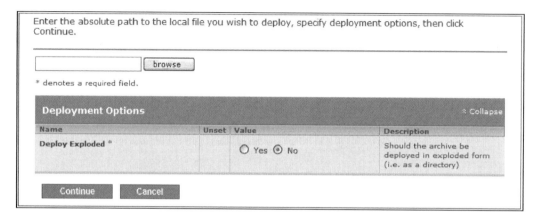

Updating an application

If your application has already been deployed and you just need to update it, there's an appropriate form that is reachable by clicking on the application name (in the application list) and then selecting the **Content** tab.

Again you just have to browse the filesystem to specify a local path for the application to be uploaded.

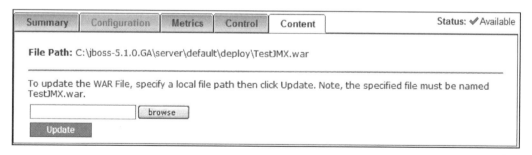

Starting/stopping/restarting an application

The next operation will be changing the application status. You need to reach the tabbed panel menu by clicking on the application name and selecting the **Control** tab.

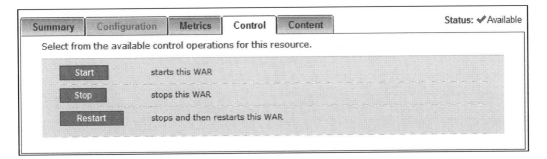

From there, you can intuitively select the available control operation by choosing the appropriate action button.

Administering resources

The administration console takes care managing application server resources in the lower part of the left frame.

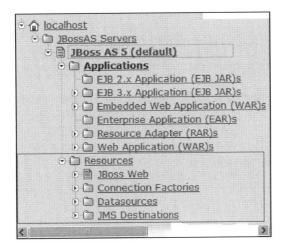

Adding a new resource

Start by expanding the type of resource you want to include. For example, if you want to add a new `local-tx-datasource`, expand the `Datasources` element, and click on the **Local tx Datasources** link. In the tabbed panel window, choose the **Add a new resource** button.

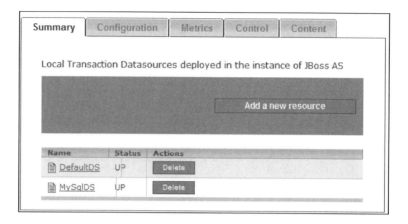

The administration console will then prompt you to choose a template, if one exists, for the resource (for example, a template for Oracle datasource) and finally will take you to a form for inserting the **Connection Properties**:

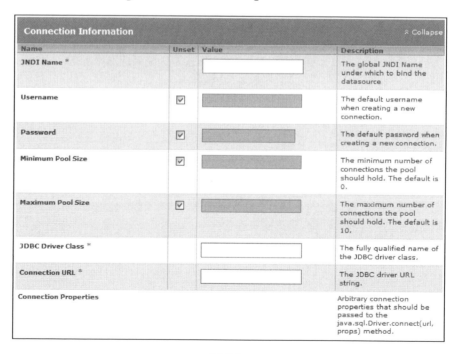

The previous connection schema will result in a new datasource definition, which will be persisted in the `server/default/deploy` directory in a file bearing the JNDI name and the `-ds.xml` extension.

Managing resources

Administering resources includes a set of operations that are specific for each resource. For example, a connection pool would require to list pool statistics and flush the connection pool. A JMS resource would need to display messages, or stopping and restarting message delivering, and so on.

Resources can be managed by clicking on an individual resource in the central frame, and then selecting the **Control** tab option. From there you can choose among the list of available control operations.

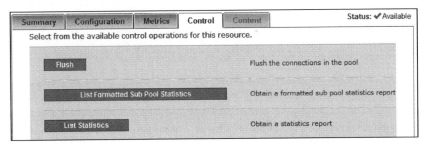

In the same tab panel, you can manage the resource configuration by selecting the **Configuration** tab. From there on, you can alter the resource configuration and persist the changes.

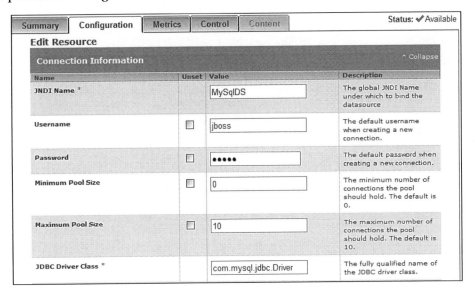

Metrics

Both applications and resources have a list of metrics associated, which can be examined by choosing the option **Metrics** in the tabbed panel. For example, the following screenshot shows the **Metrics** for **MySqlDS**:

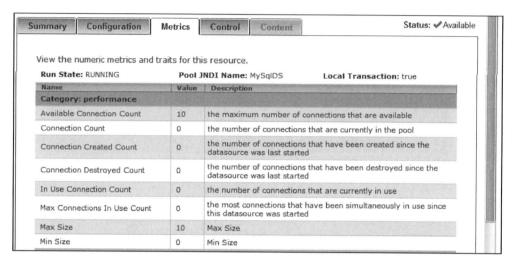

If you are curious to know where metrics configurations are stored, you need to dig a bit into the administration console structure. Precisely, you have to unzip the file `rhq-plugin.xml` that is located in the file `server/default/deploy/admin-console.war/pluginsjopr-jboss-as-5-plugin-2.3.0.EmbJopr.1.2.0-1.jar`.

For example, here's the metric for the **Available Connection Count** element:

```
<metric property="availableConnectionCount" measurementType="dynamic"
   displayType="summary" displayName="Available Connection Count"
   description="Number of available connections." defaultOn="true"
   defaultInterval="60000" dataType="measurement"
   category="performance"/>
<metric property="availableConnectionCount"
   measurementType="dynamic" displayType="summary"
   displayName="Available Connection Count" description="Number of
   available connections." defaultOn="true" defaultInterval="60000"
   dataType="measurement" category="performance"/>
```

If you want to expand your knowledge on plugins and metrics, we suggest you read this in-depth paper from Red Hat website:

`http://www.redhat.com/f/pdf/Write_A_Plugin_WP_web.pdf`

Summary

Hopefully this chapter has given you a deep immersion into the world of MBeans. As should be obvious from the examples provided, there are far more variations than we can hope to cover in this chapter.

We have provided some concrete examples of standard MBeans, illustrating their features with step-by-step examples. The good news is that JBoss 5 makes it much easier to handle services with POJO MBeans, which can be seen as an effective complementary partner of Enterprise JavaBeans.

In the latter section of this chapter, we have included a set of quick drills for the administrator who wants to approach the new JBossAS Administration Console, available as built-in application since JBoss AS 5.1.0.

In the next chapter, we are going to discuss interoperability between different technologies. As you might guess we are going to discuss Web Services.

10
Developing Applications with JBoss Web Services

Any program is only as good as it is useful. – Linus Torvalds

Web Services are defined by W3C as *a software system designed to support interoperable machine-to-machine interaction over a network.*

What makes Web Services different from other forms of distributed computing is that information is exchanged using only simple and non-proprietary protocols. This means the services can communicate with each other regardless of location, platform, or programming language. Essentially, the Web Services protocols provide a platform-independent way to perform **Remote Procedure Calls (RPCs)**.

The focus of this chapter will be on **JBossWS,** a Web Service framework developed as part of the JBoss Application Server, based on **JSR 224** (Java API for XML-based web services 2.0).

You will get your hands on the following topics:

- A short introduction to Web Services
- How to create, deploy, and test Web Services using the JBoss WS and Eclipse
- Some advanced concepts about Web Services (Handler Chains, SOAP debugging)

Web Service concepts

As stated at the beginning of this chapter, Web Services are based on the exchange of messages using non-proprietary protocol messages. The messages themselves are not sufficient to define the Web Service platform. We actually need a list of standard components, including the following:

- A language used to define the interfaces provided by a Web Service, in a manner that is not dependent on the platform on which it is running or the programming language used to implement it

- A common standard format for exchanging messages between Web Service Producers and Web Service Consumers

- A registry within which the service definitions can be placed

The **Web Service Description Language**, that is, **WSDL** (`http://www.w3.org/TR/wsdl`) is the de facto standard for providing a description of the Web Service contract exposed to clients. In particular, a WSDL document describes a Web Service in terms of the operations that it provides and the data types that each operation requires as inputs and can return in the form of results.

The communication between the service provider and service consumer happens by means of XML messages, which rely on the **SOAP** protocol specification.

A basic SOAP message consists of an **Envelope** that may contain any number of headers and a body. These parts are delimited by XML elements called Envelope, Header, and Body, which belong to a namespace defined by the SOAP specification.

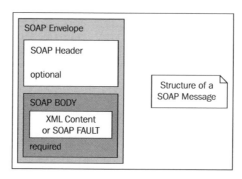

Once you have determined that your business needs to find a provider for a specific service, how do you find the businesses that offer that service, evaluate their offerings, and, if appropriate, fetch the WSDL definition for the service itself? The answer lies in the **XML-based registries** that are accessible through the Internet and contain the necessary information that allows businesses to discover and make use of the Web Services.

Strategies for building up Web Services

As we have just learned, the service description is provided by a commonly agreed document interface named the Web Service Description Language that exposes services as a collection of networks, endpoints, and ports, using the XML format.

You may logically be inclined to think that it is necessary to state at the beginning the contract of the service, and then produce the corresponding programming interfaces. Actually, you can follow two approaches for developing your web services:

- **Top-down:** This development strategy involves creating a Web Service from a WSDL file. The top-down approach is likely to be used when creating Web Services from scratch. It is the preferred choice of "purist" Web Service engineers because it's business-driven, that is, the contract is defined by business people and so the software is designed to fit the Web Service contract.

- **Bottom-up:** This approach requires generating the WSDL file from the programming interfaces. It is likely to be used when we have existing applications that we want to expose as Web Services. As it doesn't require a deep knowledge of the WSDL syntax, it's the easiest choice if you want to turn your Java classes or EJB into Web Services.

As the audience of this book is composed mainly of Java developers with little or no knowledge at all of WSDL basics, we will focus primarily on the **bottom-up** approach. However, in the following sections, we will teach the reader how to use **JBoss Web Service tools** to reverse the process of creation of Web Services, starting from a WSDL contract.

Designing top-down Web Services will require that you integrate the basic Web Services notions provided with this chapter with a comprehensive awareness of the WSDL standard.

JBoss Web Services stack

If you surf on the JBossWS project page `http://www.jboss.org/jbossws/`, you will see that three main options are available to deploy Web Services on JBoss.

- JBossWS native
- Glassfish Metro
- Apache CXF

Each of these stacks has its own specific features and you are free to develop on JBoss AS choosing the one that is closest to your needs. In this book we will use **JBoss WS Native**, which is a Web Service framework developed to be part of JBoss AS' Java EE5 offering. JBoss WS native stack is based on the new Web Service specification called **JAX WS**, and is a follow-on release of the former **JAX-RPC** specification delivered by Sun in early 2002.

JAX-WS simplifies the task of developing Web Services by supporting Java JEE annotations for declaring Web Services. This API also addresses some of the issues of JAX-RPC, providing support for multiple protocols such as SOAP 1.1, SOAP 1.2, and XML, and by providing a facility for supporting additional protocols along with HTTP.

In the next section, we will deliver a high-level picture of the JAX WS Runtime architecture from the server point of view, showing the components that are involved for processing Web Services requests and responses.

A brief look at the JAX WS architecture

When a SOAP message sent by the client enters the Web Service runtime environment, it is captured by a component named **Server endpoint listener**, which in turn uses the **Dispatcher** module to deliver the SOAP message to that Service.

At this point, the HTTP request is converted internally into a **SOAP Message**. The message context is extracted from the transport protocol and it is processed through the handler chain configured for the Web Service.

SOAP message handlers are used to intercept the SOAP messages as they make their way from the client to the endpoint service and vice versa. These handlers intercept the SOAP message for both the request and response of the Web Service. You will find this concept similar to EJB interceptors, which we have discussed in Chapter 4.

The next step is unmarshalling the SOAP message into Java objects. This process is governed by **WSDL to Java mapping** and **XML to Java Mapping**. The former is performed by the JAX-WS engine and determines which endpoint to invoke from the SOAP Message. The latter, performed by the JAXB libraries, deserializes the SOAP message so that it is ready to invoke the endpoint method.

Finally, the deserialized SOAP message reaches the actual Web Service implementation and the method is invoked.

Once the call is completed, the process is reversed. The return value from the Web Service method is marshalled into a SOAP response message using JAX-WS WSDL to Java mapping and the JAXB 2.0 XML to Java mapping.

Then the outbound message is processed by handlers before returning it to the Dispatcher and the endpoint listener, which will transmit the message as an HTTP response.

The following diagram describes how data flows from a Web Service client to a Web Service endpoint and back:

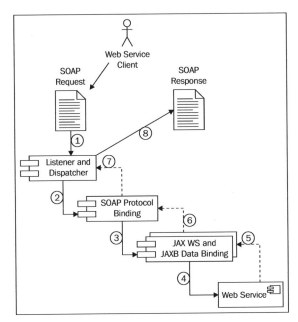

Coding Web Services with JBossWS

In the first deliverable, we will show how easily you can turn a plain Java class into a Web Service. The newly created service will be then tested using both Java and non-Java clients. The second part of this chapter will draw your attention to how EJB can be exposed as Web Service endpoints.

Developing a POJO Web Service

We will approach Web Services with a simple Java class, which will be used as **endpoint** for our Web Service. If you browse across the Eclipse menus, you will find that the Enterprise release of this IDE ships with a Wizard for Web Service creation. You can find it the **New | Other | Web Services** menu.

However, we will not use this wizard for creating our bottom-up Web Services and we encourage you to do the same. As you'll see in a while, all your effort will be adding some annotations to your classes; furthermore, using a Web Service Wizard locks you to a development environment, making it difficult for you to switch to another IDE that hasn't got the same features.

That being said, a good compromise will be starting a new **dynamic web project**; name the project as **WebServiceProject**. Now add to it a Java class named com.packtpub.webservice.example1.POJOWebService. This class has a method calculatePower that returns the power of an argument, as shown in the following highlighted code:

```java
public class POJOWebService
{
    public double calculatePower(double argument,
                                 double power)
    {
        return Math.pow(argument,power);
    }
}
```

Now we will turn this simple class into a Web Service by adding the mandatory @WebService annotation.

```java
package com.packtpub.webservice.example1;

import javax.jws.WebMethod;
import javax.jws.WebParam;
import javax.jws.WebResult;
import javax.jws.WebService;
import javax.jws.soap.SOAPBinding;

@WebService(targetNamespace = "http://www.packtpub.com/",
                              serviceName = "CalculatePowerService")
@SOAPBinding(style = SOAPBinding.Style.RPC)

public class POJOWebService
{
    @WebMethod
    @WebResult(name="result")     [1]
    public double calculatePower(@WebParam(name="base")     [2]
                                 double base,
                                 @WebParam(name="exponent")
                                 double exponent
    {
        return Math.pow(base,exponent);
    }
}
```

Inside the @WebService annotation, you can specify additional elements such as the targetNamespace element that declares the namespace used for the WSDL elements generated by the Web Service. If you don't specify this element, the Web Service container will use the Java package name to generate a default XML namespace.

You can also use the serviceName element to specify the service name. The name specified using serviceName is used for generating the name attribute in the service element in the WSDL. If you don't specify the serviceName element, the server will generate it using the default, which is the bean class name appended with Service.

In the next row, we have stated that the Web Service is of the type **Remote Procedure Call**, by using the @javax.jws.SOAPBinding annotation. Possible values are DOCUMENT and RCP, the first one being the default value.

Attaching the @WebMethod attribute to a public method indicates that you want the method exposed as part of the Web Service.

The @WebParam **[2]** annotation is used to specify the parameter's name to exhibit in the WSDL. You should always consider using a WebParam annotation, especially using multiple parameters, else the WSDL will use the default argument parameter (in this case arg0), which is meaningless for the Web Service consumers.

The @WebResult annotation **[1]** is quite similar to @WebParam in that it can be used to specify the name of the value returned by the WSDL.

What are the defaults for Web Services?

JAX WS specification mandates only a minimal set of annotations to be added to your Web Service (actually only @WebService is mandatory). If you don't provide a target namespace, your Web Service will expose the Java class package name as target namespace in reverse order (in our example, http://example1.webservice.packtpub.com/).

The serviceName, if not included, will be defaulted to the class name with "Service" appended (in the example it would be POJOWebServiceService).

Finally, if parameter names are not specified, the default is "argN", where N is replaced with the zero-based argument index. Therefore, in our example, the list of arguments would turn into "arg0" and "arg1".

Your Web Service is now completed. In order to register it on the JBossWS directory, you have to add it to your web.xml and declare it as a servlet:

```
<servlet>
  <servlet-name>POJOService</servlet-name>
  <servlet-class>com.packtpub.webservice.example1.POJOWebService</
servlet-class>
</servlet>

<servlet-mapping>
  <servlet-name>POJOService</servlet-name>
  <url-pattern>/pojoService</url-pattern>
</servlet-mapping>
```

Now deploy your web application in the usual way, that is, first add the project to your server. Then choose **Full Publish** from the **JBoss AS Server View**.

JBoss AS will provide a minimal output on the console, which informs you that the Web Service project has been deployed and the WSDL file generated.

16:36:57,224 INFO [DefaultEndpointRegistry] register: jboss.ws:context=WebServi

ceProject,endpoint=POJOService

16:36:58,068 INFO [TomcatDeployment] deploy, ctxPath=/WebServiceProject

16:37:01,427 INFO [WSDLFilePublisher] WSDL published to: file:/C:/jboss-5.0.0.G

A-1.6/server/default/data/wsdl/WebServiceProject.war/HelloWorldPOJOService.Wsdl

From this short log, you can pick up some useful information. For example, the first line states that the Web Service has been bound in the endpoint registry as "POJOService". Next is the information about the web context path, which by default has the same name as your project, that is, "WebServiceProject". The last piece of information is about the generated WSDL, which is placed in the server/default/data/wsdl/WebServiceProject.war folder.

The data directory contains a versioned list of all generated WSDL. So, you might find all the history of your Web Service tagged as CalculatePowerServiceXXX.wsdl.

Inspecting the Web Service from the console

JBossWS ships with a Web Service console, which gathers some useful information about the services deployed. In fact, its most useful option is the list of endpoint contracts available, which is needed when developing our clients.

You can access the console using the URL `http://localhost:8080/jbossws`. (Of course replace `localhost` with the actual host name when accessing from a remote browser.)

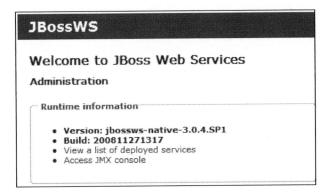

Follow the link **View a list of deployed services**, which will take you to the list of available Web Services.

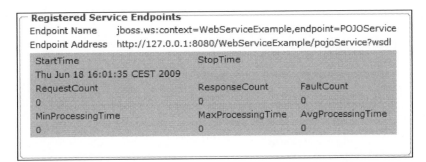

Apart from some statistics information, we have got here the **Web Service endpoint address**, which is `http://127.0.0.1:8080/WebServiceProject/pojoService?wsdl`.

If you click on the WSDL link, you will see in the browser the contract published for the Web Service.

```
<definitions name="CalculatePowerService"
targetNamespace="http://www.packtpub.com/">
  <types />
  <message name="POJOWebService_calculatePowerResponse">
  <part name="result" type="xsd:double" />
  </message>
  <message name="POJOWebService_calculatePower">
  <part name="argument" type="xsd:double" />
  <part name="power" type="xsd:double" />
  </message>
  <portType name="POJOWebService">
  <operation name="calculatePower"
    parameterOrder="argument power">
   <input message="tns:POJOWebService_calculatePower" />
   <output message="tns:POJOWebService_calculatePowerResponse" />
  </operation>
  </portType>
  <binding name="POJOWebServiceBinding" type="tns:POJOWebService">
   <soap:binding style="rpc" transport="http://schemas.xmlsoap.org/soap/http" />
   <operation name="calculatePower">
   <soap:operation soapAction="" />
   <input> <soap:body namespace="http://www.packtpub.com/" use="literal" />
   </input>
   <output> <soap:body namespace="http://www.packtpub.com/" use="literal" />
   </output>
   </operation>
  </binding>
  <service name="CalculatePowerService">
  <port binding="tns:POJOWebServiceBinding" name="POJOWebServicePort">
   <soap:address location="http://127.0.0.1:8080/WebServiceProject/pojoService" />
  </port>
  </service>
</definitions>


@WebService(targetNamespace = "http://www.packtpub.com/",
            serviceName = "CalculatePowerService")


public class POJOWebService {

@WebMethod
@WebResult(name="result")
public double calculatePower(@WebParam
            (name="argument")
            double argument,

            @WebParam
            (name="power")
            double power) {  }

}
```

In the screenshot, you can see how the required (and optional) annotations mix and match into the WSDL contract. In particular, you can appreciate the usefulness of the @WebParam annotation, which enriches the WSDL with information about the parameter, which would be otherwise named with meaningless default values.

Using JBossWS tools

If you look at the `JBOSS_HOME/bin` folder, you will find a few handy tools for Web Service development. Let's have a look at them:

Command	Action
wsprovide	Generates JAX-WS portable artifacts, and provides the abstract contract. Used for **bottom-up** development.
wsconsume	Consumes the abstract contract (WSDL and schema files), and produces artifacts for both a server and client. Used for **top-down and client** development.
wsrunclient	Executes a Java client (has a main method) using the JBossWS classpath.

The reason for using these tools resides in the **JAX-WS** specification, which requires that a Web Service stack provides some offline tools for generating Web Service wrapper classes. When you deployed your Web Service, the application server created these Wrapper classes along with the WSDL contract; however, if you need to port your Web Service to another environment, you will need to generate these artifacts offline.

For example, if you want to produce the abstract contract starting from your Java classes, you could use the `wsprovide` command, which has the following syntax:

```
usage: WSProvide [options] <endpoint class name>
```

For a detailed explanation of all `wsprovide`'s options, we suggest you to consult the JBossWS documentation. In our example, we will instruct the tool to generate the WSDL (`-w` option) and to output the file (`-o` option) in a folder of our project.

Let's first set the path to your project in a shell variable:

```
set PATH_TO_PROJECT=C:\chap08\WebServiceProject #Windows

$PATH_TO_PROJECT=/usr/eclipse/WebServiceProject #Unix
```

Then you have to launch the wsprovide shell to generate the WSDL. Again we will illustrate both the Windows version and the Unix one:

```
wsprovide -w -o %PATH_TO_PROJECT%\wsdl --classpath %PATH_TO_PROJECT%\
build\classes  com.packtpub.webservice.example1.POJOWebService  #Win

wsprovide.sh -w -o $PATH_TO_PROJECT/wsdl --classpath $PATH_TO_PROJECT/
build/classes  com.packtpub.webservice.example1.POJOWebService
#Unix
```

This `wsprovide` shell script is placed in the `JBOSS_HOME/bin` folder in the two varieties—`wsprovide.cmd` (in the case of Windows) and `wsprovide.sh` (in the case of Unix/Linux). As you might guess, you can either issue this command from this folder or you can opt for adding the `JBOSS_HOME/bin` folder in your system PATH.

The output of `wsprovide` will be as follows:

Generating WSDL:

HelloWorldPOJOService.wsdl

If you need to generate your Web Service client, you may find the **wsconsume** tool quite useful. This tool is useful because it consumes the WSDL contract and generates portable artifacts for both client and server development.

We highly recommend you to use this approach for client development because it helps you to design loosely coupled clients that are not tied to any particular environment, location, or even programming language. After all that's why we are using Web Services to cleanly decouple the client from the server, otherwise we would have stuck to RPC technologies that are tightly coupled but obviously faster.

If you are not too comfortable with shell scripts, then you can configure Eclipse to execute them directly from the IDE and even associate an icon in the toolbar to the command. Go to the option **Run | External Tools | External Tool Configurations**. The External Tools wizard is quite intuitive. You have to specify your command line tool (In the **Location** field), then you have to provide arguments just as you would do with the command line.

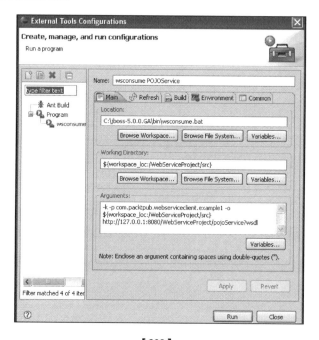

We have added a few more parameters to our script. The –k option specifies to generate Java sources. The –p parameter is used to specify the package name of our artifacts. Finally, the –o option is the output destination of our classes. Notice the use of Eclipse variables that let you use a path relative to the workspace (for a full list of all the available Eclipse variables, click on the **Variables** button).

The last argument of **wsconsume** is the WSDL document of our POJOWebService, which must be available on the server when you issue Run command.

Now refresh your **Project Explorer** view and take a look at the generated classes:

As you can see, **wsconsume** has generated two source files— POJOWebService. java and CalculatePowerService.java. The first one is merely the service interface for our Web Service as it's obtained from the WSDL. The other file, CalculatorPowerService.java, is the **client artifact**. Let's have a look at it:

```
@WebServiceClient(name = "CalculatePowerService", targetNamespace =
"http://www.packtpub.com/", wsdlLocation = "http://127.0.0.1:8080/
WebServiceProject/pojoService?wsdl") [1]

public class CalculatePowerService
    extends Service
{

    private final static URL CALCULATEPOWERSERVICE_WSDL_LOCATION;

    static {
        URL url = null;
        try {
```

```
                url = new URL("http://127.0.0.1:8080/
                        WebServiceProject/pojoService?wsdl");
            } catch (MalformedURLException e) {
                e.printStackTrace();
            }
            CALCULATEPOWERSERVICE_WSDL_LOCATION = url;
        }

        public CalculatePowerService(URL wsdlLocation, QName serviceName)
        {
            super(wsdlLocation, serviceName);
        }

        public CalculatePowerService() {
            super(CALCULATEPOWERSERVICE_WSDL_LOCATION,
                    new QName("http://www.packtpub.com/",
                    "CalculatePowerService"));
        }

        @WebEndpoint(name = "POJOWebServicePort") [2]
        public POJOWebService getPOJOWebServicePort() {
            return (POJOWebService)super.getPort(
                    new QName("http://www.packtpub.com/",
                    "POJOWebServicePort"), POJOWebService.class);
        }

    }
```

The generated class extends the `javax.xml.ws.Service` and is tagged with the `@WebServiceClient` annotation **[1]**. This annotation provides a client view of the Web Service, which is uniquely identified by the `wsdlLocation` and `targetNamespace` elements.

Performance tip

When you are running your Web Service clients in a production environment, it's advised to refer to a local copy of your WSDL. This will avoid the burden of network latency, each time you have to retrieve the WSDL from a remote location.

The other relevant annotation is `@WebEndpoint` **[2]**, which is used to specify the port name of the Web Service. By definition, a **Web Service port** is an abstract set of operations supported by one or more endpoints. Its `name` attribute provides a unique name among all port types defined within in the enclosing WSDL document. In our case, the `name` attribute (obtained from the WSDL) is `POJOWebServicePort`.

Invoking our Web Service is just a matter of requesting the Web Service port and issuing the operations, which are listed in the exposed interface. For this purpose, add a class to your project and name it com.packtpub.webserviceclient. example1.Client.

```
package com.packtpub.webserviceclient.example1;

public class Client {

    public static void main(String[] args) {
      if (args.length != 2) {
            System.err.println("usage: Client <arg> <power>");
            System.exit(1);
      }

      double arg = Double.parseDouble(args[0]);
      double power = Double.parseDouble(args[1]);

      CalculatePowerService pojo = new CalculatePowerService();
      POJOWebService pojoService = pojo.getPOJOWebServicePort();

      System.out.println("Result is " +pojoService.calculatePower(arg,
power));
    }

}
```

As you can see, the client is not aware of the Web Service location, nor does it know any details about the OS or the Web Service language.

You can execute it either from the Eclipse environment or from the **wsrunclient** shell, which is a handy tool for Web Service clients located in the JBOSS_HOME/bin folder. (Actually, it builds up for you the correct Web Service classpath for client execution.)

```
wsrunclient --classpath %PATH_TO_PROJECT%\build\classes  com.packtpub.
webservice.example1.Client 2 4  #Win

wsrunclient.sh --classpath $PATH_TO_PROJECT/build/classes  com.
packtpub.webservice.example1.Client 2 4 #Unix
```

The expected output of wsrunclient should be:

Result: 16.0

The Black art of Web Services

If you have been working with Web Services before, you have probably drawn the conclusion that they are intrinsically difficult, much more then it seems at first glance. Writing a Web Service in Java itself is not hard at all, what's difficult is to connect all the standards such as SOAP, WSDL, XML, and Java EE container services.

To make things harder we must account for a few issues with Eclipse environment and also with XML parsers library which are anyway solved in the newer JBoss 5.1.0 release.

To make your journey through Web Services as pleasant as it can be, here's a checklist of fixes you should know before diving into JBossWS.

When you add a new JBoss server runtime to your Eclipse Java EE project, a system library is created and placed in the project build path. This includes two jar files (`jaxws-rt.jar`, `jaxws-tools. jar`) that might cause a standalone client error as the JAX-WS provider is accessed by a jar service loader. Depending on which jar is in the classpath, it either loads the JBossWS one or the Sun RI one. In the latter case, a weird `java.lang.UnsupportedOperationException` is thrown to the client.

So as a general rule, use the wsclient utility to run client Web Services instead of running them through Eclipse. If you feel uncomfortable with shells, you can still mimic the behavior of the wsclient utility by having a look at its content and adding the right libraries to the Eclipse build path. A quick fix that we have tested on our examples is replacing Eclipse's JBoss Runtime libraries with JBossWS native libraries (`http://www.jboss.org/jbossws`) and then adding the single libraries required for the project.

Another advice you should consider, is switching to release 5.1.0 of the application server, which fixes some issues relative to the XML parses libraries that are now overridden in the `JBOSS_HOME/lib/endorsed` lib (see this interesting thread `http://www.jboss.org/index. html?module=bb&op=viewtopic&t=158265`).

Finally, if you still cannot run your Web Service clients, check that the JBoss variant release matches with the JDK release, for example, verify that you use the JDK 1.6 variant for running the JBoss 5.1.0.

External Web Service clients

JBoss Web Services can be consumed by a variety of external applications; you can easily find on the Web, examples of .NET or PHP Web Service clients.

If you don't have installed the required client environment on your PC, it will take a while to complete a full Web Service example. We suggest you to try the versatile Flex platform. **Flex** is a free, open source framework for building highly interactive, expressive web applications that deploy consistently on all major browsers, desktops, and operating systems. All you need is the Adobe Flex Builder 3 software, which is a highly productive, Eclipse-based IDE. You can download a trial copy of it at http://www.adobe.com/cfusion/entitlement/index.cfm?e=flex3email.

Flex uses a declarative language, **MXML**, that has many built-in functions. For our purpose we'll use the <mx:WebService> tag. It requires mainly knowing the WSDL address of the Web Service and the operation to invoke.

```
public var o:Object;

        private function callWS():void
        {
                webService.calculatePower.send();
        }

        private function displayfault(evt:FaultEvent):void
                                {ta.text+="FAULT";}

        private function getMyJobMng(evt:ResultEvent):void {

                o=evt.result;
                ta.text = "Result from operation : " + o ;

        }
]]>
</mx:Script>

<mx:WebService id="webService"
        wsdl="http://127.0.0.1:8080/WebServiceProject/
                                pojoService?wsdl"
        useProxy="false">
            <mx:operation name="calculatePower"
             resultFormat="object"
             result="getMyJobMng(event);"
             fault="displayfault(event);">
                <mx:request xmlns="" >
                    <argument>{argument.text}</argument>
                    <power>{power.text}</power>
                </mx:request>
            </mx:operation>
        </mx:WebService>
```

Running the example will invoke the `calculatePower` service that is hosted by the POJO service.

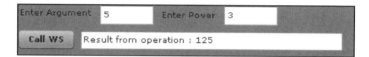

Exposing EJB as Web Services

So far we have seen how you can promote your Java classes to Web Services by merely adding some annotations at the class level; however, the JAX-WS specification also allows exposing a Stateless Session Bean as Web Services by deploying it as a JAR file in an EJB container.

For this purpose, we will create a quintessential **Account Manager** that registers user deposits and withdrawals from their accounts. In this example, we will exhibit only the Session Bean façade, which is our main concern. In the book source code, you can find the complete example including the entity classes for persisting the accounts.

Start by creating a new EJB Project **WebServiceEJBProject** and add a new Stateless Session Bean named `com.packtpub.webservice.example2.AccountManager`. The EJB Wizard will create the interface **EJBWebService** for you along with its implementation class `EJBWebServiceBean`.

In our interface, we will add three basic methods for managing the accounts plus a generic method for querying data.

```
package com.packtpub.webservice.example2;

import java.util.List;
import javax.ejb.Remote;
@Remote

public interface AccountManager {

    public void createAccount(String name);

    public void withdraw(String name, Double amount)    throws
                            AccountException;

    public void deposit(String name, Double amount);

    public List<Account> findAccounts();
}
```

The implementation class follows here:

```
package com.packtpub.webservice.example2;

import java.util.List;
import javax.ejb.*;
import javax.jws.*;
import javax.persistence.*;
import org.jboss.ejb3.annotation.*;

@Stateless
@RemoteBinding(jndiBinding="AccountManagerEJB/remote")
@WebService(targetNamespace = «http://www.packtpub.com/»,
        serviceName = «AccountManagerService») [1]

public  class AccountManagerBean implements AccountManager {

    @PersistenceContext(unitName="AppStore")
    private EntityManager em; [2]

    @WebMethod
    public void createAccount(@WebParam(name="name")
                String name) { [3]
        Account account = new Account();
        account.setName(name);
        account.setAmount(0d);
        em.persist(account);

    }

    @WebMethod
    public void withdraw(@WebParam(name="name")
                String name,
                @WebParam(name=»amount»)
                Double amount) [4]
        throws AccountException
    {

        Query query = em.createQuery("FROM Account
                            WHERE name= :name");
        query.setParameter("name", name);
        Account account = (Account)query.getSingleResult();
        double currentAmount = account.getAmount().doubleValue();
        double newAmount = currentAmount - (amount.doubleValue());
        if (newAmount < 0) {
            throw new AccountException("Unsufficient
                            funds for account
                    "+ account.getAccountId());
        }
```

```
                    account.setAmount(newAmount);
                    em.persist(account);
        }

        @WebMethod
        public void deposit(@WebParam(name="name")
                        String name,
                        @WebParam(name=»amount»)
                        Double amount) [5]
        {

                Query query = em.createQuery("FROM Account
                                        WHERE name= :name");
                query.setParameter("name", name);
                Account account = (Account)query.getSingleResult();
                double currentAmount = account.getAmount().doubleValue();
                account.setAmount(currentAmount + (amount.doubleValue()));
                em.persist(account);
        }

        @WebMethod
        public List<Account> findAccounts() [6]
        {
                Query query = em.createQuery("FROM Account");
                List <Account>items = query.getResultList();
                return items;
        }

}
```

The `AccountManager` is declared as `@Web Service` **[1]** as using the namespace `www.packtpub.com` and the service name `AccountManagerService`.

This EJB will use a `PersistenceContext`, which is injected **[2]** to provide JPA connectivity. In our sample, we are recycling the AppStore's `persistence.xml`, which we created in the Chapter 5, *Developing JPA Entities*.

The method `createAccount` **[3]** allows our client to create a new account with a starting empty account. The methods `withdraw` **[4]** and `deposit` **[5]** are conceptually used to add/remove money from the account. Finally, the method `findAccounts` **[6]** returns the list of accounts created.

Exposing all EJB methods as Web Service

In this example, we are exposing all EJB methods to Web Service clients by adding the @WebMethod annotation before each method. A shortcut to perform the same thing is by adding the @WebService annotation on the EJB interface, which automatically exposes all EJB methods.

Your EJB endpoint doesn't need any extra configuration like the POJO Web Service. Add the project to your server and deploy it to JBoss AS.

In the Web Service console, verify that your `AccountManagerService` has been added to the available services.

Registered Service Endpoints

Endpoint Name   jboss.ws:context=WebServiceEJBProject,endpoint=AccountManagerBean
Endpoint Address   http://127.0.0.1:8080/WebServiceEJBProject/AccountManagerBean?wsdl

StartTime	StopTime	
Wed Jul 01 16:03:53 CEST 2009		
RequestCount	ResponseCount	FaultCount
0	0	0
MinProcessingTime	MaxProcessingTime	AvgProcessingTime
0	0	0

Handling exceptions in Web Services

If you have kept an eye on the Web Service contract, you surely have noticed that the method `withdraw` raises a runtime exception named `AccountException`.

When implementing a Web Service using Java and JAX-WS, you might want to code your exceptions using Java natural style, that is, throwing an exception from your service operation. In terms on Web Services, this would require the runtime translation of the exception into a SOAP fault that is received on the client. For example, here's how the `AccountException` is translated into the WSDL:

```
<operation name="withdraw" parameterOrder="withdraw">
  <input message="tns:AccountManagerBean_withdraw" />
  <output message="tns:AccountManagerBean_withdrawResponse" />
  <fault message="tns:AccountException" name="AccountException" />
</operation>
```

If you don't want to rely on JAX WS default mapping of exceptions, then you can use the @WebFault annotation:

```
@WebFault(name = "AccountExceptionFault",
        targetNamespace = "http://www.packtpub.com/")
public class AccountException extends RuntimeException implements
Serializable{

    public AccountException(String error) {
        super(error);
    }
    public AccountException( ) {
        super();
    }
}
```

The fault message, as a consequence of the @WebFault annotation, would become:

```
<operation name="withdraw" parameterOrder="withdraw">
  <input message="tns:AccountManagerBean_withdraw" />
  <output message="tns:AccountManagerBean_withdrawResponse" />
  <fault message="tns:AccountExceptionFault" name="AccountExceptionFa
ult" />
</operation>
```

Generating a test client

If you have not skipped the first Web Service example, creating a client for our EJB Web Service should be a matter of seconds.

We will again use **wsconsume** to generate the client artifacts and wrapper classes. Go to **Run | External tools | External tools Configuration** and add the following configuration for the **wsconsume** tool.

```
-k -p com.packtpub.webserviceclient.example2 -o ${workspace_
loc:/WebServiceEJBProject/ejbModule} http://127.0.0.1:8080/
WebServiceEJBProject/AccountManagerBean?wsdl
```

Running the tool will generate a quite a lot of classes as shown from the **Project Explorer** view:

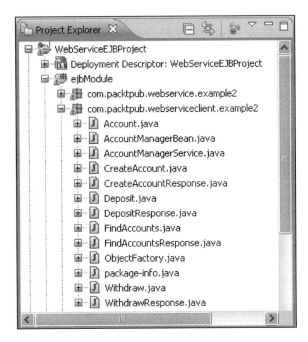

As you can see, **wsconsume** has generated both the service artifacts and the JAX WS client for the Web Service. The class `AccountManagerService` is the JAX-WS Client, which we will use to interact with the Web Service.

The class `AccountManageBean` contains the `ServiceEndpoint` interface with all exposed service methods. In this interface, each service method is wrapped by a **Request/Response wrapper**. For example, the `createAccount` method declares a wrapper Bean for the request named `CreateAccount`, along with a response wrapper Bean named `CreateAccountResponse`.

```
    @WebMethod

    @RequestWrapper(localName = "createAccount", targetNamespace
= "http://www.packtpub.com/", className = "com.packtpub.
webserviceclient.example2.CreateAccount")

    @ResponseWrapper(localName = "createAccountResponse",
targetNamespace = "http://www.packtpub.com/", className = "com.
packtpub.webserviceclient.example2.CreateAccountResponse")
    public void createAccount(String name);
```

For testing our example, we will set up a minimal client class that creates an account, performs some operations on it, and then invokes the findAccounts method that rolls out the list of accounts with their balance.

```
package com.packtpub.webserviceclient.example2;

public class Client {

    public static void main(String[] args) {
                AccountManagerService accountService = new
                                    AccountManagerService();
        AccountManagerBean ejb =
                accountService.getAccountManagerBeanPort();

        ejb.createAccount("John Nash");
        ejb.deposit("John Nash", 1000d);
        ejb.withdraw("John Nash", 500d);

        List <Account> list = ejb.findAccounts();

        for (int ii=0;ii<list.size();ii++) {
            Account acc = list.get(ii);
            System.out.println(acc.getName());
            System.out.println(acc.getAmount());
        }

    }
}
```

Running the test client will return the balance for the single account, registered in the name of professor John Nash.

Injecting Web Services

In the above example, we are creating a Service stub in the client code in order to access the Web Service. However, this is a costly operation and you might consider using the @WebServiceRef annotation, which is used to declare a reference to a Web Service.

This annotation follows the Resource pattern exemplified by the javax.annotation. Resource annotation in **JSR-250**. However, JBossWS provides some additional properties that extend the JSR specification; these include:

- Definition of the port that should be used to resolve a container-managed port
- Definition of the stub property settings for stub objects
- Definition of the URL of a final WSDL document to be used

For example, in the following EJB, we are declaring a reference to our `AccountManagerService` and injecting a service stub into the `accountService` field:

```
@Stateless
public  class  EJBWebServiceClientBean implements EJBWebServiceClient
{

  @WebServiceRef(name = "EJBWebService",wsdlLocation =
"http://127.0.0.1:8080/WebServiceEJBProject/AccountManagerBean?wsdl")

    public AccountManagerService accountService;

}
```

You can then safely use the `accountService` reference in your EJB to invoke the Web Service operations defined in `AccountManagerService`.

Web Service Handler chains

Web Services are all about messaging. A message enters the server and another is returned after the Web Service is invoked. A **Handler** is simply a class that pre-processes the message before it reaches the endpoint and also post-processes the message before it is returned to the client.

The Handler class can be used to perform core operations on the SOAP message like validations on the SOAP request message, to encrypt or decrypt the message for security reasons, or to perform logging at various points while the SOAP request is served.

We will present here a sample Handler, which performs some basic operations on the messages targeted at the `AccountManagerService`. The first step we need to do is declaring the Handler Chain in our EJB:

```
import javax.jws.HandlerChain;

@HandlerChain(file = "META-INF/jaxws-handlers-server.xml")

public  class AccountManagerBean implements AccountManager {

...
}
```

The annotation `HandlerChain` associates the Web Service with an externally defined handler chain. The chain of Web Service can be reached both from a virtual path (`http://yourhost:8080/jaxws-handlers-servers.xml`) and from a physical path (as in our case).

The next step is adding a file named `jaxws-handlers-server.xml` into the `META-INF` folder of your application. This file will contain the list of declared Handler Chains:

```
<handler-chains xmlns="http://java.sun.com/xml/ns/javaee"
                xmlns:xsi="http://www.w3.org/2001/XMLSchema-instance"
                xsi:schemaLocation="http://java.sun.com/xml/ns/javaee
javaee_web_services_1_2.xsd">

    <handler-chain>
        <protocol-bindings>##SOAP11_HTTP</protocol-bindings>
        <handler>
            <handler-name>DebugHandler</handler-name>
            <handler-class>com.packtpub.webservice.example2.
DebugHandler</handler-class>
        </handler>
    </handler-chain>
</handler-chains>
```

Here, we have declared a single Handler named `DebugHandler`, which is mapped by the class `com.packtpub.webservice.example2.DebugHandler`.

The first thing you have to know, when coding your Handler, is that you have to extend the class `GenericSOAPHandler`.

```
public class DebugHandler extends GenericSOAPHandler
{
...
}
```

Once inside your Handler, you can override the two main methods—`handleInbound` and `handleOutbound`. These methods are intuitively called for pre-processing and post-processing the message.

In this example, we will use the `handleInBound` processor to modify the SOAP message. Starting from the `MessageContext`, we will extract the SOAP message, its header (using a safe method named `getFailsafeSOAPHeader`) and body. Inside the body, we trace the parameter `name` [1], which is subsequently uppercased [2].

```
    protected boolean handleInbound(MessageContext msgContext)
    {

        try
        {
            SOAPMessage soapMessage =
            ((SOAPMessageContext)msgContext).getMessage();
            SOAPHeader soapHeader = getFailsafeSOAPHeader(soapMes
sage);
```

```
            SOAPBody soapBody = soapMessage.getSOAPBody();
            log.debug("[handleInbound]");

            SOAPBodyElement soapBodyElement =
            (SOAPBodyElement)soapBody.getChildElements().next();
            Iterator iter = soapBodyElement.getChildElements(new
                        QName("name")); [1]

            while (iter.hasNext()) {
                    SOAPElement nameElement =
                        (SOAPElement)iter.next();
                    nameElement.setValue(nameElement.getValue().
                                        toUpperCase()); [2]

            }

        }

    catch (SOAPException e)
    {
            throw  new WebServiceException(e);
    }

    return true;
}
private SOAPHeader getFailsafeSOAPHeader(SOAPMessage soapMessage)
                throws SOAPException
{

    SOAPHeader soapHeader = soapMessage.getSOAPHeader();
    if (soapHeader == null)
    {
            soapHeader =
            soapMessage.getSOAPPart().getEnvelope().addHeader();
    }
    return soapHeader;
}

    catch (SOAPException e)
    {
            throw  new WebServiceException(e);
    }
    return true;
}
  private SOAPHeader getFailsafeSOAPHeader(SOAPMessage
                soapMessage) throws SOAPException
{

    SOAPHeader soapHeader = soapMessage.getSOAPHeader();
    if (soapHeader == null)
```

```
        {
             soapHeader =
           soapMessage.getSOAPPart().getEnvelope().addHeader();
        }
        return soapHeader;
}
```

Here's the dump of the SOAP packet before and after processing the inbound message:

```
Before handleInBound

<S:Envelope xmlns:S='http://schemas.xmlsoap.org/soap/envelope/'>
  <S:Body>
    <ns2:createAccount xmlns:ns2='http://www.packtpub.com/'>
      <name>John Nash</name>
    </ns2:createAccount>
  </S:Body>
  <S:Header></S:Header>
</S:Envelope>


After handleInBound

<S:Envelope xmlns:S='http://schemas.xmlsoap.org/soap/envelope/'>
  <S:Body>
    <ns2:createAccount xmlns:ns2='http://www.packtpub.com/'>
      <name>JOHN NASH</name>
    </ns2:createAccount>
  </S:Body>
  <S:Header></S:Header>
</S:Envelope>
```

This operation is intentionally simple (and maybe a bit silly); however, once you have digested the concept of SOAP handlers, it will take little time to improve this example with an Enterprise solution.

The outbound callback also demonstrates how you can add extra payload to your message by attaching another element in the header, containing the **hostname** of the host that delivered the response.

```
protected boolean handleOutbound(MessageContext msgContext)
    {
        try
        {
            SOAPMessage soapMessage = ((SOAPMessageContext)msgContext).getMessage();
```

```
            SOAPHeader soapHeader = getFailsafeSOAPHeader
                                    (soapMessage);
            SOAPBody soapBody = soapMessage.getSOAPBody();

            SOAPFactory soapFactory = SOAPFactory.newInstance();
            javax.xml.soap.Name headerName =
                    soapFactory.createName("DeliveredBy",
                    "ns1","http://www.packtpub.com");
            SOAPHeaderElement she =
                    soapHeader.addHeaderElement(headerName);
            InetAddress localMachine =
                                    InetAddress.getLocalHost();
            she.setValue(localMachine.getHostName());

    }
    catch (SOAPException exc2)
    {
            throw  new WebServiceException(exc2);
    }

        return true;
}
```

Here is the SOAP message before and after processing:

```
Before handleOutBound

<S:Envelope xmlns:S='http://schemas.xmlsoap.org/soap/envelope/'>
<env:Header></env:Header>
<env:Body>
 <ns2:createAccountResponse xmlns:ns2="http://www.packtpub.com/" />
</env:Body>
</S:Envelope>


After handleOutBound

<S:Envelope xmlns:S='http://schemas.xmlsoap.org/soap/envelope/'>
<env:Header></env:Header>
<ns1:DeliveredBy xmlns:ns1='http://www.packtpub.com'>
   SERVERC00500
</ns1:DeliveredBy>
<env:Header>
<env:Body>
 <ns2:createAccountResponse xmlns:ns2="http://www.packtpub.com/" />
</env:Body>
</S:Envelope>
```

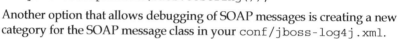

SOAP debugging

If you are curious to know how you can get a dump of the SOAP message, it's obtained by wiring the SOAP message (collected in the inbound/outbound methods) into an output stream.

```
ByteArrayOutputStream baos = new
ByteArrayOutputStream();
soapMessage.writeTo(baos);
System.out.println(baos.toString());
```

Another option that allows debugging of SOAP messages is creating a new category for the SOAP message class in your `conf/jboss-log4j.xml`.

All you have to do is add the following XML fragment in your category section:

```
<category name="jbossws.SOAPMessage">
    <priority value="DEBUG" />
</category>
```

Summary

Web Services are quickly becoming a significant technology in the evolution of the Web and distributed computing.

The main advantage that Web Services offer is data independence, by virtue of which data types and structures are not bound to the core implementations of the services. Previously, data types and structures for distributed computing were defined within individual programming languages or middleware description languages.

JBossWS uses the JBoss application server as its target container, and delivers the full JAX WS implementation, making easier even for inexperienced developers to create their Web Services.

At the end of this chapter, we have explored the full range of development topics for the standalone application server. Now it's about time to move to the clustered environment, where critical applications are deployed.

11
Clustering JBoss AS

Virtus unita fortior. Virtue united is stronger. — a Latin saying

JBoss clustering is not the product of a single library or specification, but rather a blend of technologies. On the basis of this concept, we decided to split the discussion about clustering into two sessions. In this chapter, we will introduce the rationale behind clustered programming. Here is a preview of what you will learn from this unit:

- What clustering is and how JBoss AS implements it
- The configuration of JBoss AS clustered services
- How to set up additional components required for clustering web applications

Cluster basics

A cluster of application servers consists of multiple server instances (cluster nodes) running *simultaneously* and working together to provide increased scalability and reliability. The nodes that make up the cluster can be either located on the same machine or on different machines. From the client's point of view, this is irrelevant because the cluster appears as a single server instance.

Introducing clustering in your applications will produce the following benefits:

- **Scalability:** Adding a new node to a cluster should allow the overall system to service a higher client load than that provided by the simple basic configuration. Ideally, it should be possible to service any given load, simply by adding the appropriate number of servers or machines.
- **Load balancing:** In a clustered environment, the individual nodes composing the cluster should each process a fair share of the overall client load. This can be achieved by distributing client requests across multiple servers, also known as load balancing.

- **High availability:** Applications running in a cluster can continue when a server instance fails. This is achieved because applications are deployed on multiple nodes of the cluster, and so if a server instance fails, another server instance on which that component is deployed can continue application processing.

Introducing JBoss AS cluster

JBoss AS ships with built-in clustering support, located in the "all" server configuration. To be part of a cluster, JBoss instance nodes have to be grouped together in **partitions**. The members of a cluster can be located either on the same machine or on different machines. What actually required is that they are assigned different IP address for each node.

In the following figure, you can see (on the left side) a cluster composed of two nodes running in the same partition (**DefaultPartition**), each one with its assigned IP address.

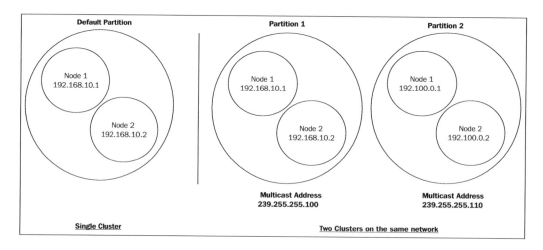

You can also have **multiple cluster** partitions running on the same network. In order to differentiate them, each cluster must have an individual **name** and **multicast** address/port. If you look at the right portion of the picture, we have a slightly more complex scenario with two partitions, namely **Partition1** and **Partition2**, each one with two cluster members and a distinct multicast address.

Multicast is a protocol where data is transmitted **simultaneously** to a group of hosts that have joined the appropriate multicast group. You can think about multicast as radio or television streaming where only those tuned to a particular frequency receive the streaming.

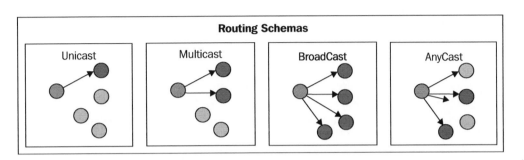

However, JBoss cluster does not deal with such low-level schemas directly; rather the communication between cluster nodes is handled by a library called **JGroups** that is a toolkit for reliable multicast communication. The basic building block of JGroups is the **Channel**, which is quite similar to a standard socket. Essentially Channels are the means by which applications connect to a cluster and send messages to each other.

At server startup, the JGroups library launches a set of Channels that have the ability to *discover each other dynamically* through the exchange of multicast packets. Nodes that join the cluster at a later time have their state automatically initialized and synchronized by the rest of the group.

All messages sent and received over the Channel have to pass through the **protocol stack**, which is the second main element of the JGroups framework.

The protocol stack is made up of a list of protocol layers in a bi-directional list. Outgoing requests go down the JGroups stack, and incoming requests climb up in the stack. For example, you might have in your protocol stack a **fragmentation layer** that might break up a message into several smaller messages, adding a header with an ID to each fragment, and re-assembling the fragments on the receiver's side.

Knowledge of the protocol stack is not required anyway, unless you need to tweak the default values and configure you own protocol stack.

JBoss AS clustering architecture

In the previous section, we have introduced some basic administrative concepts about JBoss AS clustering; as a developer, you are probably more interested to know the interaction between your client and the clustered application.

Basically, JBoss AS cluster solutions fall between two kinds of architectures—**Smart Proxy Architecture** and **External Load Balancer**. To summarize the boundary between the two architectures, we can state that the external load balancer is used by clustered web applications, while smart proxies are used for all other clusterable components.

Smart proxies

When using JBoss AS services such as JNDI, EJB, RMI, and JBoss remoting, the communication between the client and the server component is not a peer-to-peer communication. For example, when a client invokes an EJB, an object named **smart proxy** is looked up and **downloaded locally**. In a single node environment, the smart proxy must only pursue the job of routing the call from the client to the server, taking care of marshalling parameters and unmarshalling the return value of the EJB.

In a clustered environment, the smart proxy object includes an **interceptor** that understands how to route calls to multiple nodes in the cluster. The smart proxy is constantly aware of the clustering topology—for example, if one node of the cluster fails, the proxy stub is updated to reflect the latest changes in the cluster.

The following screenshot depicts (left side) how dynamic proxies enable switching from one node to another in case of failure.

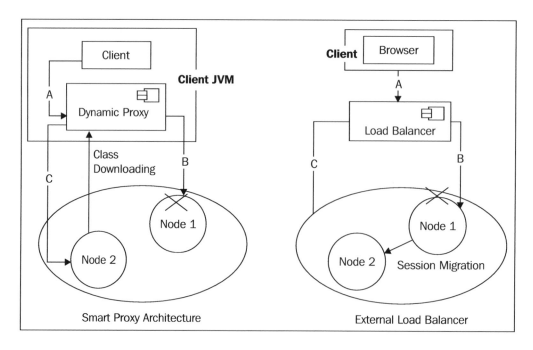

External load balancer

The HTTP service does not require downloading any component to run in a cluster. As a matter of fact, clustering the HTTP application needs configuring an external component that contains the logic to route the requests to the nodes hosting the web application. This component can either be hardware or software; however, they perform conceptually the same function—spreading the requests across the nodes, taking care of cluster configuration as well as failover policies. The section *Clustering web applications* contains the necessary information for setting up a software load balancer, namely Apache Tomcat Connection (`mod_jk`).

JBoss AS 5 cluster configuration

In earlier JBoss AS releases, the cluster configuration file was spread across the `server deploy` directory. Since JBoss AS 5, the configuration has been centralized in the new `deploy/cluster` directory.

Also, the configuration files have been ported from the older JMX configuration to the new **POJO MicroContainer**. This is evident from the view of the cluster directory that shows it doesn't contain any MBean's `*-service.xml` file.

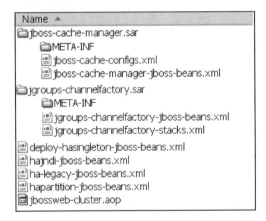

This is a short description of the configuration files. We will examine the most interesting files in more detail in the appropriate sections.

File / directory	Description
jboss-cache-manager-jboss-beans.xml	JBoss Cache configuration file. Used for HTTP and SFSB replication and for Entity cache replication.
jboss-cache-configs.xml	Additional JBoss Cache configurations using the standard JBC 3.x config format can be stored here.
jgroups-channelfactory-jboss-beans.xml	JGroups JChannelFactory configuration.
jgroups-channelfactory-stacks.xml	Standard JGroups protocol stacks definitions, used by the JChannelFactory bean.
deploy-hasingleton-jboss-beans.xml	HA Singleton configuration.
hajndi-jboss-beans.xml	HA-JNDI Configuration.
ha-legacy-jboss-beans.xml	HA Legacy services configuration.
hapartition-jboss-beans.xml	HA Partition configuration.

Starting JBoss AS in cluster mode

JBoss AS has a built-in cluster configuration named **all**. So, in order to start the AS in cluster mode, it's roughly enough to reference this server configuration. Depending on your network requirements, you can either start a JBoss AS cluster distributing the nodes on different hosts or you can have multiple nodes on a single machine. You can run multiple clusters on the same network. We shall now analyze each of these options.

Running cluster nodes on separate machines

This is the most common scenario for running a cluster and can be easily carried out with a minimal networking background.

By using the following command line, you will start a JBoss AS cluster node in the **DefaultPartition**, bound at the IP Address 192.168.10.1:

```
run -c all -b 192.168.10.1 -Djboss.messaging.ServerPeerID=1    #Windows
run.sh -c all -b 192.168.10.1 -Djboss.messaging.ServerPeerID=1    #Unix
```

Notice we have added a system property named `jboss.messaging.`
`ServerPeerID` with a unique value as required by clustered JMS Server.
More about this topic will be discussed in the *JMS clustering* section, at the
end of this chapter.

When the startup sequence has completed, group membership will be outputted on
the JBoss AS console:

INFO [GroupMember] I am (192.168.10.1:1235)

INFO [GroupMember] New Members : 1 ([192.168.10.1:1235])

INFO [GroupMember] All Members : 1 ([192.168.10.1:1235])

In order to join the cluster on the **DefaultPartition** you can start additional JBoss AS
instances from another host, using the IP Address 192.168.10.2:

```
run -c all –b 192.168.10.2 -Djboss.messaging.ServerPeerID=2
#Windows
run.sh -c all –b 192.168.10.2 -Djboss.messaging.ServerPeerID=2    #Unix
```

If you have correctly configured your Ethernet interfaces, the console will expose the
new cluster membership.

INFO [GroupMember] I am (192.168.10.2:1248)

INFO [GroupMember] New Members : 2 ([192.168.10.1:1235, 192.168.10.2:1248])

INFO [GroupMember] All Members : 2 ([192.168.10.1:1235, 192.168.10.2:1248])

Running cluster nodes on the same machine

A cluster can be run on both, separate machines or on the same machine, provided
that you have configured **multiple** IP address on it. This kind of configuration is
usually adopted on the development stage and, as far as JBoss AS is concerned,
your only requirement is to create a server configuration for each node. (See the
following resources for more details about configuring multiple nodes on the
same machine `http://support.microsoft.com/kb/157025/en-us` and
`https://www.redhat.com/docs/manuals/enterprise/RHEL-4-Manual/ref-`
`guide/s1-networkscripts-interfaces.html`)

Navigate to the JBOSS_HOME/server directory and replicate the folder **all** once for each node required. In this sample, we have created a cluster with **nodeA** and **nodeB**:

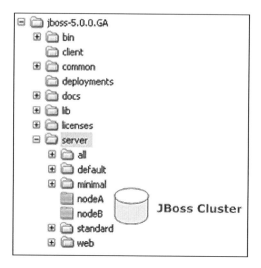

Now start each cluster passing the appropriate server configuration to the -c parameter:

```
run.sh -c nodeA -b 192.168.10.1 -Djboss.messaging.ServerPeerID=1
```

```
run.sh -c nodeB -b 192.168.10.2 -Djboss.messaging.ServerPeerID=2
```

(Replace run.sh with run for Windows users.)

From the configuration point of view, nothing will change about what you will learn here; however, consider that a single machine dedicated to the cluster will introduce **a point of failure** in your architecture. If this can impact your service level agreements, consider splitting the cluster onto multiple machines.

Running multiple clusters on the same network

You can have **multiple** cluster partitions on the same network. In order to do so, you need to isolate the JGroups channels by changing the **multicast group name and port** so that each channel has its own set of values.

In this example, we are starting a cluster named ClusterA (parameter -g), bound at the IP Address 192.168.20.1, which uses the multicast address (parameter -u) 239.255.100.100 for communication between members.

```
run.sh -c all -g ClusterA -u 239.255.100.100 -b 192.168.20.1 -Djboss.
messaging.ServerPeerID=1
```

Now, in order to join the `ClusterA` partition, we will issue the following command line, which starts up a new node bound at the IP Address 192.168.20.2:

```
run.sh -c all -g ClusterB -u 239.255.100.110 -b 192.168.20.2 -Djboss.
messaging.ServerPeerID=2
```

Running these scripts on the same network as your earlier cluster partition will produce **two distinct cluster partitions** running peacefully on the same network.

Since the release of JBoss AS 5.0.1, you are not required to change multicast ports. Actually, simply starting each cluster with a different value passed to `-u` (as described earlier) should be sufficient. Even setting different partition names via `-g` is not mandatory. (Although it's simple to do and still recommended.)

JBoss AS clustered services

As we just mentioned, the cornerstone of JBoss AS clustering architecture is the JGroups library upon which two main services are built—the first one is **JBoss Cache (JBC)** library and the second one is the **HA Partition** service. JBoss Cache is a distributed cache framework used by many clustered services, while HA Partition provides support for RPC calls among cluster members.

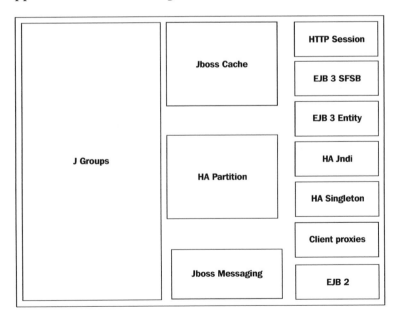

As you can see from the previous screenshot, the **HTTP Session, EJB 3 SFSB**, and **EJB 3 Entity** Bean services rely upon **JBoss Cache** architecture. On the other hand, the **HA Singleton, Client proxies** architecture, and former **EJB 2** are built upon **HA Partition** service. The distributed naming service (**HA-JNDI**) relies on both **JBoss Cache** and **HA Partition**. The only service that deals *directly* with **JGroups** protocol, is **JBoss Messaging**. We will now examine the two main JBoss AS clustering services, along with their dependent services.

JBoss Cache (JBC)

Caching is widely used for optimizing Enterprise applications. A cache is designed to reduce traffic between your application and the **Enterprise Information System** (**EIS**) by storing data fetched in a physical location or in memory.

JBoss Cache provides fully transactional features as well as a highly configurable set of options to deal with **concurrent data access** in the most efficient manner possible for your application. In addition, it is a **clustered cache** that replicates contents to other cache instances running on separate JVMs, servers, or even entire networks, using optimized and **highly configurable replication modes**.

This makes any state stored in JBoss Cache unaffected by server crashes or restarts, thus achieving high availability. Before digging into the JBoss Cache, we will explore the possible **cache replication modes** so that you will better understand the difference between the various cache configurations.

Cache modes

One of the prerequisites of a distributed cache is the **consistency of data across nodes**. This can be achieved by replicating data *constantly* across the nodes of the cluster. You can choose between the following three cache replication modes:

- **Asynchronous:** This is the default for many services such as SFSB replication and web session replication. A node that performs an asynchronous replication sends a message to other cluster members and returns *immediately* without waiting for acknowledgement of the receipt. This replication mode provides a fast data replication; however, it doesn't guarantee *data consistency* in case of node failure. This can happen if the node that fails hasn't completed the data replication to the remaining nodes. For this reason, it's not the default replication mode of Entity Caches.

- **Synchronous:** This is the least efficient mode as each node will wait for message acknowledgement from all cluster members. However, synchronous mode is needed when all the nodes in the cluster may access the cached data, resulting in a high need for consistency, for example in Entity Caches.

- **Local:** This cache mode is used for services that don't need to keep consistent data across the cluster, so cluster members don't send any messages around.

When we are looking at **data content**, another possible distinction is between data replication and data invalidation.

- **Replication**: When using data replication, each node issues messages containing a snapshot of the current state. This is a costly operation, especially if the data contains a large graph of objects; however, it is the only viable option in some scenarios such as HTTP data replication.

- **Invalidation**: A node that issues invalidating messages doesn't include the state information in the message, so the amount of data across the network is much smaller. The only information transmitted is that the session cache has gone stale, so data from the cache needs to be evicted. This is the default option for Entity Caches.

By combining these two options, you can obtain five distinct cache modes that can be used in your service configuration:

Cache mode	USED BY
REPL_SYNC	HAPartitionCache
REPL_ASYNC	Web Session cache, EJB 3 SFSB cache,
	Replicated Query cache, TimestampsCache
INVALIDATION_SYNC	Entity and Collection caches
INVALIDATION_ASYNC	None
LOCAL	Local Query cache

Cache configuration

As we have just learned, many of the standard clustered services in JBoss Application Server use JBoss Cache to maintain consistent state across the cluster. In AS 4, each cache service was shipped separately in the `deploy/` directory, which ended up in creating expensive JGroups channels also for unwanted cache services.

Since JBoss AS 5, the main configuration file for JBoss Cache services is the `deploy/cluster/jboss-cache-manager.sar/META-INF/jboss-cache-manager-jboss-beans.xml` file.

The configuration file is about 70 KB, so obviously we cannot display it here; anyway, we include the list of available configurations and their common usage:

Configuration name	Usage
standard-session-cache	Standard cache used for web sessions.
field-granularity-session-cache	Standard cache used for FIELD granularity web sessions.
sfsb-cache	Standard cache used for EJB3.0 SFSB caching.
ha-partition	Used by ClusteredSingleSignOn, HA-JNDI, Distributed State.
mvcc-entity	A config appropriate for JPA/Hibernate entity/collection caching that uses JBC's MVCC locking and READ_COMMITTED isolation level.
optimistic-entity	A configuration appropriate for JPA/Hibernate entity/collection caching that uses JBC's optimistic locking.
pessimistic-entity	A configuration appropriate for JPA/Hibernate entity/collection caching that uses JBC's pessimistic locking.
mvcc-entity-repeatable	Same as mvcc-entity but uses REPEATABLE_READ isolation level.
pessimistic-entity-repeatable	Same as "pessimistic-entity" but uses REPEATABLE_READ isolation level.
local-query	A configuration appropriate for JPA/Hibernate query result caching. Does not replicate query results.
replicated-query	A configuration appropriate for JPA/Hibernate query result caching. Replicates query results.
timestamps-cache	A configuration appropriate for the timestamp data cached as part of JPA/Hibernate query result caching.

In the previously described file, you will find additional configurations namely mvcc-shared, optimistic-shared, pessimistic-shared, and pessimistic-shared-repeatable. These configurations are maintained for **backward compatibility** with JBoss AS 4 release, but you are not advised to use them because they require cache mode REPL_SYNC, which is the least efficient mode, and a full state transfer at startup can be expensive. Use the newer JBC's MVCC/optimistic/pessimistic locking.

As you can see in the previous table, the cache configuration basically impacts the HTTP Session Cache, Entity Caches, and Stateful Session Bean Cache. You might wonder why Stateless Session Beans and Message Driven Beans are excluded from this list. The answer lies in the fact that SLSB and MDB do not hold a cache of data, as their session lifetime spans the **execution thread** invoked by the client.

Now let's see in more detail a few JBoss Cache built-in configurations.

Configuring HTTP cache management

The configuration named `standard-session-cache` is used by JBC for caching web session data. The Bean that contains the main configuration attributes is briefly introduced here:

```
<entry><key>standard-session-cache</key>
<value>
  <bean name="StandardSessionCacheConfig"
    class="org.jboss.cache.config.Configuration">
    .  .  .  .  .  .  .
  </bean>
```

The list of attributes of this Bean is quite verbose, but the following are likely to be of interest to you:

- `CacheMode`: This attribute determines *how* web session data is replicated. By default, it is replicated **asynchronously** across nodes. You can opt for a synchronous replication of the web session data by changing the attribute to `REPL_SYNC` if you need the least efficient, but safer synchronous replication.

- `SyncReplTimeout`: This is the number of milliseconds to wait until all responses for a synchronous call have been received. As the major bottleneck of synchronous replication is caused by waiting for replication ACKs from all nodes in the cluster, by changing this parameter you can greatly affect the performance of your cluster. The value of this parameter needs to be more than the `lockAcquisitionTimeout` parameter.

- `LockAcquisitionTimeout`: This property specifies the maximum number of milliseconds to wait for a synchronous lock acquisition. If a lock cannot be acquired by that time, an exception will be thrown.

- `BuddyReplicationConfig`: By default this is set to `false`. **Buddy replication** allows data replication to a limited number of nodes in a cluster rather than the entire cluster. This helps a cluster to scale by not affecting network replication traffic, or node memory usage, as more nodes are added. When set to `true`, you can configure the number of backup nodes to which a copy of the session should be replicated with the property **numBuddies**.

Additional information about HTTP session replication is contained in the section *Clustering web applications*.

Configuring EJB 3.0 Stateful Session Bean cache

The cache configuration for a clustered EJB 3.0 Stateful Session Bean is enclosed in the sfsb-cache cache descriptors. The tunable parameters of the SFSB Cache are the same as we have examined for the **standard-session-cache**; additionally, you can change the configuration of an individual SFSB by adding the name attribute on the @org.jboss.ejb3.annotation.CacheConfig annotation:

```
@Stateful
@Clustered
@CacheConfig(name="new-sfsb-cache")
@Remote(StatefulRemote.class)
```

In this example, we have created a Stateful Bean with a custom cache configuration named new-sfsb-cache. (Take care to add the custom configuration in deploy/cluster/jboss-cache-manager.sar/META-INF/jboss-cache-manager-jboss-beans.xml.)

Configuring entity caching

In EJB 3.0, entities primarily serve as a persistence data model. They do not provide remote services. Therefore, the entity clustering service in EJB 3.0 primarily deals with distributed caching and replication, instead of load balancing.

Using a distributed cache is fundamental to avoid needless round trips to the database and increase cluster performance. As you know from earlier chapters, JBoss persistence layer is implemented by means of the **Hibernate** framework, which has a support for an advanced cache system.

Basically, Hibernate uses **two different caches** for objects—the **first-level cache** that is associated with the **Session** object, and the **second-level cache** that is associated with the **Session Factory** object.

In short, the first-level cache is used at Session level to reduce the number of SQL statements **within the same transaction**. The second-level cache, on the other hand, keeps loaded objects at the Session Factory level **between transactions**. These objects are available to the whole application, not just to the user running the query. This way, each time a query returns an object that is already loaded in the cache, potentially one or more database transactions are avoided.

Entities are cached in memory areas called **regions** that can be used for caching collections, queries, and timestamps. The configuration of the second-level cache is done via your EJB 3.0 deployment's `persistence.xml`.

```
<properties>
<property name="hibernate.cache.use_second_level_cache" value="true"/>
<property name="hibernate.cache.use_query_cache" value="true"/>
<property name="hibernate.cache.region.factory_class"
value="org.hibernate.cache.jbc2.
JndiMultiplexedJBossCacheRegionFactory"/>
<property name="hibernate.cache.region.jbc2.cachefactory" value="java:
CacheManager"/>
<property name="hibernate.cache.region.jbc2.cfg.entity" value="mvcc-
entity"/>
<property name="hibernate.cache.region.jbc2.cfg.collection"
value="mvcc-entity"/>
</properties>
```

This configuration enables JBoss AS to use **Hibernate second-level cache**; however we need to specify which entities to cache. The default is not to cache anything, even with the settings shown previously. We use the `@org.hibernate.annotations.Cache` annotation at entity bean level to tag each entity that needs to be cached.

```
import javax.persistence.*;
import org.hibernate.annotations.*;

@Entity
@Cache (usage=CacheConcurrencyStrategy.TRANSACTIONAL)
@NamedQueries({
    @NamedQuery(name="calculateAccounts",
                query="select sum(users) from Account as account",
                hints={@QueryHint(name="org.hibernate.cacheRegion",
                        value="AccountRegion"),
                    @QueryHint(name="org.hibernate.cacheable",
                        value="true")})
})
public class Account implements Serializable  {
}
```

In this sample, setting the attribute `org.hibernate.cacheable` in the `@QueryHint` annotation to `true` tells Hibernate to cache the results of executing this query.

Additionally, we can specify to store the query result in a distinct cache area—`AccountRegion` in the case of our sample. This query hint is optional; if it is not specified Hibernate will create a synthetic region based on the name of the deployment and the Bean's type. The advantage of specifying a region is that you can group queries declared in multiple beans in the same region, making it easier to manage memory usage in the cache.

There's a lot of power in the clustered second-level caching in AS 5/Hibernate, far more than can adequately be discussed here. For complete details, see the *Using JBoss Cache as a Hibernate Second Level Cache* reference manual (`http://www.jboss.org/community/wiki/ClusteredJPAHibernateSecondLevelCachinginJBossAS5.pdf`).

JBoss cache and concurrency

One potential problem of cache systems is *concurrent* access to shared data. JBoss Cache is by default **thread safe** using advanced concurrency algorithms that are configurable. The two main parameters that can be tuned in JBoss Cache are the **NodeLockingScheme** and the **IsolationLevel**.

In the **NodeLockingScheme**, there are three main options that can be applied to JBoss Cache: **MVCC**, **Optimistic**, and **Pessimistic Locking**.

- **MVCC (Multi-versioned concurrency control)**: This is the default locking schema for JPA/Hibernate entity caching. MVCC ensures a high level of performance, especially for applications that mostly read data, as reader threads are completely *free of locks and synchronized blocks*. MVCC also uses custom, highly performing lock implementations for writer threads, which are tuned to multi-core CPU architectures.

- **Pessimistic locking**: This locking mode requires acquiring locks on nodes before reading and writing. As a matter fact, this locking mode carries more overhead, allowing less concurrency.

- **Optimistic locking**: This locking mode eliminates locks by using an area of memory called **workspace**, where data is temporarily copied between ongoing transactions.

Optimistic and pessimistic locking schemes are deprecated locking schemas that are kept for backward compatibility. You are strongly encouraged to use the default MVCC locking schema.

In case of the **IsolationLevel**, you can apply two possible values (`READ_COMMITTED` and `REPEATABLE_READ`) that correspond in semantic to the equivalent database isolation levels.

REPEATABLE_READ is the default isolation level used by JBoss Cache. Using this isolation lock, the transaction acquires **read locks** on all retrieved data, though phantom reads can potentially occur.

READ_COMMITTED provides a significant performance gain over REPEATABLE_READ, but data records retrieved by a query are not prevented from modification by some other transaction.

The HAPartition service

HAPartition is a general purpose service used for a variety of tasks in AS clustering. At its core, it is an abstraction built on top of JGroups Channel that provides support for making/receiving **RPC invocations** on/from one or more cluster members.

HAPartition also supports a distributed registry named DistributedReplicantManager that holds information about which clustering services are running and on which member. It also provides notifications to interested listeners when the cluster membership changes or the clustered service registry changes.

The HAPartition service is configured via the deploy/cluster/hapartition-jboss-beans.xml file. Following is the list of properties of the ClusterPartition Bean that is used to configure HAPartition Service:

Proprerty	Description
cacheHandler	References the injected cache used for state management.
partitionName	Name of the partition being built.
nodeAddress	The address used to determine the node name.
stateTransferTimeout	Maximum time (in ms) to wait for state transfer to complete. Increase for large states.
methodCallTimeout	Maximum time (in ms) to wait for RPC calls to complete.
threadPool	Optionally provide a thread source to allow async connect of our channel.
distributedStateImpl	References the bean that manages distributed state across the cluster.

You can view the current cluster information by pointing your browser to the JMX console of any application server instance in the cluster (that is http://hostname:8080/jmx-console/) and then clicking on the **jboss:service=HAPartition,partition=DefaultPartition Mbean**.

The **DistributedReplicantManager (DRM)** service is a distributed registry that allows HAPartition users to register objects under a given key, making available to callers the set of objects registered under that key by the various members of the cluster. The DRM also provides a notification mechanism, so interested listeners can be notified when the content of the registry changes.

The DistributedReplicantManager is used mainly for two purposes in JBoss AS—for letting clustered **smart proxies** communicate with other nodes and for **HA singletons**. We have discussed the clustered smart proxies earlier, we will now introduce HA singletons.

Exploring HA singletons

The **singleton** is a design pattern that allows only one instance of a class. In a clustered environment, this leads to several issues, mainly because each JVM will hold a copy of the singleton and the resource needs to be correctly synchronized across cluster members.

JBoss AS supports the concept of a singleton resource in a cluster by adding a special service called the **HASingleton** service. Since JBoss AS 5, the configuration of the HASingleton service has been moved from `deploy/deploy-hasingleton-service.xml` to `deploy/cluster/deploy-hasingleton-jboss-beans.xml`.

The simplest and most commonly used strategy for deploying an HA singleton is to take an ordinary `*.jar` deployment unit and copy it in the `$JBOSS_HOME/server/all/deploy-hasingleton` directory instead of in `deploy`.

The node running the singleton is called the **Master Node**. If the **Master Node** fails, the remaining nodes elect a new **Master Node** that keeps running the singleton service. As you can see in the next screenshot, the service is kept running on just one node.

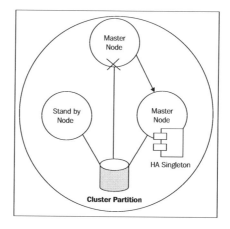

Using the `deploy-hasingleton` directory is a very straightforward approach, but it has a few drawbacks:

- First, services deployed in the folder `deploy-hasingleton` cannot take advantage of the **hot-deployment feature**, so each time you redeploy the service, a server restart is required.

- Next, each time a master node fails, the singleton service needs to go through the **whole deployment process** before being available. This can be quite expensive if your application contains many modules.

- Alternatively, if your service is implemented as an MBean, you can deploy it along with a service called **HASingletonController** in order to turn it into an HA singleton. This will solve the issues specified above. Consult JBoss clustering documentation for further information.

The HA-JNDI service

JNDI is a key component of JBoss AS server architecture. By means of the JNDI tree, client applications can look up their proxies and use them to interact with remote applications. The **HA-JNDI** module spices up the traditional JNDI services, by adding **transparent failover and load balancing** of naming operations. Furthermore, the HA-JNDI tree allows **automatic client discovery** of HA-JNDI servers (using multicast).

Each object bound into the HA-JNDI service **will be replicated** around the cluster, and a copy of that object will be available in VM on each node in the cluster. This allows a **unified view of the JNDI tree**.

On the server side, the HA-JNDI service maintains a cluster-wide context tree. Each node in the cluster retains its own local JNDI context tree. An application can bind its objects to the tree, although in practice most objects are bound into the local JNDI context tree. So what is the concrete advantage of binding a component in the HA-JNDI tree? The advantage is quite evident in a situation where the required components are not deployed on all cluster nodes (also called a **heterogeneous** cluster).

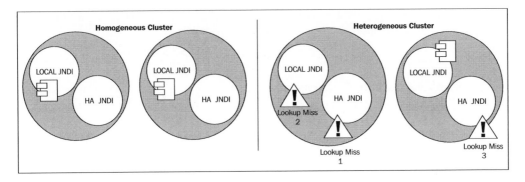

In the left side of the previous figure, a component (supposing an EJB) is deployed on the **Local JNDI** tree of all nodes of the cluster. When a remote client tries to look up the EJB through **HA-JNDI**, the **HA-JNDI** is not aware of the component and **will delegate to the Local JNDI** tree that will return the object to the client.

On the other hand, if the EJB is deployed only on one **Local JNDI** tree, (right side of the previous figure) a **Lookup Miss** will result in both the **HA-JNDI** tree and in the **Local JNDI** tree of Node A. The search for the object will continue on the remaining cluster nodes, using the same order — first inspecting the HA-JNDI tree and then the local tree.

If no local JNDI service owns such a binding, a `NameNotFoundException` is finally raised. In our example, the second node will return a copy of the object from the Local tree but the lookup process was quite expensive. Using HA-JNDI for storing the object would avoid delegating the lookup query to the local JNDI service — on the server node and, if not available, to all local JNDI services of the cluster.

Accessing HA-JNDI

If you want to perform JNDI lookups on the HA-JNDI tree, you must configure your `InitalContext` **differently** from the Local JNDI lookups. The following code shows how you can initialize `NamingContext` bound to HA-JNDI from a local client:

```
Properties p = new Properties();

p.put(Context.INITIAL_CONTEXT_FACTORY, "org.jnp.interfaces.
NamingContextFactory");

p.put(Context.URL_PKG_PREFIXES, "jboss.naming:org.jnp.interfaces");

String bindAddress = System.getProperty("jboss.bind.address",
"localhost");

p.put(Context.PROVIDER_URL, bindAddress + ":1100");
return new InitialContext(p);
```

 On a **multihomed** cluster environment, it is safer to specify the partition name instead of the provider URL — for example:

```
p.put("jnp.partitionName","DefaultPartition");
```

For clients running **outside** the application server, you can pass a comma-separated list of JNDI servers (that is the nodes in the HA-JNDI cluster) to the `java.naming.provider.url` property in the `jndi.properties` file.

```
java.naming.provider.url=server1:1100,server2:1100,server3:1100,serve
r4:1100
```

When performing lookups, the JNP client code will try to get in touch with each server node from the list, one after the other, stopping as soon as one server has been reached. It will then download the HA-JNDI stub from this node.

HA-JNDI configuration

The configuration of HA-JNDI is located in the `deploy/cluster/hajndi-jboss-beans.xml` file.

The following table summarizes the configurable parameters of the `HANamingServiceBean`:

Parameter	Description
bindAddress	The address to which the HA-JNDI server will bind to listen for naming proxy download requests from JNP clients. (Default `jboss.bind.address` property.)
port	Specifies the port to which the HA-JNDI server will bind to listen for naming proxy download requests from JNP clients. (Default 1100.)
backlog	The maximum queue length for incoming connection indications for the TCP server socket on which the service listens for naming proxy download requests from JNP clients (default 50).
rmiBindAddress	Specifies the address to which the HA-JNDI server will bind to listen for RMI requests (for example JNDI lookups) from naming proxies. Default value is `jboss.bind.address` system property.
rmiPort	Specifies the port to which the server will bind to communicate with the downloaded stub. Default value is 1101.
discoveryDisabled	A Boolean flag that disables configuration of the auto discovery multicast listener. Default is `false`.
autoDiscoveryAddress	Specifies the multicast address to listen to for JNDI automatic discovery. Default value is the `jboss.partition.udpGroup` system property, or 230.0.0.4 if that is not set.
autoDiscoveryGroup	Specifies the port to listen on for multicast JNDI automatic discovery packets. Default value is 1102.
autoDiscoveryBindAddress	Sets the interface on which HA-JNDI should listen for auto-discovery request packets. If this attribute is not specified and a `bindAddress` is specified, the `bindAddress` will be used.

Parameter	Description
`autoDiscoveryTTL`	Specifies the TTL (time-to-live) for autodiscovery IP multicast packets.
`loadBalancePolicy`	Specifies the class name of the `LoadBalancePolicy`implementation that should be included in the client proxy.
`clientSocketFactory`	An optional attribute that specifies the fully qualified classname of the `java.rmi.server.RMIClientSocketFactory` that should be used to create client sockets. Default is null.
`serverSocketFactory`	An optional attribute that specifies the fully qualified classname of the `java.rmi.server.RMIServerSocketFactory` that should be used to create server sockets. Default value is null.

Clustering web applications

The configuration of a clusterable web application is slightly more complex than other components, so it deserves a section on its own. In order to achieve a scalable and consistent state for a web application across the cluster, two distinct functions are required:

- Session state replication
- Load-balancing of incoming invocations

Session state replication occurs when we replicate the information (that is session attributes) stored in your **HttpSession** across the nodes of the cluster. **Load balancing**, on the other hand, is *not directly* handled by JBoss AS and requires an external load balancer, either hardware or software. The following section explains how you can configure and possibly override the default web container parameters.

Configuring HTTP replication

Configuring HTTP session replication on a web application has a mandatory requirement as per JEE specification, that is, adding the `<distributable />` tag in your application's `web.xml`.

```
<web-app>
    . . . . .
    <distributable />
</web-app>
```

Next, you can apply JBoss AS-specific configuration both at server level and at application level. The server-wide configuration is located at `server\all\deployers\jbossweb.deployer\META-INF\war-deployers-jboss-beans.xml`.

It is a good practice to configure your HTTP session on a web application basis, by adding to your web archive, a JBoss AS specific deployment descriptor, `jboss-web.xml`.

```
<!DOCTYPE jboss-web PUBLIC
    -//JBoss//DTD Web Application 5.0//EN
    http://www.jboss.org/j2ee/dtd/jboss-web_5_0.dtd>
<jboss-web>
    <replication-config>
        <cache-name>custom-web-cache</cache-name>
        <replication-trigger>SET</replication-trigger>
        <replication-granularity>ATTRIBUTE</replication-granularity>
        <max-unreplicated-interval>30</max-unreplicated-interval>
        <snapshot-mode>instant</snapshot-mode>
        <snapshot-interval>1000</snapshot-interval>
    </replication-config>
</jboss-web>
```

In the previous example, we have configured our application to use the `custom-web-cache` that can be defined in the file `deploy/cluster/jboss-cache-manager.sar/META-INF/jboss-cache-manager-jboss-beans.xml`.

Additionally, we have set a few custom attributes for the HTTP Session Replication:

- `replication-trigger`: Determines when the HTTP session is considered eligible for replication (also known as "dirty"). The following table depicts the three possible values for this field:

Attribute	Description	Speed
SET	This is the best option for performance. The session is replicated only if an attribute is explicitly modified with the `setAttribute` method.	good
SET_AND_GET	With this option any attribute that is `get`/`set` is marked as dirty even if it's not written back to the session. This leads to a significant performance degradation.	slow
SET_AND_NON_PRIMITIVE_GET	This is the default option. It works the same as SET_AND_GET except for primitive system types (String, Integer, Long). Since they are immutable objects they are not replicated when a `get` is issued.	average

- In practice, the default option (**SET_AND_NON_PRIMITIVE_GET**) considers the session "dirty" when a `session.setAttribute()` is issued on an object or when a `session.getAttribute()` is issued on an object that is mutable. The following table summarizes the effect on session invalidation of the replication-trigger attribute using an immutable Object (String) or a mutable Object (MyPOJO)

Command	SET	SET_AND_NP_GET	SET_AND_GET
`HttpSession session;`	NO	NO	NO
`String s = (String)session.getAttribute("x");`	NO	NO	YES
`MyPOJO p = (MyPOJO)session.getAttribute("p");`	NO	YES	YES
`MyPOJO p = (MyPOJO)session.getAttribute("p"); session.setAttribute(p);`	YES	YES	YES

- `replication granularity`: Determines which part of the stored objects needs to be replicated. Supported values are:

  ○ **ATTRIBUTE**: Replication is only for the dirty attributes in the session plus some session data such as the last-accessed timestamp.

  ○ **SESSION**: The entire session object is replicated if any attribute is dirty. The entire session is serialized in one unit, so shared object references are maintained on remote nodes. This is the default setting.

  ○ **FIELD**: Replication is only for individual changed data fields inside session attribute objects. Shared object references will be preserved across the cluster.

  If your sessions are generally small, SESSION is the better policy. If your session is larger and some parts are infrequently accessed, ATTRIBUTE replication will be more effective. If your application has very big data objects in session attributes and only fields in those objects are frequently modified, the FIELD policy would be the best.

- `max-unreplicated-interval`: Specifies the maximum interval between requests (in seconds) after which the session's timestamp will be written. Such replication ensures that other nodes in the cluster are aware of the most recent value for the session's timestamp and will not incorrectly expire an unreplicated session upon failover.

If you need session metadata to be written whenever the session is accessed, you can set this parameter to 0. A value of -1 means the metadata will be replicated only if some attributes have been modified during the request.

- `snapshot-mode`: Defines the way sessions are replicated to the other nodes. Possible values are:

  - `instant` (the default): The default value "instant" replicates changes to the other nodes synchronously, that is, at the end of requests. Using this option, the "snapshot-interval" property is ignored.

  - `interval`: Using the "interval" mode, a background task takes care of checking for modified sessions and then triggering replication.

- `Snapshot-interval`: If you are using the interval snapshot mode, this parameter specifies how often (in milliseconds) the interval background task kicks in.

HttpSession passivation/activation

Session passivation is the process of controlling memory usage by removing relatively unused sessions from memory, while storing them in persistent storage. Until now, the only component that could benefit from session passivation was the Stateful Session Bean. Beginning with JBoss AS 5, an analogous mechanism is available also for the HTTP Session.

In the same way as SFSB, a web session can be **temporarily passivated** and, when requested by a client, it can be "activated" back into memory and removed from the persistent store. Support for session passivation is available for a web application whose web.xml includes the `<distributable/>` tag.

In order to be passivated, one of the following conditions must evaluate to `true`:

- The session has been idle for a period of time (in seconds) greater than a configurable maximum idle time (`passivation-max-idle-time`).

- The number of active sessions exceeds the `max-active-session` parameter and the session has been idle for a period (in seconds) greater than a configurable minimum idle time (passivation-min-idle-time).

The configuration is applied on the file `jboss-web.xml` at application level.

```
<max-active-sessions>20</max-active-sessions>
<passivation-config>
   <use-session-passivation>true</use-session-passivation>
   <passivation-min-idle-time>60</passivation-min-idle-time>
   <passivation-max-idle-time>600</passivation-max-idle-time>
</passivation-config>
```

Whatever event triggers the session passivation, single sessions are passivated on a **Least Recently Used (LRU)** basis.

Configuring load balancing

A load balancer tracks the HTTP requests and, depending on the session to which the request is linked, dispatches it to the appropriate node. In the following excerpt, we will briefly illustrate how to set up the popular `mod_jk` balancer. A complete description of `mod_jk` can be found at the Tomcat website: `http://tomcat.apache.org/connectors-doc/`.

In the following section, we assume that a stable **Apache Web Server** 2.X has been installed on your host. The next step in the checklist is downloading the latest stable release of Tomcat `mod_jk`, available at `http://www.apache.org/dist/tomcat/tomcat-connectors/jk/binaries/`.

At the time of writing, the latest release is **1.2.28** that mainly fixes a few bugs found in the earlier 1.2.27. Once downloaded, the module `mod_jk.so` should be copied in your Apache module directory (usually located in the `APACHE_ROOT/modules` directory). Check your Apache documentation if you cannot locate it.

Windows users are encouraged to rename the binary file to `mod_jk.dll` if the downloaded Windows module bears the `.so` extension. This way you will not confuse this library with a compiled library for Unix.

The configuration of `mod_jk` can be included into the Apache `httpd.conf` file or held in an external file, which is a good practice:

```
# Load mod_jk module
  LoadModule    jk_module modulesc/mod_jk.so  # UNIX
# LoadModule    jk_module modules/mod_jk.dll # WINDOWS

# Where to find workers.properties
 JkWorkersFile /etc/httpd/conf/workers.properties

# Where to put jk shared memory
 JkShmFile     /var/log/httpd/mod_jk.shm
```

```
# Where to put jk logs
JkLogFile      /var/log/httpd/mod_jk.log

# Set the jk log level [debug/error/info]
JkLogLevel     info

# Select the timestamp log format
JkLogStampFormat "[%a %b %d %H:%M:%S %Y] "

# Send everything for context /jbossApplication to mod_jk
loadbalancer
JkMount  /jbossApplication/* loadbalancer
```

The module is loaded in memory by the `LoadModule` directive; the configuration of the single nodes is contained in a separate file named `workers.properties`, which will be examined in a moment.

The **JkMount** directive tells Apache which URLs it should forward to the `mod_jk` module. Supposing we have deployed on JBoss AS a web application reachable at the web context *jbossApplication*, with the above JKMount directive all requests with URL path `/jbossApplication/*` are sent to the `mod_jk` load balancer. This way, you actually split the requests either on Apache directly (static contents) or on the load balancer for Java applications.

> If you want your web application served directly by JBoss Web Server you would need to point the browser to this location:
>
> `http://localhost:8080/jbossApplication`
>
> The same web context, proxied by Apache Web server can be reached at:
>
> `http://localhost/jbossApplication`

Additionally, you can use the **JkMountFile** directive that allows dynamic updates of mount points at runtime. When the mount file is changed, `mod_jk` will reload its content.

```
# Load mount points
JkMountFile conf/uriworkermap.properties
```

The format of the file is `/url=worker_name`. To get things started, paste the following example into the file you created:

```
# Mount the Servlet context to the ajp13 worker
/jmx-console=loadbalancer
/jmx-console/*=loadbalancer
/jbossApplication=loadbalancer
/jbossApplication/*=loadbalancer
```

This will configure `mod_jk` to forward requests to `/jmx-console` and `/jbossApplication` to JBoss web container.

Next, you need to configure the workers file `conf/workers.properties`. A worker is a process that defines a communication link between Apache and the Tomcat container.

This file specifies where the different nodes are located and how to balance the calls between the hosts. The configuration file is made up of global directives (that are generic for all nodes) and the individual worker's configuration. This is a sample two-node configuration:

```
# Define list of workers that will be used
worker.list=loadbalancer,status
# Define Node1
worker.node1.port=8009
worker.node1.host=jbossNode1
worker.node1.type=ajp13
worker.node1.lbfactor=1
worker.node1.cachesize=10
# Define Node2
worker.node2.port=8009
worker.node2.host= jBossNode2
worker.node2.type=ajp13
worker.node2.lbfactor=1
worker.node2.cachesize=10
# Load-balancing behaviour
worker.loadbalancer.type=lb
worker.loadbalancer.balance_workers=node1,node2
worker.loadbalancer.sticky_session=1
# Status worker for managing load balancer
worker.status.type=status
```

In this file, each node is defined using the `worker.xxx` naming convention where XXX represents an arbitrary name you choose for each of the target servlet containers. For each worker, you must specify the host name (or IP address) and the port number of the AJP13 connector running in the servlet container.

`balance_workers` is a comma-separated list of workers that the load balancer need to manage.

`sticky_session` specifies whether requests with SESSION IDs should be routed back to the same Tomcat worker. If `sticky_session` is set to `true` or `1`, sessions are **sticky**, otherwise `sticky_session` is set to `false`. (The default is `true`.)

Finally, we must configure the JBoss Web instances on all clustered nodes so that they can expect requests forwarded from the `mod_jk` load balancer. Edit the `JBOSS_HOME/server/all/deploy/jboss-web.deployer/server.xml` file by locating the `<Engine>` element and adding an attribute `jvmRoute`:

```
<Engine name="jboss.web" defaultHost="localhost" jvmRoute="node1">
... ...
</Engine>
```

The same attribute is required on node2:

```
<Engine name="jboss.web" defaultHost="localhost" jvmRoute="node2">
... ...
</Engine>
```

You also need to be sure the AJP Connector definition is uncommented. By default, it is enabled.

```
<!-- Define an AJP 1.3 Connector on port 8009 -->
<Connector port="8009" address="${jboss.bind.address}"
protocol="AJP/1.3"
emptySessionPath="true" enableLookups="false" redirectPort="8443" />
```

> Since JBoss AS 5, there is no longer a need to configure a `UseJK` property on the JBoss HTTP service configuration to enable failover handling when AJP is used. By default, the session manager treats the presence of a `jvmRoute` attribute on the **Engine** element of `server.xml` as an indication that the specialized handling is needed.

Now test your installation by requesting the JMX Console using Apache port (instead of JBoss AS's default 8080), for example:

```
http://jbossNode1/jmx-console
```

```
http://jbossNode2/jmx-console
```

JMS clustering

JBoss Messaging has built-in support for clustering so that you can smoothly move your single-node applications to a clustered solution. The only crucial step is assigning at server startup an unique peer that should remain consistent across server restarts. A simple naming scheme is just fine (for example, 1, 2, 3 and so on).

```
run.sh  -c  node1  -g  PartitionA  -u  239.255.100.100  -b  192.168.10.1
-Djboss.messaging.ServerPeerID=1
```

JBoss Messaging clusters JMS queues and topics **transparently** across the cluster. Messages sent to a distributed queue or topic on one node are consumable on other nodes. To designate that a particular destination is clustered, simply set the `Clustered` attribute in the destination deployment descriptor to `true`:

```
<mbean code="org.jboss.jms.server.destination.QueueService"
       name="jboss.messaging.destination:service=Queue,name=clusteredQ
ueue"
       xmbean-dd="xmdesc/Queue-xmbean.xml">
       <depends optional-attribute-name="ServerPeer">
                 jboss.messaging:service=ServerPeer
       </depends>
       <depends>jboss.messaging:service=PostOffice</depends>
       <attribute name="Clustered">true</attribute>
</mbean>
```

Summary

JBoss clustering is an advanced cluster solution for Java Enterprise Applications. In spite of the vast number of features available, it is designed to run out of the box with minimal (or no) additional configuration.

JBoss AS 5 introduced cutting-edge clustering features such as simplified cluster isolation, improved Hibernate JPA/Hibernate caching, Web session passivation, and a better-organized configuration repository of services.

In the next chapter, we will show how you can smoothly turn your single node application to a clustered environment.

12
Developing a Clustered Application

Don't worry. As long as you hit that wire with the connecting hook at precisely 88 mph the instant the lightning strikes the tower... everything will be fine. – Dr. Emmett Brown, Back to the Future

Clustering an application with JBoss AS is much easier than driving an old DeLorean across time! Speaking in a general context, if your application has minimal requirements, it might just be a matter of adding a few tags to your components and/or some deployment descriptors. If you're an impatient reader and have already jumped ahead here for the code, feel free to do it. However, we have a recommendation for you — when your application is going to be rolled out, it is essential that you have acquired a rock-solid background of JBoss clustering theory; otherwise, with the default values provided, it's not guaranteed that your application will benefit from clustering.

In this chapter, we will build some concrete examples of clustering based on the abstract concepts disclosed in the earlier chapter. Specifically we will address the following topics:

- How to cluster session beans
- How to apply caching strategies to entities beans
- How to cluster a web application

Clustering Stateless Session Beans

In Chapter 4, we introduced the **Stateless Session Bean** (**SLSB**), while talking about Enterprise Java Beans. By now, you should be aware that they do not hold state between client invocations, so the main benefit of clustering an SLSB is to balance the load between an array of servers. Consequently, the clustering policies are pretty simple. The following is a bare-bones clustered SLSB:

```
@Stateless
@Clustered
public class ClusteredBean implements ClusteredInt
{
  public void doSomething()
  {
    // Do something
  }
}
```

The @Clustered annotation needs to be added before the class declaration level. That's all you need to make a clustered Stateless Session Bean.

If you don't want to stick to clustering defaults, you can configure some additional elements. Here's the same ClusteredBean with customized clustering parameters:

```
@Stateless
@Clustered(loadBalancePolicy="FirstAvailable",partition="ClusterA")
public class ClusteredBean implements ClusteredInt
{
  public void doSomething()
  {
    // Do something
  }
}
```

Following is a detailed explanation about the annotation elements:

- loadBalancePolicy: This element allows you to choose the load balance policy to be applied to your bean. Possible alternatives are shown in the following table:

Load balance policy	Description
RoundRobin	Default load balance policy. The smart proxy cycles through a list of JBoss Server instances in a fixed order.
RandomRobin	Each request is redirected by the smart proxy to a random node in the cluster.

Load balance policy	Description
FirstAvailable	Implies a random selection of the node, but subsequent calls will stick to that node until the node fails. The next node will again be selected randomly.
FirstAvailableIdenticalAllProxies	Same as FirstAvailable, except that the random node selection will then be shared by all dynamic proxies.

- partition: This element allows you to choose the cluster name where the SLSB will be exposed. If not specified, the DefaultPartition will be used.

The @Clustered annotation can also be applied by means of a jboss.xml deployment descriptor, located in the META-INF folder of your application. The only variation is the configuration parameter names, which use the XML element style. Therefore, loadBalancePolicy will be load-balance-policy and partition will be partition-name.

```
<jboss>
  <enterprise-beans>
    <session>
      <ejb-name>ClusteredBean</ejb-name>
      <clustered>true</clustered>
      <cluster-config>
        <partition-name>MyPartition</partition-name>
        <load-balance-policy>org.jboss.ha.framework.interfaces.
          RandomRobin</load-balancepolicy>
      </cluster-config>
    </session>
  </enterprise-beans>
</jboss>
```

Clustering Stateful Session Beans

Stateful Session Beans (SFSBs) deserve a bit more attention than their SLSB counterparts, as this component is able to retain client state between calls. In order to build a concrete example, we will use our BlackJackBean example that we introduced in Chapter 4.

Create a new EJB project named ClusteredSFSB and add a new Stateful Session Bean in it named com.packtpub.clustering.example1.BlackJack. This will include the BlackJack interface and the BlackJackBean implementation class in your project.

Don't rewrite it from scratch!

You can simply copy the sources from Chapter 4 into the source folder of your new project. Then simply refactor the sources, by moving them from the package `com.packtpub.ejb.example2` to `com.packtpub.clustering.example1`.

Now, before the class declaration, add the `@Clustered` annotation as in the SLSB counterpart, as follows:

```
@Stateful
@Clustered
public class BlackJackBean implements BlackJack {
  // code stays the same
}
```

The only difference between specifying the `@Clustered` annotation on an SFSB rather than on an SLSB is that you can't use a load balancing policy other than `FirstAvailable` with Stateful Session Beans. This value is set by default, so you don't need to specify the load balancing policy.

You can further customize your SFSB caching behavior by adding the `@org.jboss.ejb3.annotation.CacheConfig` annotation.

```
@Stateful
@Clustered
@CacheConfig(idleTimeoutSeconds=6000,removalTimeoutSeconds=18000)
public class BlackJackBean implements BlackJack {
  // code stays the same
}
```

The `@CacheConfig` parameter controls the replication and passivation policy of the SFSB. You might wonder how these two operations are connected. Actually SFSB replication involves serialization of the bean. Therefore, by default, replication of the bean will trigger its passivation through `@PrePassivate` and `@PostActivate` callback methods respectively. This default policy can be changed by setting the element `replicationIsPassivation` to `false`.

The `idleTimeoutSeconds` element specifies that the SFSB will be passivated if it is idle for over 6000 seconds. If you don't want to passivate your SFSB on the basis of time, but rather on the basis of size of the cache, then you can alternatively set the `maxSize` element. You can even use both of them, but you must be aware that the `idleTimeoutSeconds` will prevail over the `maxSize` attribute.

The `removalTimeoutSeconds` specifies the maximum period of time a bean can be unused before it is removed from the cache.

As discussed in the earlier chapter, you can reference a custom cache configuration by adding the `name` element to the `@CacheConfig` annotation.

```
@Stateful
@Clustered
@CacheConfig(name="new-sfsb-cache")
```

The configuration needs to be registered in the **CacheManager** bean in the file `deploy/cluster/jboss-cache-manager.sar/META-INF/jboss-cache-manager-jboss-beans.xml`.

As an example, we include a cache configuration, which exhibits a fairly small `synchReplTimeout` (number of milliseconds to wait until all responses for a synchronous call have been received) and `lockAcquisitionTimeout` (number of milliseconds to wait for a synchronous lock acquisition).

```
<entry><key>new-sfsb-cache</key>
  <value>
    <bean name="StandardSFSBCacheConfig"
      class="org.jboss.cache.config.Configuration">
      <property name="clusterName">${jboss.partition.name:
        DefaultPartition}-SFSBCache</property>
      <property name="multiplexerStack">${jboss.default.jgroups.
        stack:udp}</property>
      <property name="fetchInMemoryState">true</property>
      <property name="nodeLockingScheme">PESSIMISTIC</property>
      <property name="isolationLevel">REPEATABLE_READ</property>
      <property name="useLockStriping">false</property>
      <property name="cacheMode">REPL_ASYNC</property>
      <property name="syncReplTimeout">7500</property>
      <property name="lockAcquisitionTimeout">10000</property>
      <property name="stateRetrievalTimeout">60000</property>
    </bean>
  </value>
</entry>
```

Deploying a clustered SFSB

Java EE application servers are usually equipped with a component named **farming service** that is used to deploy and undeploy applications cluster-wide. JBoss AS farming service is quite easy to manage, as all you have to do is copy your deployments in the `JBOSS_HOME\server\all\farm` folder and the application will immediately be distributed to the cluster and deployed on each node.

In release 5.0.0 of the AS, the farming service is not available. Therefore, you need to either copy the archived applications manually in the `deploy` folder or have a script doing it for you. The reason for this incompatibility lies in the new JBoss 5.0.0 AS profile service implementation. In short, a profile represents a named collection of deployments on a server and the 5.0.0 release of the AS allows just one global profile managing deployments.

Since the release 5.1.0 CR1 of the AS, the farming service has been restored with a few nice add-ons, such as the capability to deploy your applications as exploded archives in the `farm` directory. (In the 4.X release, only packaged archives could be copied in the `farm` directory.)

So, if you are running JBoss AS 5.1.0 release, you can safely copy your deployment units in the `JBOSS_HOME\server\all\farm` folder and your application will be spread to all cluster nodes. Alternatively, we will show how you can deploy your SFSB from inside the Eclipse environment, using a very simple and intuitive approach.

First, you have to define your clustered environment as described in the previous chapter. Start with a simple two-node configuration by replicating the `all` configuration in the `nodeA` and `nodeB` directories.

Then add two new servers from the **JBoss Server View** (or alternatively from the menu: **New | Other | Server**). For each server, configure the runtime environment.

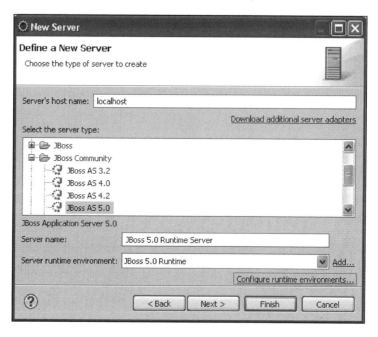

In the next window, select **Edit** on the standard configuration and, in the subsequent applet, point to **nodeA** for the first server and **nodeB** for the second one.

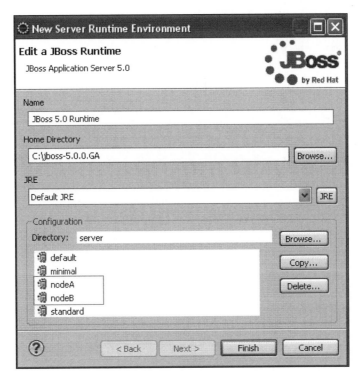

Your new server configuration should look like this:

Now, start the cluster using the available IP addresses. In this sample, we are binding the two nodes respectively on the IP addresses 192.168.10.1 and 192.168.10.2. (Windows XP is used for this demonstration; change `run` to `run.sh` for Unix machines.)

```
run -c nodeA -b 192.168.10.1 -Djboss.messaging.ServerPeerID=1
run -c nodeB -b 192.168.10.2 -Djboss.messaging.ServerPeerID=2
```

You might as well start JBoss AS nodes from inside the Eclipse environment. However, we do recommend starting the server nodes with a separate shell. This can avoid crashing the servers if Eclipse gets locked and will also keep the development environment lighter and more responsive.

When the cluster is up and running, deploy your clustered application by first choosing **Add and Remove Projects** on the individual servers. Then publish the application by selecting **Full Publish** on the SFSB clustered application for each node.

Testing the clustered SFSB

Here, we will again recycle some code from Chapter 4. Add a new class named `com.packtpub.clustering.example1.BlackJackClient` to your project. This is identical to the equivalent `BlackJackClient` class of Chapter 4. However, it needs to use a different JNDI lookup policy.

As this application is deployed on a cluster of servers, the JNDI lookup includes the extended node list, rather than the single server address/port. Create a new folder named `client-config` for your project and include the following `jndi.properties` in it:

```
java.naming.factory.initial=org.jnp.interfaces.NamingContextFactory
java.naming.provider.url=jnp://192.168.10.1:1100,192.168.10.2:1100
java.naming.factory.url.pkgs=org.jnp.interfaces
```

Now, add the folder `client-config` to the classpath (refer to Chapter 4 if you don't remember how to do it). Add a little debug information in the `deal()` method; this will be helpful to know your game score and the server handling the game.

```
public int deal() {
  Random randomGenerator = new Random();
  int randomInt = (randomGenerator.nextInt(13)) + 1;
  if (randomInt > 10) randomInt = 10; // Q - J - K
  score+=randomInt;
  if (score > 21){
    score = 0;
    throw new BustedException("You Busted!");
  }
  System.out.println("Current score: "+score);
  return score;
}
```

Your client is ready to run.

Launch the `BlackJackClient` and observe the output on both—the Eclipse client console and the server console.

You will notice the message **Player score: xx** on the server, which we have added for debugging purposes in the `deal()` method. This message indicates which server has been hit by the smart proxy. The subsequent calls will stick to that server as a result of the `FirstAvailable` load balancing policy. Now crash this server using your preferred shutdown hook (*Ctrl + C*, `shutdown` script, or `kill -9`). At this point continue your Black Jack game by requesting another deal.

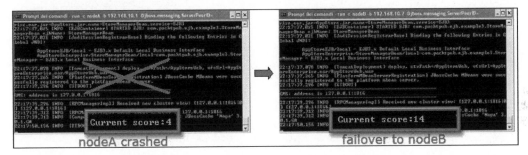

If you have carefully followed our instructions, the remaining node will retain the player score and continue the game. Session replication ensured that the Black Jack deck could be continued.

Programmatic replication of the session

So far we have shown how the session can be replicated on a configuration basis. It is also possible to override the cache strategy by implementing the `org.jboss.ejb3.cache.Optimized` interface. The optimized interface contains a method `isModified()` that can spell the final word about replication. If this method returns `true`, then session replication can be carried on, otherwise it will not occur.

In practice, you can define a class-level Boolean variable, which will be checked in the `isModified()` method:

```
@Stateful
@Clustered
public class BlackJackBean implements BlackJack {
  // all prior code
  boolean replicateSession;
  public boolean isModified()  {
    if (replicateSession)
      return true;
    else
      return false;
  }
}
```

As you can see in the last code snippet, by using the `isModified()` method, you can programmatically decide whether your session data needs to be replicated or not.

Clustering entities

Entities do not provide remote services like session beans, so they are not concerned with the load balancing logic or session replication. JBoss EJB 3.0 persistence layer is based on the Hibernate framework and, as we have learned, this framework has a complex cache mechanism, which is implemented both at **Session** level and at **SessionFactory** level.

The latter mechanism is called second-level caching. The key characteristic of the second-level cache is that it can be used across sessions. This differentiates it from the session cache, which only (as the name says) has session scope.

Hibernate provides a flexible way to define cache providers, using the property `hibernate.cache.provider_class`, when dealing with a clustered solution. However, we need a provider that is able to keep the set of data synchronized across the cluster. So which provider is fit for this purpose? Well, the answer is **JBoss Cache**.

The configuration of the second-level cache is broken into two steps. First, you have to declare the use of the second-level cache in the `persistence.xml` file of your application. Then, at bean level, you have to declare that the bean will use the cache for storing entities, queries, or timestamps.

Revisiting the AppStore example

Our AppStore described in Chapter 5 was able to load and persist some entities, chiefly `Customers` and `Items`. Here, we will show how you can cache some of this data using the second-level cache feature.

Create a new JPA project named **ClusteredAppStore** and copy the source files from Chapter 5 into the project.

The first change we do is updating the `persistence.xml` file, located in the `META-INF` folder of your ClusteredAppStore project.

```
<persistence version="1.0" xmlns="http://java.sun.com/xml/ns/
persistence" xmlns:xsi="http://www.w3.org/2001/XMLSchema-instance"
xsi:schemaLocation="http://java.sun.com/xml/ns/persistence http://
java.sun.com/xml/ns/persistence/persistence_1_0.xsd">
  <persistence-unit name="AppStore" transaction-type="JTA">
    <provider>org.hibernate.ejb.HibernatePersistence</provider>
    <jta-data-source>java:/MySqlDS</jta-data-source>
```

```
<properties>
  <property name="hibernate.dialect"
    value="org.hibernate.dialect.MySQLDialect"/>
  <property name="hibernate.cache.use_second_level_cache"
    value="true"/>
  <property name="hibernate.cache.use_query_cache" value="true"/>
  <property  name="hibernate.cache.region.factory_class"
    value="org.hibernate.cache.jbc2.
    JndiMultiplexedJBossCacheRegionFactory"/>
  <property name="hibernate.cache.region.jbc2.cachefactory"
    value="java:CacheManager"/>
  <property name="hibernate.cache.region.jbc2.cfg.entity"
    value="mvcc-entity"/>
  <property name="hibernate.cache.region.jbc2.cfg.collection"
    value="mvcc-entity"/>
</properties>
</persistence-unit>
</persistence>
```

By setting the property `hibernate.cache.use_second_level_cache` to `true` we are turning on the second-level cache mechanism. The cache, by default, is activated only for entities, so we also need to explicitly set `hibernate.cache.use_query_cache` to `true` if we want to cache queries as well.

The second-level cache can be implemented using several different schemas—open source and commercial. In the next property, `hibernate.cache.region.factory_class`, we are telling Hibernate to use JBoss Cache as the second-level cache implementation.

The next parameter, `hibernate.cache.region.jbc2.cachefactory`, is specific to the JBoss Cache implementation. It specifies the JNDI name under which the CacheManager to be used is bound. There is no default value, thus the user must specify the property.

The `hibernate.cache.region.jbc2.cfg.collection` property is also specific to JBoss Cache and details the name of the configuration that should be used for collection caches (in our configuration, `mvcc-entity`). Refer to the previous chapter for additional information about MVCC policy.

Having uncovered the configuration details, it's now time to learn how to tell Hibernate which entities or queries we are going to cache. Suppose we want to test caching the customer objects.

```
import org.hibernate.annotations.Cache;

@Entity
@Table(schema="appstore", name="CUSTOMER")
@Cache(usage = CacheConcurrencyStrategy.TRANSACTIONAL, region =
"customers")    [1]
```

```
@NamedQueries(
{
  @NamedQuery(
    name = "listCustomers",
    query = "FROM Customer c WHERE c.name = :name",
    hints = { @QueryHint(name = "org.hibernate.cacheable", value =
      "true") }   [2]
  )
})
public class Customer implements Serializable {
  // Entity code stays the same
}
```

As you can see, we have chosen to cache customer data [1] assigning a caching region named customers. If you do not specify a cache region for an entity class, all instances of this class will be cached in the /_default region.

Next, we decided to cache the parameterized query called listCustomers, by using the property org.hibernate.cacheable inside the @QueryHint annotation [2].

Hibernate is now able to cache customer data and one query across different sessions. Let's see what happens under the hood when we start querying the Customer table.

Inside the second-level cache

We are confident that the above changes will produce remarkable performance gains to our application. However, we need some kind of instruments to inspect the content of the cache. Luckily, Hibernate ships with a complete statistics and metrics API that allows you to figure out everything that is happening under the covers. In order to retrieve statistics, you have to enable them at first. This can be done by means of configuration, by adding the following property to your persistence.xml file:

```
<property name="hibernate.generate_statistics">true</property>
```

Alternatively, the statistics can be enabled programmatically by setting the setStatisticsEnabled() method of the class org.hibernate.stat.Statistics to true.

```
SessionFactory factory;
Statistics stats = factory.getStatistics();
stats.setStatisticsEnabled(true);
```

As you can see from the last code snippet, the statistics are retrieved from the `SessionFactory` class. In our AppStore example, the persistence layer is handled by the `StoreManagerBean` façade, so we will first make the factory available through injection.

```
public  class StoreManagerBean implements StoreManager {
   @PersistenceUnit(unitName="AppStore")
   SessionFactory factory;
}
```

We will then add some utility methods to display the second-level cache statistics. In order to retrieve statistics, you have to request the cache region you are interested in. The cache region name is made up of a set of elements, including the persistence unit name and also the custom region name that we have chosen for our entities (if we chose any). We will include the following utility method in our `StoreManagerBean` that will actually display the list of region names on the console:

```
public void displayRegions() {
   Statistics stats = factory.getStatistics();
   stats.setStatisticsEnabled(true);
   String regions[] = stats.getSecondLevelCacheRegionNames();
   for (String s: regions) {
   System.out.println(s);
   }
}
```

The following is taken from the standard output displayed on the console:

```
Prompt dei comandi - run.bat -c nodeA -b 192.168.10.1 -Djboss.messaging.ServerPeerID=...

10:05:24,686 INFO  [Http11Protocol] Starting Coyote HTTP/1.1 on http-127.0.0.1-8
080
10:05:24,827 INFO  [AjpProtocol] Starting Coyote AJP/1.3 on 192.168.10.10-8009
10:09:58,214 INFO  [TomcatDeployment] deploy, ctxPath=/ClusteredAppStoreWeb, vfs
Url=ClusteredAppStoreEnterprise.ear/ClusteredAppStoreWeb.war
10:10:06,480 INFO  [PlatformMBeanServerRegistration] JBossCache MBeans were succ
essfully registered to the platform mbean server.
10:10:06,526 INFO  [STDOUT]
GMS: address is 192.168.10.10:3804
10:10:08,542 INFO  [RPCManagerImpl] Received new cluster view: [192.168.10.10:38
] [127.0.0.1:3804]
10:10:08,542 INFO  [RPCManagerImpl] Cache local address is 192.168.10.10:3804
10:10:08,573 INFO  [ComponentRegistry] JBoss Cache version: JBossCache 'Naga' 3.
0.1.GA
10:10:08,658 INFO persistence.unit:unitName=ClusteredAppStoreEnterprise.ear/Clus
teredAppStore.jar#ClusteredAppStore.customers
10:10:08,756 INFO persistence.unit:unitName=ClusteredAppStoreEnterprise.ear/Clus
teredAppStore.jar#ClusteredAppStore.org.hibernate.cache.StandardQueryCache
10:10:09,124 INFO persistence.unit:unitName=ClusteredAppStoreEnterprise.ear/Clus
teredAppStore.jar#ClusteredAppStore.org.hibernate.cache.UpdateTimestampsCache
```

The former region, **ClusteredAppStore.customers**, is where the data copied from `Customer` entity (and not the entity itself) will be cached.

The **StandardQueryCache**, which is not on by default, stores the result of the set of queries issued to the database.

The **UpdateTimestampsCache** keeps track of database changes, by updating a timestamp each time a table is modified.

In order to collect statistics, we will add a generic method to our StoreManagerBean that will output some information on the console.

```
public void displayMemoryStats(String regionName) {
  Statistics stats = factory.getStatistics();
  SecondLevelCacheStatistics cacheStats =
  stats.getSecondLevelCacheStatistics(regionName);
  System.out.println("Objects cached:"
    +cacheStats.getElementCountInMemory());
}
```

The SecondLevelCacheStatistics object is the key to our statistics. It contains plenty of useful methods for inspecting the cache. For our purpose, it's sufficient to retrieve the count of elements cached in the memory. Consult the Hibernate documentation for further information about all the methods available.

The ClusteredAppStore application can now be redeployed across the cluster. Follow the same procedure as explained for the SFSB and check that the application server has deployed all components correctly.

We will add a standalone client to the project, deferring the job of clustering the Web tier to the last section of this chapter.

```
public class Client {
  static String CUSTOMER_REGION="persistence.unit:
    unitName=AppStoreEnterprise.ear/AppStore.jar#AppStore.customers";
  static String QUERY_REGION="persistence.unit:
    unitName=AppStoreEnterprise.ear/AppStore.
    jar#AppStore.org.hibernate.cache.StandardQueryCache";
  public static void main(String args[])throws Exception {
    Context ctx = new InitialContext();
    StoreManager store =
      (StoreManager)ctx.lookup("AppStoreEJB/remote");
    List <Customer> list = store.findAllCustomers();
    store.displayMemoryStats(CUSTOMER_REGION);
    store.displayMemoryStats(QUERY_REGION);
    List <Customer> list2 = store.findCustomerByName("Acme ltd");
    store.displayMemoryStats(CUSTOMER_REGION);
    store.displayMemoryStats(QUERY_REGION);
  }
}
```

The following diagram depicts what happens in the cache when you run this client:

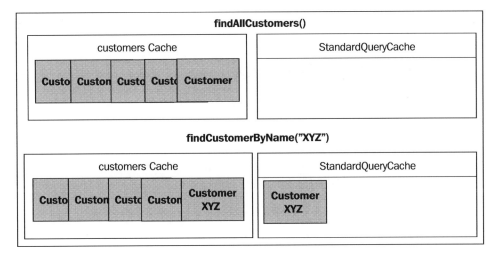

The first query, findAllCustomers, loads the list of customers into the customers cache, as specified by the @Cache directive. The query cache is empty as we haven't specified any directive to cache the result of this query.

The second query, findCustomerByName, returns a single customer (**XYZ**), which is already loaded into the customer cache. As this query has been tagged as cacheable with the @QueryHint directive, an entry will also be inserted into the StandardQueryCache.

In between the two queries, we are issuing two calls for displayMemoryStats (one for the customer region and the other for the query region) to get our statistics on the console.

What's in the QueryCache?

What is actually inserted into the QueryCache is not the object data but rather a map object. The key of the map contains the query string itself (and bind parameters if any). The value consists of the primary key identifiers for all the entities returned by the query. When a query hits the query cache, the entities are retrieved through the first or second-level caches using the primary key stored.

The above example is fairly trivial; however, it should give a clear perspective of how Hibernate stores the individual entities in the different cache regions. This is quite important to understand, especially if we plan to manage the eviction of objects programmatically, as shown in the next section.

Evicting entities from the cache

The cache of data stored by Hibernate doesn't reside in memory forever. The cache is continuously updated if there are too many/less used entries around, as specified in the `jboss-cache-manager-jboss-beans.xml` configuration file.

You can also evict data from the cache programmatically, if you want to fine tune your application to suit your needs. Removing an entry from the cache is quite simple; you only need to reference the entity by its primary key, as in the following code snippet:

```
public void evictCustomer(Integer key) {
    factory.evict(com.packtpub.jpa.example3.Customer.class,key);
}
```

You can also evict the content of data contained in the `QueryCache`:

```
public void evictQueries() {
    factory.evictQueries();
}
```

General guidelines for a good cache

Generally speaking, the use of cache should not be applied before an accurate analysis of your objects. Therefore, first, you should examine the class diagram of your objects and their dependencies before applying any cache strategy.

The basic rule of thumb is that any data that is frequently read but seldom updated is an ideal candidate for caching.

The second rule is to turn on the second-level cache only for one entity at a time—for instance, in the previous example, we have activated it only for the `Customer` object. Then measure the performance; if it is satisfying, you are on the right road and you can move on to other entities.

The third important advice is to use the `QueryCache` with caution because it might have a bad impact on your application if used blindly. First of all the `QueryCache` will increase the memory requirements, if your queries (stored as key in the `QueryCache`'s map) are made up of hundreds of characters.

Another important reason is that the result of the `QueryCache` is constantly invalidated, each time there's a change in the underlying database. This will lead to a very poor hit ratio of the `QueryCache`, if entities are constantly modified. Therefore, it is advisable to, turn on the `QueryCache` only when you have a read application.

If there are chances that your application data is read but never modified, you can apply an extreme CacheConcurrencyStrategy that does not evict data from the cache (unless performed programmatically).

```
@Entity
@Table(name="Customer")
@Cache(usage=CacheConcurrencyStrategy.READ_ONLY)
```

Clustering web applications

The configuration of a clustered web application is broken into two steps:

- The **load balancer** configuration
- The **session replication** configuration

Here, we suppose that you have correctly installed Apache Web Server and mod_jk as described in the previous chapter. Therefore, we will just highlight what is needed to adapt the configuration to our specific example, the AppStore.

First, specify the mount point that will be passed to mod_jk:

```
JkMount /ClusteredAppStoreWeb/* loadbalancer
```

Then, in the workers.properties, detail the list of nodes:

```
# Define nodeA
worker.nodeA.port=8009
worker.nodeA.host=192.168.10.1
worker.nodeA.type=ajp13
worker.nodeA.lbfactor=1
# Define nodeB
worker.nodeB.port=8009
worker.nodeB.host=192.168.10.2
worker.nodeB.type=ajp13
worker.nodeB.lbfactor=1
# Load-balancing behaviour
worker.loadbalancer.type=lb
worker.loadbalancer.balance_workers=nodeA,nodeB
worker.loadbalancer.sticky_session=1
# Status worker for managing load balancer
worker.status.type=status
```

Then, you should set the jvmRoute property for the Engine attribute. In the JBOSS_HOME/server/node[A-b]/deploy/jboss-web.deployer/server.xml file, locate the Engine element and add the attribute jvmRoute:

```
<Engine name="jboss.web" defaultHost="localhost" jvmRoute="nodeA">
</Engine>
```

And for nodeB add the equivalent:

```
<Engine name="jboss.web" defaultHost="localhost" jvmRoute="nodeB">
</Engine>
```

The last step needs to be performed at application level, by adding the `<distributable/>` tag to the web.xml file:

```
<web-app>
  <distributable />
</web-app>
```

At this stage, the AppStore application is ready to be deployed cluster-wide. Restart Apache Web Server, and then from the **JBoss Server View** choose to redeploy the application on both nodes. If you have completed all the above steps, the application will be served correctly through Tomcat's mod_JK plugin: http://apache.host. name/ClusteredAppStoreWeb.

Testing HTTP session replication

The AppStore web application doesn't store any information in the HttpSession at the moment. We can enrich the StoreManagerJSFBean with a simple method that dumps the SessionId of the current session.

```
public void dumpSession() {
  FacesContext ctx = FacesContext.getCurrentInstance();
  HttpSession session =
    (HttpSession)ctx.getExternalContext().getSession(true);
    String serverName = System.getProperty("jboss.server.name");
    FacesMessage fm =
      new FacesMessage("Running Session  "+session.getId()+ " on
      server "+serverName);
    FacesContext.getCurrentInstance().addMessage("Message", fm);
  }
```

The `dumpSession()` will be triggered in the `home.jsp` page, by means of a `commandButton`.

```
<h:commandButton action="#{manager.dumpSession}" value="DumpSession"
    styleClass="buttons" />
```

Again redeploy your application on both nodes and request the homepage. Suppose that the load balancer redirected the request to **nodeA**. Click on the **DumpSession** button and take a look at the session ID. A message will inform you about the node where the session is stuck. Now shut down this node (in our example **nodeA**) and reload the page.

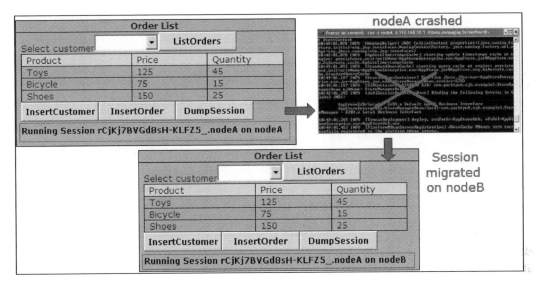

If the homepage displays correctly, then we just need a final check. Hit the **DumpSession** button again. The session ID should stay the same, meaning that the session has successfully migrated.

Sticky sessions or not sticky sessions ?

By configuring the parameter `sticky_sessions=1` in your `workers. properties`, you have instructed the load balancer to continue serving the request with the same host where the session started. However, it is possible to turn off sticky sessions, by setting this property to `0`. We really don't advise this practice — why? Let's see an example. In the following code snippet, executed by a web application, we write some text using the `response.getWriter()` method:

```
PrintWriter out = response.getWriter();
out.print(header);
out.flush(); //flush the header
```

 When the web application calls `flush()` (or `close()`) on the `PrintWriter` stream, the response is considered *committed*. The JBoss Web Server then sends all request headers to the browser before sending the Writer/OutputStream content.

That's the real critical path. If you switch to another node before the replication completes, this will lead to a request that is handled partially by two nodes. That's a violation of the Servlet 2.4 specification, section 7.7.2.7, which states: *Within an application marked as distributable, all requests that are part of a session must be handled by one Java Virtual Machine (JVM) at a time.*

Additionally, if you chose to disable a sticky session when using a cache replication mode ASYNC (default), you'll get an even higher chance of retrieving stale data because of the asynchronous nature of the replication.

Summary

This chapter concludes our journey through the world of clustered applications. Here, we have shown the robust clustering features of JBoss AS applied to some basic examples, and ultimately to the Enterprise application introduced in Chapter 5.

The number of topics related to clustering might be expanded to cover a full book of its own; however, we decided to stress some features. In particular, we have learned about JBoss Cache — a key component of clustering in JBoss AS 5. This topic was further expanded to analyze Hibernate/JBoss Cache integration for second-level caching, which is one of the big improvements in the clustering area of JBoss AS 5.

In the next chapter, we will add the last piece of the puzzle that's missing in our Enterprise applications, JBossSX, the security framework.

13
JBoss AS Security

The prince who relies upon their words, without having otherwise provided for his security, is ruined – Niccoló Machiavelli (*The Prince*).

Today, networks provide a potential avenue of attack to any computer hooked to them and thus, security is a fundamental part of any Enterprise application. The Java platform was designed from the ground up with a strong emphasis on security. Its security APIs span a wide range of areas—interfaces for performing authentication and access control that protect applications against unauthorized access to protected resources, and cryptographic infrastructures that supply the underlying basis for developing secure applications.

A necessary preamble of this chapter will be an introduction to the **Java Security API** and how these interfaces are implemented in **JBoss Security Extension (JBossSX)**. Then, in the core section of the chapter, we will deliver:

- A systematic guide for configuring JBoss security domains that can be used for providing standard authentication and authorization
- The cryptographic interfaces and tools available in the Java SE to secure the communication between users and the application server

Approaching Java Security API

Java EE security services provide a robust and easily configured security mechanism for authenticating users and authorizing access to application functions and associated data.

Authentication is the process by which the user of an application (any type of Java program, including EJB, servlets, and so forth) is verified.

Authorization is about managing access to protected system resources based on the rights of a user or class of users. Authorization, therefore, assumes that authentication has occurred; otherwise it would be impossible to grant any access control if you don't know who the user is.

In Java EE, the component containers are responsible for providing application security. A container, basically, provides two types of security — **declarative** and **programmatic**. Let's see them:

- **Declarative security**: This expresses an application component's security requirements by means of deployment descriptors, whose information is contained in an external file, and can be changed without the need to modify the source code.

  For example, Enterprise JavaBeans components use an EJB deployment descriptor that must be named `ejb-jar.xml` and placed in the `META-INF` folder of the EJB JAR file.

  Web components use a web application deployment descriptor named `web.xml` located in the `WEB-INF` directory.

  Web Services components use a `jaxrpc-mapping-info.xml` deployment descriptor defined in JSR 109. This deployment descriptor provides deployment time mapping functionality between Java and WSDL and needs to be placed in the `META-INF` folder of your JAR file.

> Since Java EE 1.5 you can apply declarative security by means of **annotations**. Annotations are specified within a class file and, when the application is deployed, this information is translated internally by the Application Server.
>
> By using annotations, you are exempted from writing boilerplate useless code, as this can be generated by external tools from the source code. This leads to a declarative programming style, where the programmer says what should be done and tools emit the code to do it. It also eliminates the need for maintaining side files that must be kept up-to-date with changes in source files. Instead, the information is maintained in the source file.

- **Programmatic security**: This is embedded in an application and is used to make security decisions. It can be used when declarative security alone is not sufficient to express the security model of an application. The Java EE security API allows the developer to test whether the current user has access to a specific role using these calls:

  ° `isUserInRole()` for servlets, JSPs

  ° `isCallerInRole()` for EJBs

Additionally, there are other API calls that provide access to the user's identity:

- ° `getUserPrincipal()` for Servlets, JSPs
- ° `getCallerPrincipal()` for EJBs

Using these APIs, you can develop arbitrarily complex authorization models.

- **Annotation security** encompasses both the declarative and programmatic security concepts.

The JAAS security model

The framework that provides an API for the authentication and authorization of users is called **Java Authentication and Authorization Service (JAAS)**.

JAAS uses a **service provider** approach for its authentication features, meaning that it is possible to configure different login modules for an application without changing any code. The application remains unaware of the underlying authentication logic. It's even possible for an application to contain multiple login modules, somewhat like a stack of authentication procedures.

The **Login Module** is the key element of JAAS authentication, which is based on information provided through `CallbackHandler`. Custom login modules must implement the methods defined by the `javax.security.auth.spi.LoginModule` interface.

Clients interact with JAAS through a `LoginContext` object that provides a way to develop applications independent of the underlying authentication technology. The `LoginContext` class describes the methods used to authenticate subjects. A **Subject** is an identity in a system that you want to authenticate and assign access rights to.

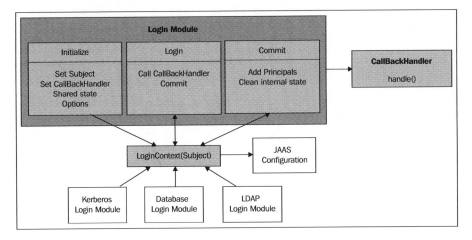

In the following example, a `LoginContext` is created by using the login module name as the first argument of the constructor and the callback handler as the second argument for passing login information to the **Login Module**.

Each **CallbackHandler** implements a `handle` method that transfers the required information to the **Login Module**. The `login` method in the `LoginContext` is used to start the login process. Following is a sample servlet that challenges the JAAS authentication process:

```
public class LoginServlet extends HttpServlet {
  public void doGet (HttpServletRequest req,
                     HttpServletResponse res)
    throws ServletException, IOException
  {
    PrintWriter out = res.getWriter();
    LoginContext ctx = null;
    try {
      ctx = new LoginContext("SampleLogin", new MyCallbackHandler());
    } catch(LoginException le) {
      throw new RuntimeException("Login failed!");
    }
    try {
      ctx.login();
    } catch(LoginException le) {
      throw new RuntimeException("Authentication failed!");
    }
    out.println("Authentication succeeded.");

  }
```

After its successful completion, LoginModules add instances of `java.security.Principal` to the **Subject**, and the application can retrieve the **Subject** from the `LoginContext` using the `getSubject()` method.

Introducing JBossSX

JBossSX uses **JAAS** as the underlying security infrastructure. The central point of JBossSX is the **SecurityDomain** that acts a bit like a customs office for foreigners. Before the request crosses JBoss AS borders, the SecurityDomain performs all the required authorization and authentication checks and eventually notifies the caller if he/she can proceed.

Security domains are generally configured at server startup and subsequently bound into the JNDI tree under the key `java:/jaas/`. The security service configuration is declared in the `server/xxx/deploy/security/security-jboss-beans.xml` file. This is the most relevant portion of it:

```
<bean name="XMLLoginConfig" class="org.jboss.security.auth.login.
XMLLoginConfig">
        <property name="configResource">login-config.xml</property>
</bean>

<bean name="SecurityConfig" class="org.jboss.security.plugins.
SecurityConfig">
        <property name="mbeanServer"><inject bean="JMXKernel" property="
mbeanServer"/></property>
        <property name="defaultLoginConfig"><inject
bean="XMLLoginConfig"/></property>
</bean>
```

The `org.jboss.security.plugins.SecurityConfig` bean handles the security service configuration, delegating the job of loading security policies to `XMLLoginConfig`. The property `configResource` of the `XMLLoginConfig` service contains a pointer to the configuration file for security policies, which is by default in `server/xxx/conf/login-config.xml`.

Instead of listing the whole login configuration file, we will summarize the default available login policies in the following table:

Application policy	Description
client-login	Used by clients within the application server VM such as MBeans and servlets that access EJBs
HsqlDbRealm	Security domains for testing the new JCA framework using the DefaultDS Factory name
JmsXARealm	Security domains for testing the new JCA framework using the JmsXA Factory name
jmx-console	Security domain for the JMX console
web-console	Security domain for the web console application
JBossWS	Security domain for the JBossWS framework
JMSRealm	Security domain for JMS
other	Login configuration used by any security domain that does not have an application-policy entry with a matching name

Securing the JMX console

The `jmx-console` security policy is a good starting point to learn about login modules. Seek for "jmx-console" in the `login-config.xml`:

```
<application-policy name = "jmx-console">
    <authentication>
        <login-module code="org.jboss.security.auth.spi.
UsersRolesLoginModule"
            flag = "required">
        <module-option name="usersProperties">props/jmx-console-
users.properties</module-option>
        <module-option name="rolesProperties">props/jmx-console-
roles.properties</module-option>
        </login-module>
    </authentication>
</application-policy>
```

As you can see, each security policy is made up of three main elements:

- `name`: This is the unique policy name for the security domain and it is directly referenced by applications that want to use the security domain.

- `code`: This is the login module class that will be used by the domain. Most security domains default to the `UsersRolesLoginModule` that verifies authentication against a simple property file.

- `module-options`: Depending on the login module selected in the `code` attribute, a list of options will be available to configure the security domain.

In order to switch on this security domain in the JMX console application you have to activate security constraints both on the standard `web.xml` file and on the JBoss-specific deployment descriptor (`jboss-web.xml`).

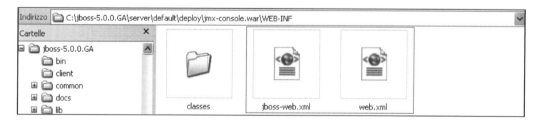

In `server\xxx\deploy\jmx-console.war\WEB-INF\web.xml`, uncomment the `security-constraint` block that restricts access to users with the role **JBossAdmin**:

```
<security-constraint>
  <web-resource-collection>
    <web-resource-name>HtmlAdaptor</web-resource-name>
    <description>An example security config that only allows users
with the
       role JBossAdmin to access the HTML JMX console web
application
    </description>
    <url-pattern>/*</url-pattern>
    <http-method>GET</http-method>
    <http-method>POST</http-method>
  </web-resource-collection>
  <auth-constraint>
    <role-name>JBossAdmin</role-name>
  </auth-constraint>
</security-constraint>
```

Then, in the same folder, modify the `jboss-web.xml` file by uncommenting the `security-domain` block.

```
<jboss-web>
    <security-domain>java:/jaas/jmx-console</security-domain>
</jboss-web>
```

The security domain value maps the application-policy name in the `login-config.xml` JAAS configuration file that defines how authentication and authorization are done.

As this security domain uses the `UsersRolesLoginModule`, you have to provide the users and roles allowed in two separate configuration files. As specified in the login module options, they are located in `server/default/conf/props/jmx-console-users.properties` and `server/default/conf/props/jmx-console-roles.properties`.

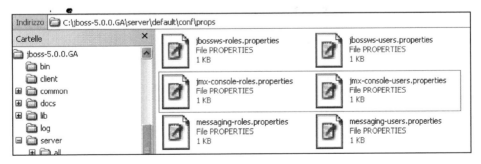

For example, if you want to set the combination of username/password to john/
smith, granting him the JBossAdmin role, here's the corresponding configuration:

```
#  users.properties file for use with the UsersRolesLoginModule
john=smith

# A sample roles.properties file for use with the
UsersRolesLoginModule
john=JBossAdmin
```

With this configuration, your JMX console will prompt for username and password,
which will be checked against the users and roles files.

The UserRolesLoginModule can be used for applications that don't have strict
security requirements; in real-world scenarios you would rather use a more
robust login module class. The following list, taken from JBoss AS documentation
(http://www.jboss.org/community/wiki/LoginModule), contains all the available
login modules, which can be assigned to your login policies:

Login module	Description
UsersRolesLoginModule	Loads user/role information from properties files.
DatabaseServerLoginModule	Loads user/role information from a database.
SimpleServerLoginModule	A testing login module that allows any role with a null password to authenticate.
IdentityLoginModule	A testing login module that causes all users to authenticate with the same credentials.
LdapLoginModule	Loads user/role information from an LDAP server.
LdapExtLoginModule	Loads user/role information from a hierarchical structure in an LDAP server.
BaseCertLoginModule	Authenticates client certificates; must be stacked with another login module that does authorization.
CertRolesLoginModule	An extension of BaseCertLoginModule that authenticates against client certificates and authorizes against properties files.
DatabaseCertLoginModule	An extension of BaseCertLoginModule that authenticates against client certificates and authorizes against a database.
RunAsLoginModule	Can be stacked with other login modules to define the <run-as>; status that they use while they are authenticating. Useful if you need to call a secured EJB that is responsible for authenticating users.

Login module	Description
SRPCacheLoginModule	Used to authenticate users using the **Secure Remote Password** (SRP) protocol.
SRPLoginModule	Used by standalone clients that want to authenticate using the SRP protocol.
ClientLoginModule	Used by standalone clients that want to login to a secure server (use with another LoginModule to perform client-side authentication).

An exhaustive explanation of all the individual login modules is beyond the scope of this book; however, in the next chapter we will show in detail how you can apply a **DatabaseServerLoginModule** to secure access to our AppStore application.

Dynamic login configuration

The JAAS login configuration introduced in the earlier section is static and needs a server restart each time you modify login-config.xml. You can pack a login module along with your application so that you will not need to modify any JBoss AS configuration file.

The traditional way to perform a dynamic login configuration is by means of the org.jboss.security.auth.login.DynamicLoginConfig MBean that loads the XML configuration at service startup and unloads it when the service is stopped. (See http://www.jboss.org/community/wiki/DynamicLoginConfig for a detailed explanation about this component.)

Since JBoss AS 5, a simpler solution is available that can be accessed using a Microcontainer configuration file. As an example, add the following jmxconsole-jboss-beans.xml to the \jmx-console.war\WEB-INF folder.

This file defines an alternative security policy (named "jmx-dynamic") for the JMX console:

```
<?xml version="1.0" encoding="UTF-8"?>

<deployment xmlns="urn:jboss:bean-deployer:2.0">

  <application-policy xmlns="urn:jboss:security-beans:1.0" name="jmx-dynamic">
    <authentication>
     <login-module code = "org.jboss.security.auth.spi.
UsersRolesLoginModule"
flag = "required">
```

```
        <module-option name = "unauthenticatedIdentity">anonymous</
module-option>
        <module-option name="usersProperties">u.properties</module-
option>
        <module-option name="rolesProperties">g.properties</module-
option>
      </login-module>
    </authentication>
  </application-policy>

  </deployment>
```

Now place the u.properties and g.properties configuration files at the
same level as that of the configuration file (or anywhere reachable by the web
application classpath).

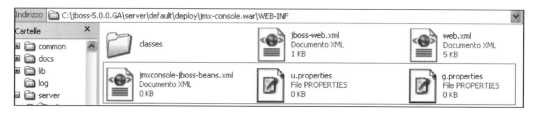

You don't need a server restart; just update your jboss-web.xml configuration file
so that it points to the new *dynamic* security domain:

```
<jboss-web>
      <security-domain>java:/jaas/jmx-dynamic</security-domain>
</jboss-web>
```

 The previously mentioned jmxconsole-jboss-beans.xml can be
added into the deploy folder of JBoss, thus making it available to all
applications requesting that security domain.

Finally, using dynamic login configuration you can add users and roles to
your security domain at any time and they will be picked up immediately from
the application server without server restart.

Stacked login configuration

If your authentication repository is not centralized into a single database, the previous configuration procedure might not be sufficient. For example, suppose that your username and password are stored in an **LDAP** server and the corresponding application roles are maintained into a relational database; how do you link the two things?

In this scenario, you have to configure which module allows authentication and which one needs to provide the supplemental roles.

Here's an example of a login module that uses LDAP as authentication repository and a database as role repository:

```
<application-policy name="stackedLogin">
    <authentication>
        <login-module code="org.jboss.security.auth.spi.
                    LdapLoginModule"
                    flag="required">
        <module-option name="password-stacking">
            useFirstPass</module-option>
        <module-option name="java.naming.factory.initial">
            com.sun.jndi.ldap.LdapCtxFactory </module-option>
        <module-option name="java.naming.provider.url">
            ldap://localhost/
        </module-option>
        <module-option name="java.naming.security.
                    authentication">
            simple
        </module-option>
        <module-option name="principalDNPrefix">
            uid=
        </module-option>
        <module-option name="principalDNSuffix">
            ,ou=People,o=jbossAsBook
        </module-option>
    </login-module>
    <login-module code="org.jboss.security.auth.spi.
                    DatabaseServerLoginModule"
        flag="required">
        <module-option name="password-stacking">useFirstPass
            </module-option>
        <module-option name="dsJndiName">java:/MySQLDS
            </module-option>
        <module-option name="rolesQuery">
```

```
            select role, 'Roles' from USER_ROLES where login=?
        </module-option>
    </login-module>
  </authentication>
</application-policy>
```

The magic trick here is done by the `password-stacking` option that is set to `useFirstPass`. In practice, it will first require authentication on the LDAP server and defer role querying to the next login module.

A possible alternative scenario can be depicted if both repositories can issue a complete authentication and role management. Imagine, for example, an application that can be executed both in the development environment and in the production environment, using a different relational database for storing credentials.

In this case, it is enough that **just one of the two repositories** completes the authentication process. What are the changes in our login module? You just have to skip the `password-stacking` option and mark each login module with the `sufficient` flag:

```
<!-Development environment
<login-module code=" org.jboss.security.auth.spi.
DatabaseServerLoginModule"
            flag="sufficient">
<!-Production environment
<login-module code="org.jboss.security.auth.spi.
DatabaseServerLoginModule"
            flag="sufficient">
```

Logging and auditing

The routine analysis and review of security logs benefits organizations by identifying fraudulent activity, operational problems, policy violations, and security incidents, as well as providing the necessary information to help resolve these problems. Logs can also be useful for establishing baseline activity, exposing long-term problems, performing auditing, and tracking operation trends.

By default, JBoss Application Server's `log4j` file (located in `server/xxx/conf/jboss-log4j.xml`) dumps some basic information about the **JaasSecurityManager** in the `server.log` file:

```
<category name="org.jboss.security.plugins.JaasSecurityManager.
jbossmq">
    <priority value="TRACE" class="org.jboss.logging.XLevel"></
priority>
</category>
```

You can further enrich the `server.log` by switching on Tomcat security logs:

```
<category name="org.jboss.web.tomcat.security">
        <priority value="TRACE" class="org.jboss.logging.XLevel"/>
</category>

<category name="org.apache.catalina">
        <priority value="DEBUG"/>
</category>
```

Auditing is a little different from the above logging categories because it covers a larger set of data; besides tracing successful/failed invocation of secured methods, it includes a great deal of information related to the *context* of your application. For example, if you are in the context of a web application, you might request a dump of objects such as cookies, headers, requests, and parameters.

In order to activate auditing, you first have at to uncomment the `log4j` **Audit appender**:

```
<appender name="AUDIT" class="org.jboss.logging.appender.
DailyRollingFileAppender">
. . . .
    </appender>
```

and then its corresponding **Category**:

```
<category name="org.jboss.security.audit.providers.
LogAuditProvider" additivity="false">
    <priority value="TRACE"/>
    <appender-ref ref="AUDIT"/>
</category>
```

The previous configuration will enable auditing for all EJB invocations. If you need to inspect the web tier, a few additional steps are required. First, add the attribute `enableAudit=true` in the `JBossWebRealm`, defined in the `deploy/jbossweb.sar/server.xml` file:

```
<Realm className="org.jboss.web.tomcat.security.JBossWebRealm"
certificatePrincipal="org.jboss.security.auth.certs.SubjectDNMapping"
allRolesMode="authOnly" enableAudit="true" />
```

Then, add in your JBoss startup script an argument that includes the objects we want to dump in the audit log file:

```
set JAVA_OPTS=%JAVA_OPTS% -Dorg.jboss.security.web.
audit=headers,cookies
```

Accepted parameters are:

Parameter	Description
off	Turn it off
headers	Audit the headers
cookies	Audit the cookie
parameters	Audit the parameters
attributes	Audit the attributes

Securing the transport layer

If you were to create a mission-critical application with just the bare concepts we have learned until now, you would not be guaranteed to be shielded from all security threats. For example, if you need to design a payment gateway, where the credit card information is transmitted by means of an EJB or Servlet, using just the Authorization and Authentication stack is really not enough.

In order to prevent disclosure of critical information to unauthorized individuals or systems, you have to use a protocol that provides encryption of the information. **Encryption** is the conversion of data into a form that cannot be understood by unauthorized people. Conversely, **decryption** is the process of converting encrypted data back into its original form, so it can be understood.

The protocols that are used to secure the communication are **SSL** and **TLS**, the latter being considered a replacement for the older SSL.

 The differences between the two protocols are minor and very technical. In short, TLS uses *stronger* encryption algorithms and has the ability to work on different ports. For the rest of our chapter we will refer to SSL for both protocols.

There are two basic techniques for encrypting information: **symmetric encryption** (also called secret key encryption) and **asymmetric encryption** (also called public key encryption.)

Symmetric encryption is the oldest and best-known technique. It is based on a secret key that is applied to the text of a message to change the content in a particular way. As long as both sender and recipient know the secret key, they can encrypt and decrypt all messages that use this key. These encryption algorithms typically work fast and are well suited for encrypting blocks of messages at once.

One significant issue with symmetric algorithms is the requirement of a safe administrative organization to distribute keys to users. This generally results in more overhead from the administrative aspect while the keys remain vulnerable to unauthorized disclosure and potential abuse.

For this reason, a mission-critical enterprise system usually relies on the asymmetric encryption algorithms, which tend to be easier to employ, manage, and ultimately more secure.

Asymmetric cryptography, also known as **public key cryptography**, is based on the concept that the key used to encrypt is not the same used to decrypt the message. In practice, each user holds a couple of keys— the **public key** that is distributed to other parties and the **private key** that is kept secret. Each message is encrypted with the **Recipient's Public Key** and can only be decrypted by the recipient with his/her private key (**Recipient's Private Key**).

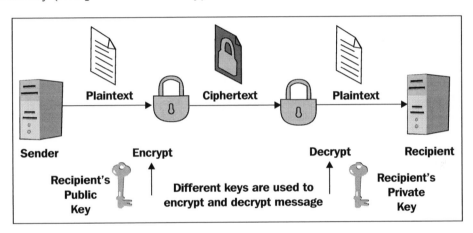

Using asymmetric encryption you can be sure that your message cannot be disclosed by a third party, however you *still* have one vulnerability.

Suppose you want to exchange some valuable information with a business partner and so you are requesting his public key by telephone or by e-mail. A fraudulent user intercepts your e-mail or simply listens to your conversation and quickly sends you a fake mail with his public key. Now, even if your data transmission is secured, it will be directed to the wrong person!

In order to solve this issue we need a document that verifies whether the public key belongs to an individual. This document is called a **Digital Certificate** or public key certificate. A digital certificate consists of a formatted block of data that contains the name of the certificate holder (which may be either a user or a system name) and the holder's public key, as well as the digital signature of a **Certification Authority (CA)** for authentication. The **Certification authority** attests that the sender's name is the one associated with the public key in the document.

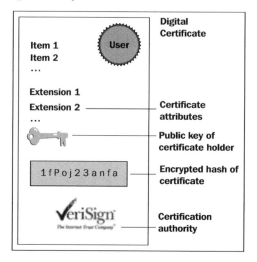

Public key certificates are commonly used for **secure interaction with websites**. By default, the web browser ships with a set of predefined CAs; they are used to verify that the public certificate served to your browser when you enter a secure site has been actually issued by the owner of the website. In short, if you connect your browser to https://www.abc.com and your browser doesn't give any certificate warning, then you can be sure to interact with the entity in charge of the site (unless the site or your browser has been hacked, but this is another story).

Simple authentication and client authentication

In the previous example, we have depicted a simple authentication (also called server authentication). In this scenario, the only party that needs to prove its identity is the server.

SSL, however, is able to perform a **mutual authentication** (also called client or two way authentication) where the server requests a client certificate during the SSL handshake over the network.

Client authentication requires a client certificate in **X.509** format from a CA. The X.509 format is an industry-standard format for SSL certificates. In the next section we will explore which are the available tools to generate digital certificates and how to have your certificates signed by a CA.

Enabling the Secure Socket Layer on JBoss AS

JBoss AS uses the **Java Secure Socket Extension** (JSSE) which is bundled in the J2SE to leverage the SSL/TLS communication.

An Enterprise application can be secured at two different locations—at HTTP level and RMI level. HTTP communication is handled, as we have learned, by the embedded Tomcat web container so the configuration changes are restricted to the Tomcat's `server.xml` file.

Securing the RMI transport is, on the other hand, not always a compelling requirement of your applications: Actually, in most production environments, **JBoss AS** is placed behind a **Firewall**. As you can see in the following screenshot; this implies that your EJBs are not directly exposed to untrusted networks, which usually connect through the Web Server placed in a *demilitarized* zone.

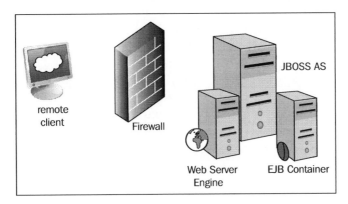

However, if your application grants access to Java SE clients or to any application that *directly* connects to JBoss AS through RMI, then you need to enable your RMI socket factories to support SSL.

In order to get started with JBoss AS and SSL we need, first of all, a tool that generates a public key/private key pair in the form of an X.509 certificate for use by the SSL server sockets.

Certificate management tools

One tool that can be used to set up a digital certificate is **keytool**, a key and certificate management utility that ships with the Java SE. It enables users to administer their own public/private key pairs and associated certificates for use in self-authentication (where the user authenticates himself or herself to other users or services) or data integrity and authentication services, using digital signatures. It also allows users to cache the public keys (in the form of certificates) of their communicating peers.

The `keytool` stores the keys and certificates in a file termed a `keystore`, a repository of certificates used for identifying a client or a server. Typically, a keystore contains one client or one server's identity, which is protected by using a password. Let's see an example of keystore generation:

```
keytool -genkey -keystore jboss.keystore -storepass mypassword
-keypass mypassword -keyalg RSA -validity 180  -alias jbossbook
-dname "cn=Francesco Marchioni,o=PacktPub,c=GB"
```

This command creates the keystore named `jboss.keystore` in the working directory, and assigns it the password `mypassword`. It generates a public/private key pair for the entity whose "distinguished name" has a common name of `Francesco Marchioni`, organization of "*PacktPub*" and two-letter country code of `GB`.

The aftermath of this action will be a **self-signed** certificate (using the RSA signature algorithm) that includes the public key and the distinguished name information. This certificate will be valid for 180 days, and is associated with the private key in a keystore entry referred to by the alias `jbossbook`.

 A **self-signed certificate** is a certificate that has not been not verified by a CA and thus leaves you vulnerable to the classic **man-in-the-middle** attack. A self-signed certificate is only suitable for in-house use or for testing while you wait for your real one to arrive

Securing the HTTP communication with a self-signed certificate

Now let's see how you can use this keystore file to secure your JBoss web channel. Open the `server.xml` file located in `server\xxxx\deploy\jbossweb.sar`.

Uncomment the following section and update the `keystoreFile` and `keyStorePass` information with data from your certificate.

```
<Connector protocol="HTTP/1.1" SSLEnabled="true"
        port="8443" address="${jboss.bind.address}"
        secure="true" clientAuth="false"
            keystoreFile="${jboss.server.home.dir}/conf/jboss.
keystore"
            keystorePass="mypassword" keyAlias="jbossbook"
            sslProtocol="TLS" />
```

You have to restart JBoss AS to activate changes. You should see at the bottom of your console the following log that informs you about the new HTTPS channel running on port 8443:

13:21:49,915 INFO [Http11Protocol] Starting Coyote HTTP/1.1 on http-127.0.0.1-8443

The following screen is what will be displayed by the Internet Explorer browser if you try to access any web application on the secured channel:

```
https://localhost:8443/jmx-console
```

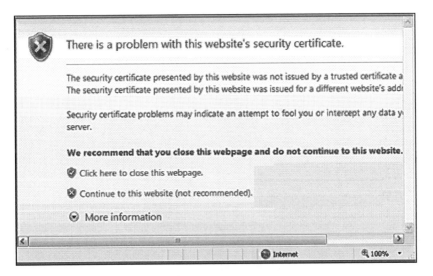

Now that you have established a secure connection with the Web Server, the server certificate has been sent to the browser. As the certificate has not been signed by any recognized CA, the browser security sandbox warns the user about the potential security threat.

This is an in-house test so we can safely proceed to JBoss AS JMX console by choosing **Continue to this website**. That's all you need to do in order to activate the Secure Socket Layer with a self-signed certificate.

Securing the HTTP communication with a certificate signed by a CA

Having your certificate signed requires issuing a **Certificate Signing Request (CSR)** to a CA that will return a signed certificate to be installed on your server. This implies a cost for your organization, which depends on how many certificates you are requesting, the encryption strength and other factors (at the time of writing the cost ranges from a minimum of around $200 to a maximum of $1300 per certificate).

So, first generate a **CSR** using the newly create `keystore` and `keyentry`:

```
keytool -certreq -keystore jboss.keystore -alias jbossbook -storepass
mypassword -keypass mypassword  -keyalg RSA  -file certreq.csr
```

This will create a new certificate request named `certreq.csr`, bearing the format:

```
-----BEGIN NEW CERTIFICATE REQUEST-----
. . . . . .
-----END NEW CERTIFICATE REQUEST-----
```

The preceding certificate needs to be transmitted to the CA. For example supposing you have chosen Verisign as CA:

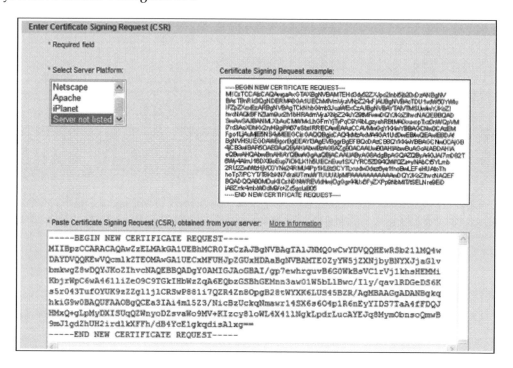

At the end of the enrollment phase, the CA will return a signed certificate that needs to be imported into your keychain. Supposing that you have saved your CA certificate in a file named `signed_ca.txt`:

```
keytool -import -keystore jboss.keystore -alias testkey1 -storepass
mypassword -keypass mypassword -file signed_ca.txt
```

Now your web browser will recognize your new certificate as being signed by a CA, so it won't complain that it cannot validate the certificate.

The command interface for keytool changed in Java SE 6.

Some commands have simply been renamed, and other commands deemed obsolete are no longer listed in Java SE documentation. The obsolete commands are, however, still supported in this release and will continue to be supported in future releases. The following summarizes all of the changes made to the keytool command interface:

Renamed commands:

`-export`, renamed to `-exportcert`

`-genkey`, renamed to `-genkeypair`

`-import`, renamed to `-importcert`

Securing the RMI transport

Remote Method Invocation (RMI) is the basis for EJB transport. With JSSE working and a keystore with the certificate you will use for the JBoss application server, you are ready to configure JBoss AS to use SSL for EJB access.

The first step to secure the RMI transport is creating an SSL-aware security domain. For this purpose, we need to use `org.jboss.security.plugins.JaasSecurityDomain`, an extension of the `JaasSecurityManager`, which adds the notion of a keystore, along with JSSE `KeyManagerFactory` and `TrustManagerFactory` for supporting SSL and other cryptographic use cases.

The following MBean definition creates a domain named `SSLDomain` that points to the `keystore` we created earlier. (The keystore file is searched for through the server classpath, with the `conf` folder being the first directory scanned.)

```
<mbean code="org.jboss.security.plugins.JaasSecurityDomain"
        name="jboss.security:service=JaasSecurityDomain,domain=SSLDo
main">
    <constructor>
        <arg type="java.lang.String" value="SSLDomain"/>
    </constructor>
    <attribute name="KeyStoreURL">jboss.keystore</attribute>
    <attribute name="KeyStorePass">mypassword</attribute>
</mbean>
```

The preceding file needs to be placed in the `deploy` folder of your server, using the `xxx-service.xml` filename pattern.

The next step will be performed on the protocol transport, which is handled by the JBoss Remoting framework. **JBoss Remoting** is a standalone project that enables you to very easily design, implement, and deploy services that can be remotely invoked by clients using several different transport mechanisms transparently. In practice, every different protocol is wrapped by an interface named **Invoker** that is used by the Remoting framework to build the full stack required to send and receive remote invocations.

By default EJB uses a standard socket-based invoker as defined in `ejb3-connectors-jboss-beans.xml`.

```
<bean name="org.jboss.ejb3.RemotingConnector"
    class="org.jboss.remoting.transport.Connector">
. . . .
            <parameter>socket://${jboss.bind.address}:${port}</
parameter>
          . . . .
    </bean>
```

All you need to do is add another transport invoker that will be used for secured EJB communication:

```
<mbean code="org.jboss.remoting.transport.Connector"
          name="jboss.remoting:type=Connector,transport=sslsocket3843,
handler=ejb3">
        <attribute name="InvokerLocator">sslsocket://${jboss.bind.
address}:3843</attribute>
        <attribute name="Configuration">
          <config>
           <handlers>
             <handler subsystem="AOP">org.jboss.aspects.remoting.
AOPRemotingInvocationHandler</handler>
           </handlers>
          </config>
        </attribute>
</mbean>
```

The preceding MBean definition adds a new Remoting connector using the `sslsocket` protocol. You can merge this MBean definition with the `JaasSecurityDomain` MBean into a single `deploy/ssl-service.xml`.

The server configuration is almost completed. We need to set up just a couple of server properties that contain a reference to the server `keystore` and `password`. Open the startup script and add the following properties to your "JAVA_OPTS":

```
-Djavax.net.ssl.keyStore=../server/default/conf/jboss.keystore -
Djavax.net.ssl.keyStorePassword=mypassword
```

Adding a client truststore

Now the server is configured to communicate through a secure channel. However, as it is, the SSL handshake will not complete successfully. This is because of the fact that as soon the server replies using its certificate (containing the server's public key), the client will fail to authenticate as the certificate wasn't verified against a list of known CAs.

You have two available options to solve this issue:

- Import the server certificate into the client's JDK bundle of certificates.
- Create a new repository of certificates trusted by the client (truststore).

Whatever your choice is, you first have to *export* your server `keytool` into a **truststore** that will be used by the client. This can be achieved using the `export` option of the `keytool` command:

```
keytool -export -alias jbossbook -file rmissl.cer -keystore jboss.
keystore -storepass mypassword
```

What is the difference between a keystore and a truststore?

JSSE differentiates between regular keystores and truststores. A **keystore** consists of a database containing a private key and an associated certificate, or an associated certificate chain. The certificate chain consists of the client certificate and one or more Certification Authority (CA) certificates.

A **truststore** contains only the certificates trusted by the client (a "trust" store). These certificates are CA root certificates, that is, self-signed certificates.

Adjust the path of the JDK with the one used by your Java environment. (Notice, the default password of JDK keystore is "changeit".)

```
keytool -import -alias myserver -file rmissl.cer -keystore C:/jdk1.6.0_
10/jre/lib/security/cacerts
```

Otherwise, if you want to *import* the certificate into a newly created truststore, just substitute the `cacerts` destination with your client truststore (that will be created):

```
keytool -import -alias jbossbook -file rmissl.cer -keystore jboss.
truststore -storepass mypassword
Owner: CN=Francesco Marchioni, O=PackPub, C=UK
Issuer: CN=Francesco Marchioni, O=PackPub, C=UK
    Serial number: 4a93f927
```

```
    Valid from: Tue Aug 25 16:18:29 CEST 2009 until: Sun Feb 21 15:18:29
CET 2010
    Certificate fingerprints:
        MD5:   10:80:BF:7D:2B:18:85:60:B5:31:01:59:AC:A9:CA:72
        SHA1: B0:A3:19:12:57:D7:4D:DF:A2:AF:56:2F:78:ED:FB:F0:B6:6E:6B:AC
    Trust this certificate? [no]:  yes
    Certificate was added to keystore
```

A last note—if you choose the latter option, you need to add to your client's JDK arguments the following properties, which will override the default JDK truststore:

```
java -Djavax.net.ssl.trustStore=<truststorefile>
     -Djavax.net.ssl.trustStorePassword=<password>
```

Summary

This chapter has introduced you to the Java Security framework and its JBossSX implementation. Security is a broad topic and it demands more than a single chapter for a detailed description. This chapter answered the most common questions related to the server configuration by explaining how to create login modules, self-signed and CA certificates as well as other core security topics.

In the next chapter, we will again look at security, but from the perspective of the developer; specifically, we will be learning how to secure the HTTP and EJB layer of our AppStore application and, as well, a Web Service application.

14
Securing JBoss AS Applications

The problem with designing something completely foolproof is to underestimate the ingenuity of a complete fool. – D. Adams, *The Hitchhiker's Guide to the Galaxy.*

One of the most striking claims of Java is the secure programming language that it provides. However, few people understand how to write secure applications correctly. This is because it requires a comprehensive and technical background. In this chapter, we will continue our in-depth exploration, providing concrete examples of secure programming, which can be an excellent resource for developers as well as system administrators who are interested in mastering JBoss security framework.

In this chapter, we will cover how to:

- Apply authentication policies to web applications and EJB middle tier
- Encrypt their HTTP and RMI data transmission
- Secure Web Services

Securing the AppStore application

We initially designed our AppStore application as a single node Enterprise. Later in Chapter 12, we upgraded it as a clustered application. The only thing missing now is an adequate security infrastructure for it.

Before planning security, you have to analyze what exactly needs to be secured. For example, the AppStore application was made up of a JSF frontend layer and an EJB middle tier that consisted of a session bean and two entity beans.

In such a scenario, if you don't plan to directly expose the EJB layer to your clients, then it's usually enough to apply security only on the HTTP layer, which is the only point reachable by untrusted entities. On the other hand, if chances are that your middle tier will be available straight to your clients, then you have to apply security at this level too. Let's start by creating an access control list to the AppStore web layer; later we will analyze how to secure EJB access.

HTTP role authentication

In the last chapter, we learned that user authentication can be configured by adding a login module in your `server\default\conf\login-config.xml` file.

Let's assume that our company's security policy expects to store the user's credentials on a relational database. So, we will add the following module to the `login-config.xml` file.

```
<application-policy name="mysqlLogin">
  <authentication>
    <login-module
      code="org.jboss.security.auth.spi.DatabaseServerLoginModule"
        flag="required">
      <module-option name="dsJndiName">java:/MySqlDS
      </module-option>
      <module-option name="principalsQuery">
        select passwd from USERS where login=?
      </module-option>
      <module-option name="rolesQuery">
        select role, 'Roles' from USER_ROLES where login=?
      </module-option>
    </login-module>
  </authentication>
</application-policy>
```

This module uses the `org.jboss.security.auth.spi.DatabaseServerLoginModule` that is configured here to store users in the USERS table and roles in the USER_ROLES table.

The module relies on the datasource named `MySqlDS`, which we have configured earlier. To get working with this configuration, you have to first create the required tables and insert some sample data into them.

```
CREATE TABLE USERS(login VARCHAR(64) PRIMARY KEY, passwd VARCHAR(64))
CREATE TABLE USER_ROLES(login VARCHAR(64), role VARCHAR(32))
INSERT into USERS values('admin', 'admin')
INSERT into USER_ROLES values('admin', 'TheBoss')
```

Here we have defined just one user account as admin/admin, which maps to the role name TheBoss. The server configuration is complete. Restart JBoss AS and check that the new login module has been correctly registered in the JNDI tree under the java:/jaas context.

Let's move on to the application configuration. Open the web application configuration (web.xml) and add the following <security-constraints> block:

```
<web-app>
  <security-constraint>
  <web-resource-collection>
    <web-resource-name>HtmlAdaptor</web-resource-name>
    <description>AppStore security constraints
    </description>
    <url-pattern>/*</url-pattern>
    <http-method>GET</http-method>
    <http-method>POST</http-method>
  </web-resource-collection>
  <auth-constraint>
    <role-name>TheBoss</role-name>
  </auth-constraint>
</security-constraint>
  <login-config>
    <auth-method>BASIC</auth-method>
    <realm-name>AppStore Realm</realm-name>
  </login-config>
  <security-role>
    <role-name>TheBoss</role-name>
  </security-role>
</web-app>
```

Security constraints are a declarative way to define the protection of web content. A security constraint is used to define access privileges to a collection of resources using their URL mapping.

As shown in the previous example, a security constraint is composed of several elements.

- web-resource-collection: A web resource collection is a list of URL patterns and HTTP operations describing a set of resources to be protected. In our example, we are restricting access to all resources using GET and POST HTTP methods.

- `auth-constraint`: An authorization constraint establishes a requirement for authentication and names the roles authorized to access the URL patterns and HTTP methods declared by this security constraint. In our example, the only role authorized to access the URL patterns is the `TheBoss` role. The wildcard character (*) can be used here as well to specify all role names defined in the deployment descriptor.

- `login-config`: This element specifies the authorization method to be used by the web application. It can contain the following methods:

    ◦ **Basic authentication**: Relies on the web server for authentication to protected areas. The username and password combination is then encoded (base 64) and passed in an unencrypted form to the web server. The web server compares the encoded value against values stored in a flat file, a database, or a directory server.

    ◦ **Form-based authentication**: Allows you to control the look and feel of the login page. Form-based authentication works like basic authentication, except that you specify a login page that is displayed, instead of a dialog, and an error page that's displayed if login fails.

    ◦ **Digest authentication**: Indicates that the web server expects digest authentication. A digest authentication requires computing a hash value of the user's password. However, this requires a repository in clear text where passwords are stored. This is rarely the case in most Enterprise environments, so this has not been widely adopted.

- `security-role`: The last element lists all of the security roles used in the application. In our example, there's only one role named `TheBoss`.

We're done with `web.xml`. The last configuration tweak needs to be performed on the JBoss web deployment descriptor: `WEB-INF/jboss-web.xml`. There you need to declare the security domain that will be used to authenticate the users. The `security-domain` name matches the `application-policy` name attribute, `mysqlLogin`, defined in the `login-config.xml` file. Provide the full JNDI name of the resource, as in the following example:

```
<jboss-web>
  <security-domain>java:/jaas/mysqlLogin</security-domain>
</jboss-web>
```

The following diagram summarizes the relation between server configuration files and web deployment descriptors:

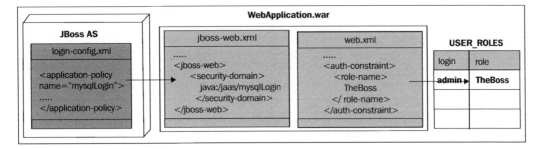

Now redeploy your application and surf on the initial page:
`http://localhost:8080/AppStoreWeb`. The outcome of this action should be a blocking pop up, requesting user authentication.

Logging in with **admin/admin** will grant access to the application.

Encrypting passwords

Storing passwords in the database as clear text strings is not considered a good practice. As a matter of fact, a database has even more potential security holes than a regular file system—for example, a database administrator who added a public synonym for some tables, forgetting that one of those tables was holding sensitive information like application passwords! You therefore need to be sure that no potential attackers will ever be able to deliver the result shown in the following screenshot:

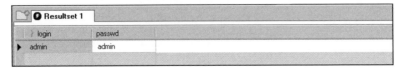

Fortunately, securing application passwords is relatively easy. You can add a few extra options to your login module, specifying that the stored passwords are encrypted using a **message digest algorithm**. For example, in the `mysqlLogin` module, you should add the following options at the bottom:

```
<application-policy name="mysqlLogin ">
  <authentication>
    <login-module
      code="org.jboss.security.auth.spi.DatabaseServerLoginModule"
      flag="required">
    <module-option name="hashAlgorithm">MD5</module-option>
    <module-option name="hashEncoding">BASE64</module-option>
    </login-module>
  </authentication>
</application-policy>
```

Here we have specified that the password will be hashed against a **Message-Digest algorithm 5 (MD5)**, which is a widely used cryptographic hash function with a 128-bit hash value. You can alternatively use any other algorithm such as **Secure Hash Algorithm (SHA)** allowed by your JCA provider.

For the sake of completeness, we include a small application here, which uses the `java.security.MessageDigest` to provide the functionality of a message digest algorithm and the `org.jboss.security.Base64Util` class to generate the base-64 hashed password to be inserted in the database.

```
public class Hash {
  public static void main(String[] args) {
    String password = args[0];
    MessageDigest md = null;
    try
    {
      md = MessageDigest.getInstance("MD5");
    }
    catch(Exception e)
    {
      e.printStackTrace();
    }
    byte[] passwordBytes = password.getBytes();
    byte[] hash = md.digest(passwordBytes);
    String passwordHash = org.jboss.security.Base64Utils.tob64(hash);
    System.out.println("password hash: "+passwordHash);
  }
}
```

So, here's what the attacker would display if he or she gained access to our database:

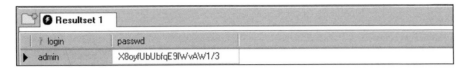

EJB role authorization

In the previous example, we have secured our AppStore application by restricting access to authenticated users by means of a login form. This is a good starting point and may be all that you need for simple applications; nevertheless you can further refine your security policies by selecting which methods are restricted and which are not.

One vast area of improvement in EJB 3.0 concerns the declarative security. You can check if the authenticated **principal** is authorized to execute a single method by simply adding an annotation on top of it. There are five annotations available, which are as follows:

- `@org.jboss.ejb3.annotation.SecurityDomain`: Specifies the security domain that is associated with the class/method.

- `@javax.annotation.security.RolesAllowed`: Specifies the list of roles permitted to access method(s) in an application.

- `@javax.annotation.security.RunAs`: Assigns a role dynamically to the EJB during the invocation of the method. Can be used in cases such as if we need to allow a temporary permission to access certain methods.

- `@javax.annotation.security.PermitAll`: Specifies that an EJB can be invoked by any client. The purpose of this annotation is to widen security access to some methods, in situations where you don't know what role will access the EJB. (Imagine that some modules have been developed by a third party and they access your EJB with some not well-identified roles.)

- `@javax.annotation.security.DenyAll`: Specifies that an EJB cannot be invoked by external clients. The same considerations apply as for `@PermitAll`.

So, if we want to restrict access to all `StoreManagerBean`'s methods to the authorized role `TheBoss`, it can be done as follows:

```
@Stateless
@SecurityDomain("mysqlLogin")
@RolesAllowed( { "TheBoss" })
public class StoreManagerBean implements StoreManager {
}
```

Be careful! There is a more than one `SecurityDomain` class in Java EE packages. As just mentioned in the list, you have to include `org.jboss.ejb3.annotation.SecurityDomain`.

As we have granted this role in the login stage, we should not have any problem executing the EJB methods from the web application. If you are not satisfied with this approach, you can apply the annotations individually before each method. For example, if we need a special role named `SuperUser` for inserting a new customer, then we will tag the method as follows:

```
@RolesAllowed( { "SuperUser" })
public void createCustomer(String country,String name) {
  Customer customer = new Customer();
  customer.setCountry(country);
  customer.setName(name);
  em.persist(customer);
}
```

You should update the database by adding the entries for the new `SuperUser` role:

```
INSERT into USERS values('guru', 'guru')
INSERT into USER_ROLES values('guru', 'SuperUser')
```

After adding the additional role `SuperUser`, your `web.xml` file appears as follows:

```
<web-app>
  <security-constraint>
    <web-resource-collection>
    </web-resource-collection>
    <auth-constraint>
      <role-name>TheBoss</role-name>
    </auth-constraint>
    <auth-constraint>
      <role-name>SuperUser</role-name>
    </auth-constraint>
  </security-constraint>
  <login-config>.
  </login-config>
  <security-role>
    <role-name>TheBoss</role-name>
  </security-role>
  <security-role>
    <role-name>SuperUser</role-name>
  </security-role>
</web-app>
```

What if you don't want to use annotations for establishing security roles? Suppose you have a security role that is used crosswise by all your EJB, and perhaps it is simpler to use plain old XML configuration instead of tagging all EJB with annotations. In this scenario, you have to first declare the security constraints in the generic META-INF/ejb-jar.xml file.

```
<method-permission>
  <role-name>TheBoss</role-name>
  <method>
    <ejb-name>*</ejb-name>
    <method-name>*</method-name>
  </method>
</method-permission>
```

Then, inside the META_INF/jboss.xml configuration file, just add a reference to your security domain, as follows:

```
<jboss>
  <security-domain>mysqlLogin</security-domain>
</jboss>
```

Here's a snapshot summarizing the EJB role configuration:

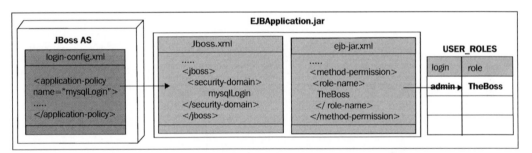

Java EE programmatic security

With the configuration just discussed, we have secured our application without writing a single line of code. If your security policy is quite complex and cannot be fully expressed with a declarative approach, then you can switch to programmatic security. Java EE programmatic security will not be discussed in detail here, as it's not a JBoss-specific topic; however, we will give some useful advice about it.

In short, using programmatic security, you exploit **EJB context variables** to check dynamically whether a user is authorized to execute a method. If you don't want to mix the security constraints with business rules, then a good place to add programmatic security is inside **EJB interceptors**. We have already used the `MailInterceptor` earlier in Chapter 4; a secure version of it would verify in the `checkMail` method whether the user is granted the role to send a mail.

```
public class MailInterceptor {
  @Resource SessionContext context;
  @AroundInvoke
  public Object checkMail(InvocationContext ctx) throws Exception
  {
    if (!context isCallerInRole("admin")) {
    throw new SecurityException("Unauthorized user!");
    try
    {
      return ctx.proceed();
    }
    catch(Exception e)
    {
      throw e;
    }
  }
}
```

Notice that in the first highlighted line, we are injecting a reference to the `SessionContext` by means of the `Resource` annotation. The `SessionContext` is used to provide access to several container services such as transaction or security. In our example, we are using its `isCallerInRole` method to check for a specific role in the running thread.

As you can see, adding programmatic security to individual resources gives you the finest-grained control over access to those resources. It can be extended to the web tier as well, by using the following methods of the `HttpRequest` object:

*   `request.isUserInRole("admin");`
*   `request.getUserPrincipal();`

Writing secure Java SE clients

Java EE authentication and authorization can be performed at any tier. Until now, we have shielded our application with an HTTP login module that grants application roles. What about Java SE clients? Standard Java clients can exploit plain Java Authentication and Authorization Service standard API or they can use a JBoss custom solution.

Using JAAS is recommended for ensuring portable applications. However, JAAS is rather invasive to implement, as it requires the creation of a `CallbackHandler` class and lots of boilerplate code in your client. Actually, JBoss AS provides a proprietary solution based on the `org.jboss.security.client.SecurityClient` class and the associated `SecurityClientFactory`.

In the simplest form, the `SecurityClient` once created invokes the `setSimple` method passing the user credentials, which are stored as `ThreadLocal` variables when you invoke the `login` method:

```
SecurityClient client = SecurityClientFactory.getSecurityClient();
client.setSimple("admin", "admin");
client.login();
```

As we don't reference any JBoss AS security policy using this strategy, the EJB client will switch to the `other` login policy, which is used as a last option security domain. So all we have to do is provide an `other` security definition that uses an appropriate client login module:

```
other {
   org.jboss.security.ClientLoginModule required;
};
```

The `org.jboss.security.ClientLoginModule` is an implementation of a `LoginModule` used by JBoss clients for the establishment of the caller identity and credentials. The above configuration needs to be stored in an `auth.conf` file whose directory is included into the client classpath.

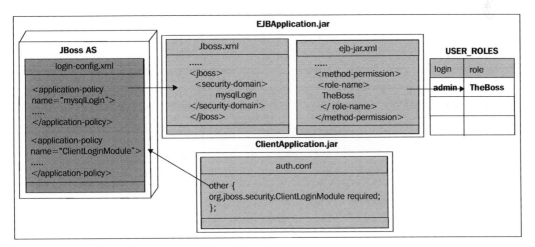

Note that this login module does not perform any authentication. It merely copies the login information provided to it into the JBoss server EJB invocation layer for subsequent authentication on the server. If you need to perform client-side authentication of users, you would need to configure another login module in addition to the `ClientLoginModule`.

The `SecurityClient` class can also be configured to use JAAS with the `SecurityClient`. As we said, this approach requires creating a `CallBackHandler` class that is used to retrieve authentication information (such as usernames, passwords, and so on) interactively.

```
SecurityClient client = SecurityClientFactory.getSecurityClient();
client.setJAAS("security-policy", new JAASCallBackHandler("admin","ad
min"));
client.login();
```

In this case, we are checking the user credentials against the security domain `security-policy`. The policy will also be declared in an `auth.conf` file.

```
security-policy {
  org.jboss.security.ClientLoginModule required;
};
```

The above example needs a `CallBackHandler` class that implements the `handle` method as shown in the following code snippet:

```
import java.io.IOException;
import javax.security.auth.callback.*;
public class JAASCallBackHandler implements CallbackHandler {
  private String user,pass;
  public JAASCallBackHandler(String user, String pass) {
    this.user = user;
    this.pass = pass;
  }
  public void handle(Callback[] callbacks) throws IOException,
    UnsupportedCallbackException {
    int len = callbacks.length;
    Callback cb;
    for(int i=0;i<len;i++) {
      cb = callbacks[i];
      if(cb instanceof NameCallback) {
        NameCallback ncb = (NameCallback)cb;
      ncb.setName(user);
      }
```

```
    else
      if (cb instanceof PasswordCallback) {
        PasswordCallback pcb = (PasswordCallback)cb;
        pcb.setPassword(pass.toCharArray());
      }
      else {
        throw new UnsupportedCallbackException(cb, "Don't know what
        to do with this!!");
      }
    }
  }
}
```

Securing applications at transport level

Authentication and authorization is only one aspect of security. Any application that communicates through a clear text channel with its customers is potentially unsafe. For example, it's not only possible to capture a session cookie reading the HTTP header, but also possible to change a financial transaction by hacking the application context.

In the following sections, we will describe how to secure an application at transport level, starting from the HTTP protocol and then moving to the RMI transport layer.

Running the AppStore with HTTPS

Your AppStore application communicates with its client through clear text HTTP protocol. In order to take advantage of secure connections, you have to configure your JBoss Web Server with an associated certificate for each external interface (IP address) that accepts secure connections. The certificate states which company the site is associated with, along with some basic contact information about the site owner or administrator.

A self-signed certificate can be created with the keytool command utility; we will briefly summarize here what we have learned in the previous chapter:

```
keytool -genkey -keystore jboss.keystore -storepass mypassword -
keypass mypassword -keyalg RSA -validity 180  -alias jbossbook -dname
"cn=Francesco Marchioni,o=PackPub,c=GB"
```

Here we have created a new public/private key pair and wrapped the keys into a keystore named jboss.keystore using the alias jbossbook and the key algorithm RSA.

Then update your `server\xxx\deploy\jbossweb.sar\server.xml` with the information about the keystore just created:

```
<Connector protocol="HTTP/1.1" SSLEnabled="true"
  port="8443" address="${jboss.bind.address}"
  secure="true" clientAuth="false"
  keystoreFile="${jboss.server.home.dir}/conf/jboss.keystore"
  keystorePass="mypassword" keyAlias="jbossbook" sslProtocol="TLS" />
```

With this configuration, your web connection will take place over a secure channel, even if by means of a self-signed certificate. Here's a trace of the HTTP and HTTPS data transmission:

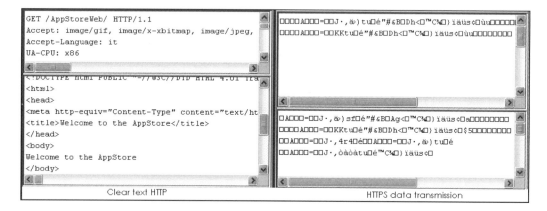

Clear text HTTP | HTTPS data transmission

If you want to get rid of the certificate warning, you have to install a certificate on your server signed by a recognized CA. Please refer to the previous chapter for a detailed explanation about it.

Securing the RMI-IIOP transport: SSL BlackJack

EJB clients interact with the Enterpirse EJB tier using the **RMI-IIOP** protocol. The RMI-IIOP protocol has been developed by Sun to combine the RMI programming model with the IIOP underlying transport.

Securing the EJB transport is required for applications that are accessible by Java SE clients. Earlier in this book we illustrated a sample **BlackJack** SFSB that is reachable by a Java client. Assuming that your SFSB is the core component of a virtual casino, you wouldn't be safe with a clear text transmission. Let's make it rock-solid safe.

Your server checklist requires you to deploy the `ssl-service.xml` that contains the **JaasSecurityDomain MBean** definition along with an **SSL transport invoker** that will be used for secured EJB communication.

You can place this file either in the `deploy` folder of your JBoss AS or in the `META-INF` directory of your application, as shown in the following screenshot:

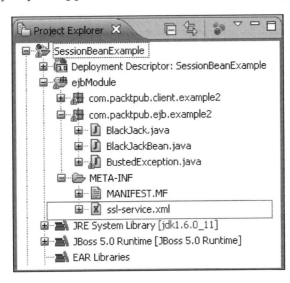

Then, at application level, you can reference your SSL transport by adding the element `clientBindURL` to your JNDI binding annotation.

```
@Stateful
@RemoteBindings(
   {
      @RemoteBinding(jndiBinding="BlackJack/remote"),
      @RemoteBinding(clientBindUrl="sslsocket://127.0.0.1:3843",
         jndiBinding="BlackJackSSL/remote")
   }
)
public class BlackJackBean implements BlackJack {
}
```

As you can see, the `BlackJackBean` now contains an array of bindings; the first one allows plain RMI-IIOP communication, while the second element references the SSL transport through the `clientBindUrl` property.

At the client level, you would need to reference the `BlackJackSSL/remote` binding to carry on a secure RMI-IIOP transmission:

```
Context ctx = new InitialContext();
BlackJack b = (BlackJack) ctx.lookup("BlackJackSSL/remote");
```

This is all that is needed to secure your EJB communication. Remember that your client needs to be started with either of the following properties:

```
java -Djavax.net.ssl.trustStore=<truststorefile>
  -Djavax.net.ssl.trustStorePassword=<password>
```

Or, if you prefer, by importing the server certificate into the client repository of certificates (also known as CAcert):

```
keytool -import -alias myserver -file rmissl.cer -keystore
  C:/jdk1.6.0_10/jre/lib/security/cacerts
```

Securing Web Services

Security is a key element of every Enterprise application, but in the recent years it has become even more important for Web Services. The reasons for all this hype on the Web Service security is due to the fact that the exposure of Web Services is rapidly moving from secure intranets to the insecure Internet. In addition, the kind of business around these services is often engaged without any prior human relationship, leaving all security issues to be addressed by the underlying technology.

Released by the **OASIS** consortium in 2004, the **Web Services Security (WS-Security)** specification (`http://www.oasis-open.org/committees/tc_home.php?wg_abbrev=wss`) provides a set of mechanisms to help developers of Web Services to secure **Simple Object Access Protocol (SOAP)** message exchanges. Specifically, WS-Security describes enhancements to the existing SOAP messaging to provide quality of protection through the application of message integrity, message confidentiality, and single message authentication to SOAP messages. These basic mechanisms can be combined in various ways to accommodate a wide variety of security models using a variety of cryptographic technologies.

In the following section, we will first describe how JAAS authentication can be applied to POJO and EJB Web Services. We will then illustrate how the SOAP messages can be encrypted and eventually signed using the WS-Security API.

Web Services authorization

Web Services authorization can basically be carried out in two ways, depending on whether we are dealing with a POJO-based Web Service or an EJB that exposes some of its methods as Web Services.

Changes to POJO Web Services are quite intuitive. You have to provide the required roles in the web.xml configuration file. For example, in the CalculatePowerService demonstrated in Chapter 10, add the following security block to the WEB-INF/web.xml file, just after the <servlet-mapping> section:

```
<web-app>
  <!—SERVLET MAPPING HERE -->
  <security-constraint>
    <web-resource-collection>
      <web-resource-name>HtmlAdaptor</web-resource-name>
      <description>My security constraints
      </description>
      <url-pattern>/pojoService</url-pattern>
      <http-method>POST</http-method>
    </web-resource-collection>
    <auth-constraint>
      <role-name>TheBoss</role-name>
    </auth-constraint>
  </security-constraint>
  <login-config>
    <auth-method>BASIC</auth-method>
    <realm-name>Calculator Realm</realm-name>
  </login-config>
  <security-role>
    <role-name>TheBoss</role-name>
  </security-role>
</web-app>
```

Here, we are authorizing the Web Service access using the same TheBoss role described earlier. Notice we are specifying a security constraint only on the POST HTTP method, as we want to make the **Web Services Description Language (WSDL)** contract available (through a GET request) to any user requesting it.

The security role is checked in the WEB-INF/jboss-web.xml descriptor.

```
<jboss-web>
  <security-domain>java:/jaas/mysqlLogin</security-domain>
</jboss-web>
```

The Web Service is now usable only by users authorized on the `mysqlLogin` module. Republish the application by selecting the **Full publish** option from inside the **JBoss Server View**.

The remaining changes are only in the client, which needs to use a **Java API for XML Web Services (JAX-WS)** interface, namely the `javax.xml.ws.BindingProvider` interface, to provide the associated credentials by means of context objects.

```
public class AuthorizedClient {
  public static void main(String[] args) {
    if (args.length != 2) {
      System.err.println("usage: EchoClient <message>");
      System.exit(1);
    }
    double arg = Double.parseDouble(args[0]);
    double power = Double.parseDouble(args[1]);
    CalculatePowerService pojo = new CalculatePowerService();
    POJOWebService pojoService = pojo.getPOJOWebServicePort();
    BindingProvider bp = (BindingProvider)pojoService;
    Map<String, Object> rc = bp.getRequestContext();
    rc.put(BindingProvider.USERNAME_PROPERTY, "admin");
    rc.put(BindingProvider.PASSWORD_PROPERTY, "admin");
    System.out.println("Result is " +pojoService.
      calculatePower(arg,power));
  }
}
```

If you have completed the entire configuration correctly, the Web Service will return the `java.lang.Math`'s power for the chosen arguments.

The recommended way to run the sample is by means of the `wsrunclient` utility that is located in the `JBOSS_HOME/bin` folder. The advantage of using this command tool is that it automatically configures for you the client library PATH of JBoss WS. You just have to feed the classpath of the application class files to `wsrunclient`, as shown in the following code snippet:

```
wsrunclient -classpath %PATH_TO_CLASSES%
  com.packtpub.webserviceclient.example1.AuthorizedClient 2 4
```

On a Unix/Linux machine it would be:

```
Wsrunclient.sh -classpath $PATH_TO_CLASSES
  com.packtpub.webserviceclient.example1.AuthorizedClient 2 4
```

Here's the expected output on the console:

```
Prompt dei comandi                                        _ □ ×

C:\Chap14>wsrunclient -classpath %PATH_TO_CLASSES%;. com.packtpub.webserviecl
ient.example1.AuthorizedClient 2 4

Result is 16
C:\Chap14>_
```

Notice that we are executing the `AuthorizedClient` by means of the `wsrunclient` utility introduced in Chapter 10, which requires just pointing to the correct application classpath. Alternatively, you can run this sample from within the Eclipse environment like any other Java class.

What about EJB-based Web Services? The configuration is slightly different; as the security domain is not specified in web descriptors, we have to provide it by means of annotations.

```
@Stateless
@RemoteBinding(jndiBinding="AppStoreEJB/remote")
@WebService(targetNamespace = "http://www.packtpub.com/",
  serviceName = "AccountManagerService")
@WebContext(authMethod = "BASIC",
  secureWSDLAccess = false)
@SecurityDomain(value = "mysqlLogin")
public class AccountManagerBean implements AccountManager {
}
```

As you can see, the `@WebContext` annotation basically reflects the same configuration options as POJO-based Web Services, with BASIC authentication and unrestricted WSDL access.

The `@SecurityDomain` annotation should be familiar to you, as we introduced it at the beginning of this chapter to illustrate how to secure an EJB. As you can see, it's a replacement for the information contained in the `jboss-web.xml` file, except that the security domain is referenced directly by `mysqlLogin` instead of `java:/jaas/mysqlLogin`.

> The above security configuration can also be specified by means of the `META-INF/ejb-jar.xml` and `META-INF/jboss.xml` files, if you prefer using standard configuration files. Have a look at the EJB role authorization section, to see how to set up the files correctly.

Web Services encryption

The Web Services technology is based on the exchange of messages between a **service consumer** and a **service provider** using a commonly agreed protocol such as HTTP. From this definition, it's clear that Web Services encryption can be performed at two different levels:

- **Security at the transport level**: This level uses the in-built security features of transport technologies such as HTTPS. Using this option requires configuring the web server for HTTPS and specifying the use of a CONFIDENTIAL transport in the web.xml file.

- **Security at the SOAP or messaging level**: This level is independent of the transport level and involves use of digital signatures, certificates, and so on at the **XML document level**. In practice, instead of encrypting the client-server communication, we just cipher the SOAP message content.

You might wonder which approach is better for securing Web Services. Generally, when you are dealing with point-to-point Web Services, where clients communicate directly with the endpoint, the transport level is sufficient.

On the other hand, if there are multiple SOAP intermediaries and the SOAP message needs to cross several hops before reaching the endpoint, then securing at the message level is the preferred approach.

In this section, we will focus on the message-level encryption that has been implemented in JBossWS, based on the WS-Security specifications.

The process of encrypting SOAP messages requires both parties to generate their **keystores** (containing public keys and their signed certificate) and **truststores** (holding the public keys of the other subjects).

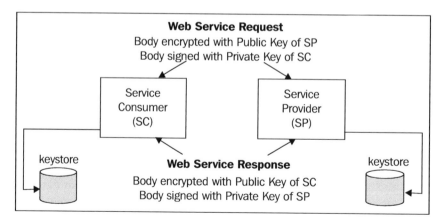

As you can see, the sender uses the receiver's public key (stored in the keystore) to encrypt the message. The receiver uses its certificate that contains both its public and private keys to decrypt the message.

In order to accomplish this, we will first generate a key pair (a public key and associated private key) for the service producer **[1]** and the service consumer **[2]**.

```
keytool -genkey -alias serverkeys -keyalg RSA -keystore
    server.keystore -storepass mypassword -keypass mypassword -dname
    "CN=localhost, OU=MYOU, O=MYORG, L=MYCITY, ST=MYSTATE, C=MY"  [1]

keytool -genkey -alias clientkeys  -keyalg RSA -keystore
    client.keystore -storepass mypassword -keypass mypassword -dname
    "CN=localhost, OU=MYOU, O=MYORG, L=MYCITY, S=MYSTATE, C=MY"  [2]
```

The keystores are then exported into a X.509 certificate **[3]**, **[4]**. This is the certificate that authenticates the server's and client's public key.

```
keytool -export -alias serverkeys -keystore server.keystore -
    storepass mypassword -file server.cer  [3]

keytool -export -alias clientkeys -keystore client.keystore -
    storepass mypassword -file client.cer  [4]
```

As the next step, each profile needs to import the other's public key in the local keystore. Therefore, the client will import the server's public key into its keystore **[6]** and use this key to encrypt the message. The server will also import the client public key into its keystore **[5]** and will use this key to decrypt the message.

```
keytool -import -alias serverkeys -keystore client.keystore -
    storepass mypassword -keypass mypassword -file server.cer  [5]

keytool -import -alias clientkeys -keystore server.keystore -
    storepass mypassword -keypass mypassword -file client.cer  [6]
```

At this point, the configuration is almost complete. As you are using self-signed certificates, each party needs to import its own certificate into the truststore **[7]**, **[8]**:

```
keytool -import -alias clientkeys -keystore client.truststore -
    storepass mypassword -keypass mypassword -file client.cer  [7]

keytool -import -alias serverkeys -keystore server.truststore -
    storepass mypassword -keypass mypassword -file server.cer  [8]
```

The following diagram depicts the configuration built so far:

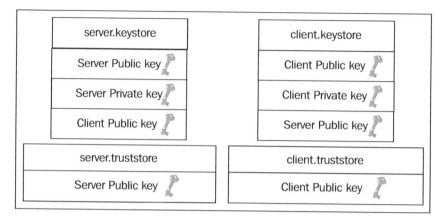

Client and server configuration files

So far, we have generated keystores and truststores for both the service producer and the service consumer. In order to enable Web Services encryption, we need to add two deployment descriptors that contain a reference to the client and server keystore and truststore:

- `jboss-wsse-server.xml`: The security configuration used on the server side. This contains a reference to the server keystore and truststore and applies to all incoming requests to a Web Service endpoint, as well as the outgoing responses sent by the Web Service endpoint.

  Here's a dump of it:

```
<jboss-ws-security xmlns="http://www.jboss.com/ws-security/config"
    xmlns:xsi="http://www.w3.org/2001/XMLSchema-instance"
    xsi:schemaLocation="http://www.jboss.com/ws-security/config
    http://www.jboss.com/ws-security/schema/jboss-ws-
        security_1_0.xsd">
    <key-store-file>WEB-INF/server.keystore</key-store-file>
    <key-store-password>mypassword</key-store-password>
    <trust-store-file>WEB-INF/server.truststore</trust-store-file>
    <trust-store-password>mypassword</trust-store-password>
    <key-passwords>
        <key-password alias="server" password="mypassword" />
    </key-passwords>
    <config>
        <encrypt type="x509v3" alias="clientkeys" />
        <requires>
```

```
      <encryption />
    </requires>
  </config>
</jboss-ws-security>
```

- `jboss-wsse-client.xml`: The security configuration used on the client-side. This contains a reference to the client keystore and truststore and applies to all outgoing requests sent by a client, as well the response messages that are received by the client.

```
<jboss-ws-security xmlns="http://www.jboss.com/ws-security/config"
  xmlns:xsi="http://www.w3.org/2001/XMLSchema-instance"
  xsi:schemaLocation="http://www.jboss.com/ws-security/config
  http://www.jboss.com/ws-security/schema/jboss-ws-
    security_1_0.xsd">
<key-store-file>META-INF/client.keystore</key-store-file>
<key-store-password>mypassword</key-store-password>
<trust-store-file>META-INF/client.truststore</trust-store-
  file>
<trust-store-password>mypassword</trust-store-password>
<key-passwords>
  <key-password alias="clientkeys" password="mypassword" />
</key-passwords>
<config>
  <encrypt type="x509v3" alias="serverkeys" />
  <requires>
    <encryption />
  </requires>
</config>
</jboss-ws-security>
```

The correct location for the above WS deployment descriptors varies depending on the type of application. The following table describes the correct location where descriptors need to be placed, depending on the type of application where Web Services are implemented:

Application type	Location
Web application archive (WAR)	Place `jboss-wsse-server.xml` in the `WEB-INF` folder.
EJB archive	Place `jboss-wsse-server.xml` in the folder `META-INF`.
Java EE application client	Place `jboss-wsse-client.xml` in the `META-INF` folder.

Encrypting the POJOWebService

In Chapter 10, *Developing Applications with JBoss Web Services*, we have coded two simple Web Services. The first one, POJO Web Service, was in charge of simply calculating a math power of an argument.

In this section, we will encrypt the SOAP communication between the client and the server. A prerequisite to this example is that you should have successfully created client and server certificates and also the `jboss-wsse-server.xml` and `jboss-wsse-client.xml` configuration files.

Securing the Web Service

Let's first start with the server. You just have to state that the Web Service will use a **handler** that is able to encrypt the content of the message. (For additional details about Web Services handlers, please refer to the *Web Service handler chains* section in Chapter 10.)

The list of available chain handlers resides in the `server/xxx/deployers/jbossws.deployer/META-INF/standard-jaxws-endpoint-config.xml` file. The handler we are interested in is **Standard WSSecurity Endpoint**. We will reference this handler by means of the `org.jboss.ws.annotation.EndpointConfig` annotation that needs to be placed at class level.

```
@WebService(targetNamespace = "http://www.packtpub.com/", serviceName
    = "CalculatePowerService")
@SOAPBinding(style = SOAPBinding.Style.RPC)
@EndpointConfig(configName = "Standard WSSecurity Endpoint")
public class POJOWebService {
}
```

Having completed the coding, let's see how our project looks like from the **Project Explorer** window. The following is the server configuration:

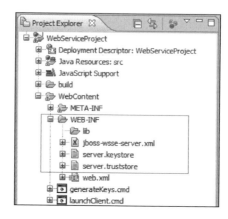

As you can see, the Web Service expects to find the `jboss-wsee-server.xml` file into the **WEB-INF** folder. This file also contains references to the server keystore and truststore, which are placed in the same folder.

> Notice that along with the source code of this example, we have also added two batch scripts to generate the keystores and truststores and to execute the client.

Securing the client

The client class does not require any change, so you can use the same `CalculatePowerService` class to access to the Web Service port and invoke the `calculatePower` method.

```
public static void main(String[] args) {
    if (args.length != 2) {
            System.err.println("usage: EchoClient <message>");
            System.exit(1);
    }
    double arg = 5;//Double.parseDouble(args[0]);
    double power = 2;//Double.parseDouble(args[1]);

    CalculatePowerService pojo = new CalculatePowerService();

    POJOWebService pojoService = pojo.getPOJOWebServicePort();

    System.out.println("Result is " +pojoService.calculatePower(arg,
power));

}
```

You might wonder how the client knows that this Web Service expects to run on a secure channel ? The answer is in the META-INF folder, which, if found in the client classpath, shapes up the Web Service for secure socket transmission. Here the client will look for the `jboss-wsse-client.xml` and `standard-jaxws-client-config.xml` files containing the secure configuration.

The file `standard-jaxws-client-config.xml` can be copied from the `server/xxx/deployers/jbossws.deployer/META-INF` directory. This file contains the list of available Web Services client configuration. The configuration you are interested in is "Standard WSSecurity Client" so take care to remove all other available configurations except this one.

Here's a snapshot of the client configuration:

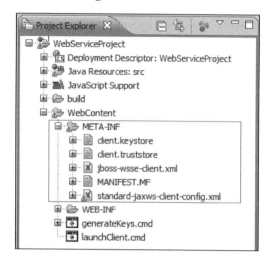

As you can see, we have placed the client keystore and trustore as well into the META-INF folder. However, this is not mandatory, you can place it in any location you like; remember to update this information in the jboss-wsse-client.xml.

Running the example

Your example is complete. The recommended way to run the sample is by means of the wsrunclient command utility that requires simply the location of the application classes and the configuration files on a Windows box.

```
wsrunclient -classpath %PATH_TO_CLASSES_AND_META_INF% com.packtpub.
webserviceclient.example1.Client
```

On a Unix/Linux machine it would be:

```
Wsrunclient.sh -classpath $PATH_TO_CLASSES_AND_META_INF. com.packtpub.
webserviceclient.example1.Client
```

In our example %PATH_TO_CLASSES_AND_META_INF% resolves to the path WEB-INF/ classes, so this is the expected output:

Signing SOAP messages

XML encryption is certainly important as it guarantees the confidentiality of the message. However, in network environments, there may be unreliable or malicious computers; the creator of a message is not always the same as the sender of the message. A digital signature applied on the message guarantees that the message has been actually sent from the subject we expect.

Technically speaking, if we want to digitally sign the SOAP message, we need to add the other party's public key in the truststore. Therefore, the client will import the server public key into its truststore **[9]** and the server will import the client public key as well, into its trustore **[10]**.

```
keytool -import -alias server -keystore client.truststore -file
   server.cert   [9]
keytool -import -alias client -keystore server.truststore -file
   client.cert   [10]
```

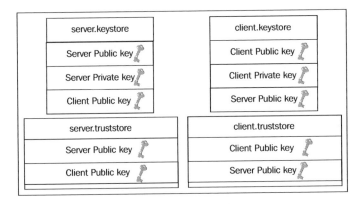

In addition, we have to configure the XML descriptors to sign messages using the other party's public key. We need to update the `jboss-wsse-server.xml` by adding the following `<config>` section at the bottom of the file.

```
<jboss-ws-security>
  <config>
    <sign type="x509v3" alias="serverkeys" />
    <encrypt type="x509v3" alias="clientkeys" />
    <requires>
      <signature />
        <encryption />
    </requires>
  </config>
</jboss-ws-security>
```

As highlighted in the last code snippet, we have specified to sign the message using an X.509 certificate. The certificate needs to be signed by a trusted entity, and so we have imported the other party's public key into the truststore.

Analogously, the `jboss-wsse-client.xml` client needs to be updated by adding a `<config>` element containing the `<sign>` and `<signature>` element relative to client and server keys.

```
<jboss-ws-security>
  <config>
    <sign type="x509v3" alias="clientkeys" />
    <encrypt type="x509v3" alias="serverkeys" />
    <requires>
      <signature />
        <encryption />
    </requires>
  </config>
</jboss-ws-security>
```

A digitally signed SOAP message will bear some additional elements, namely the `<ds:Signature>` and `<ds:SignedInfo>`, containing the digest algorithm used to sign the message and the signature along with the digest value.

```
<SOAP-ENV:Envelope >
  <ds:Signature xmlns:ds="http://www.w3.org/2000/09/xmldsig#">
  <ds:SignedInfo>
    <ds:DigestMethod
      Algorithm="http://www.w3.org/2000/09/xmldsig#sha1"/>
    <ds:DigestValue>j6lwx3rvEPO0vKtMup4NbeVu8nk=</ds:DigestValue>
  </ds:SignedInfo>
  <ds:SignatureValue>MC0CFFrVLtRlk=...</ds:SignatureValue>
</SOAP-ENV:Envelope>
```

Debugging SOAP messages

SOAP messages can be verified by turning on logs for the appender (see Chapter 3 for more information about it). However, if you need a valuable tool for debugging and testing Web Services, we suggest you to download a copy of Apache's **TCPMon** utility at `http://ws.apache.org/commons/tcpmon/download.cgi`.

Configure it to listen on an available TCP port and choose Tomcat's HTTP port (default 8080) as the destination.

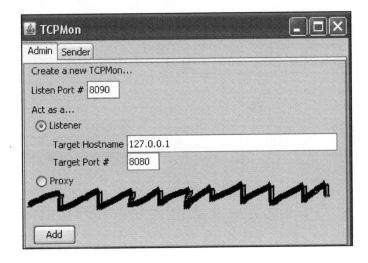

Now, in the client stub, modify the endpoint destination so that it points to the TCPMon listening port—for example, `http://127.0.0.1:8090/WebServiceProject/pojoService?wsdl`.

In the TCPMon main window, you can debug SOAP messages that have been sent to the Web Service and their response.

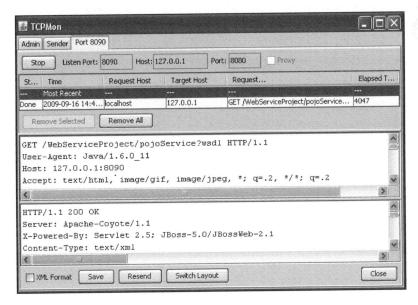

Summary

This chapter has covered a number of different topics related to the core idea of creating secure applications. We went through our examples and applied security at different layers. However, the application exposed just the web layer to the clients, so we have added an access control list to it and encrypted its HTTP traffic.

In the next section, we illustrated how to protect middle-tier components, such as EJB and Web Services, applying authentication and authorization techniques, as well as encryption of the RMI/HTTP data transmission.

We have finished learning JBoss. If you are serious about learning JBoss AS (and sure that you have completed all the chapters!) you will reap big dividends in the years to come. As a proof of it, the number of people joining the community of developers is steadily growing and also the opportunities for expert developers and architects.

I hope that this book has given you the right instruments to improve your knowledge of the application server, whether you are a learner or you are an expert Java EE technician.

Today, businesses are consumed with making their operations as efficient as possible, so most of the effort put in this book was devoted to improving your productivity, taking your assets to an outstanding level. I personally feel that being a smart developer, who's able to meet programming deadlines at every stage, is the best insurance for your working career.

May your career be rewarding, successful, and abundant, rich in opportunities for you to absorb the best of all your circumstances.

Index

POJOWebService encryption
about 378
SOAP messages, signing 381
Prepared Statement cache size parameter 67
probe level, JMX architecture 222

Q

QueryCache 325
QueueSize parameter 50

R

realm element 150
Remote Method Invocation. *See* **RMI**
removalTimeoutSeconds 314
replication-trigger attribute 303
replication granularity attribute 304
resource adapter 60
ResourceRollbackCount attribute 77
RMI 163
RMI-IIOP 32
RMI transport
about 351
client truststore, adding 353, 354
securing 351, 352
rolling file appender
about 54
file, rolling by size 55
root category configuration 57
runtime environment 21

S

sample application, JMS
creating 175-181
MDB singletons, creating 182
SAR extension 226
saveOrder() method 141
scheduled delivery 173
secure Java SE clients
about 364
writing 364, 366
Secure Socket Layer, JBoss AS
certificate management tools 347
enabling 347

HTTP communication, securing with
certificate signed by a CA 349, 350
HTTP communication, securing with
self-signed certificate 348, 349
RMI transport, securing 351, 352
security-domain 62
SecurityClient class
writing 366
security constraint
about 357
elements 357
selectOneMenu element 143
self-signed certificate 348
server element 150
server thread dump 51
service element 150
Service POJOs
about 237, 238
dependency 242
service, exposing 241
web test client, creating 239, 240
servlet API 133
session bean client
creating 124-129
Session Beans
about 81
developing 81
SFSB 81
SLSB 81
types 81
sessions, JMS 166
SFSB
about 81, 96
clustering 313, 314
developing 97-100
diagrammatic representation 96
life cycle 96
singleton 182
SLSB
about 81
application, deploying 89, 90
clustering 312
diagrammatic representation 82
interceptors, adding 93-95
life cycle 81

W

web application
  assembling 145
  clustering 327, 328
  deploying 146, 147
  store, running 148
web configuration, JBoss AS 5.0
  about 33
  limitations 33
web layout
  developing 133
  JSF managed bean, adding 139, 141
  navigation rules, setting up 137, 138
  view, setting up 142-144
weblog. *See* **blog**
Web Service concepts
  about 252
  building strategies 253
  JBoss Web Services stack 253
Web Service Handler chains 275
WebServiceProject 256
Web Services
  securing 370
Web Services, coding with JBossWS
  about 255
  EJB, exposing 268
  POJO Web Service, developing 255-258

Web Services authorization 371-373
Web Services encryption
  about 374
  jboss-wsse-client.xml 377
  jboss-wsse-server.xml 376
  levels 374
  security, at messaging level 374
  security, at transport level 374
Web Services security
  about 370
  Web Services authorization 371, 373
  Web Services encryption 374
wsconsume tool
  about 262
  arguments 263
  CalculatePowerService.java file 263
  POJOWebService.java file 263
WSDL 252
wsprovide tool 262

X

XML-based registries 252

Thank you for buying
JBoss AS 5 Development

Packt Open Source Project Royalties

When we sell a book written on an Open Source project, we pay a royalty directly to that project. Therefore by purchasing JBoss AS 5 Development, Packt will have given some of the money received to the JBoss Application Server project.

In the long term, we see ourselves and you—customers and readers of our books—as part of the Open Source ecosystem, providing sustainable revenue for the projects we publish on. Our aim at Packt is to establish publishing royalties as an essential part of the service and support a business model that sustains Open Source.

If you're working with an Open Source project that you would like us to publish on, and subsequently pay royalties to, please get in touch with us.

Writing for Packt

We welcome all inquiries from people who are interested in authoring. Book proposals should be sent to author@packtpub.com. If your book idea is still at an early stage and you would like to discuss it first before writing a formal book proposal, contact us; one of our commissioning editors will get in touch with you.

We're not just looking for published authors; if you have strong technical skills but no writing experience, our experienced editors can help you develop a writing career, or simply get some additional reward for your expertise.

About Packt Publishing

Packt, pronounced 'packed', published its first book "Mastering phpMyAdmin for Effective MySQL Management" in April 2004 and subsequently continued to specialize in publishing highly focused books on specific technologies and solutions.

Our books and publications share the experiences of your fellow IT professionals in adapting and customizing today's systems, applications, and frameworks. Our solution-based books give you the knowledge and power to customize the software and technologies you're using to get the job done. Packt books are more specific and less general than the IT books you have seen in the past. Our unique business model allows us to bring you more focused information, giving you more of what you need to know, and less of what you don't.

Packt is a modern, yet unique publishing company, which focuses on producing quality, cutting-edge books for communities of developers, administrators, and newbies alike. For more information, please visit our website: www.PacktPub.com.

PUBLISHING

Drools JBoss Rules 5.0

Developer's Guide
ISBN: 978-1-847195-64-7   Paperback: 320 pages

Develop rules-based business logic using the Drools platform

1. Discover the power of Drools as a platform for developing business rules

2. Build a custom engine to provide real-time capability and reduce the complexity in implementing rules

3. Explore Drools modules such as Drools Expert, Drools Fusion, and Drools Flow, which adds event processing capabilities to the platform

4. Execute intelligent business logic with ease using JBoss/Drools, a stronger business-rules solution

JBoss Tools 3 Developer's Guide
ISBN: 978-1-847196-14-9   Paperback: 408 pages

Develop JSF, Struts, Seam, Hibernate, jBPM, ESB, web services, and portal applications faster than ever using JBoss Tools for Eclipse and the JBoss Application Server

1. Develop complete JSF, Struts, Seam, Hibernate, jBPM, ESB, web service, and portlet applications using JBoss Tools

2. Tools covered in separate chapters so you can dive into the one you want to learn

3. Manage JBoss Application Server through JBoss AS Tools

4. Explore Hibernate Tools including reverse engineering and code generation techniques

Please check **www.PacktPub.com** for information on our titles

PACKT
PUBLISHING

Business Process Management with
JBoss jBPM

A Practical Guide for Business Analysts

Develop business process models for implementation in a
business process management system

Matt Cumberlidge

PACKT

Business Process Management with JBoss jBPM

ISBN: 978-1-847192-36-3   Paperback: 300 pages

Develop business process models for implementation
in a business process management system.

1. Map your business processes in an efficient,
   standards-friendly way

2. Use the jBPM toolset to work with business
   process maps, create a customizable user
   interface for users to interact with the process,
   collect process execution data, and integrate
   with existing systems.

3. Use the SeeWhy business intelligence toolset
   as a Business Activity Monitoring solution,
   to analyze process execution data, provide
   real-time alerts regarding the operation of the
   process, and for ongoing process improvement

JBoss Portal
Server Development

Create dynamic, feature-rich, and robust enterprise
portal applications

Ramanujam Rao

PACKT

JBoss Portal Server Development

ISBN: 978-1-847194-10-7   Paperback: 257 pages

Create dynamic, feature-rich, and robust enterprise
portal applications

1. Complete guide with examples for building
   enterprise portal applications using the free,
   open-source standards-based JBoss portal
   server

2. Quickly build portal applications such as B2B
   web sites or corporate intranets

3. Practical approach to understanding concepts
   such as personalization, single sign-on,
   integration with web technologies, and
   content management

Please check **www.PacktPub.com** for information on our titles

6770943R0